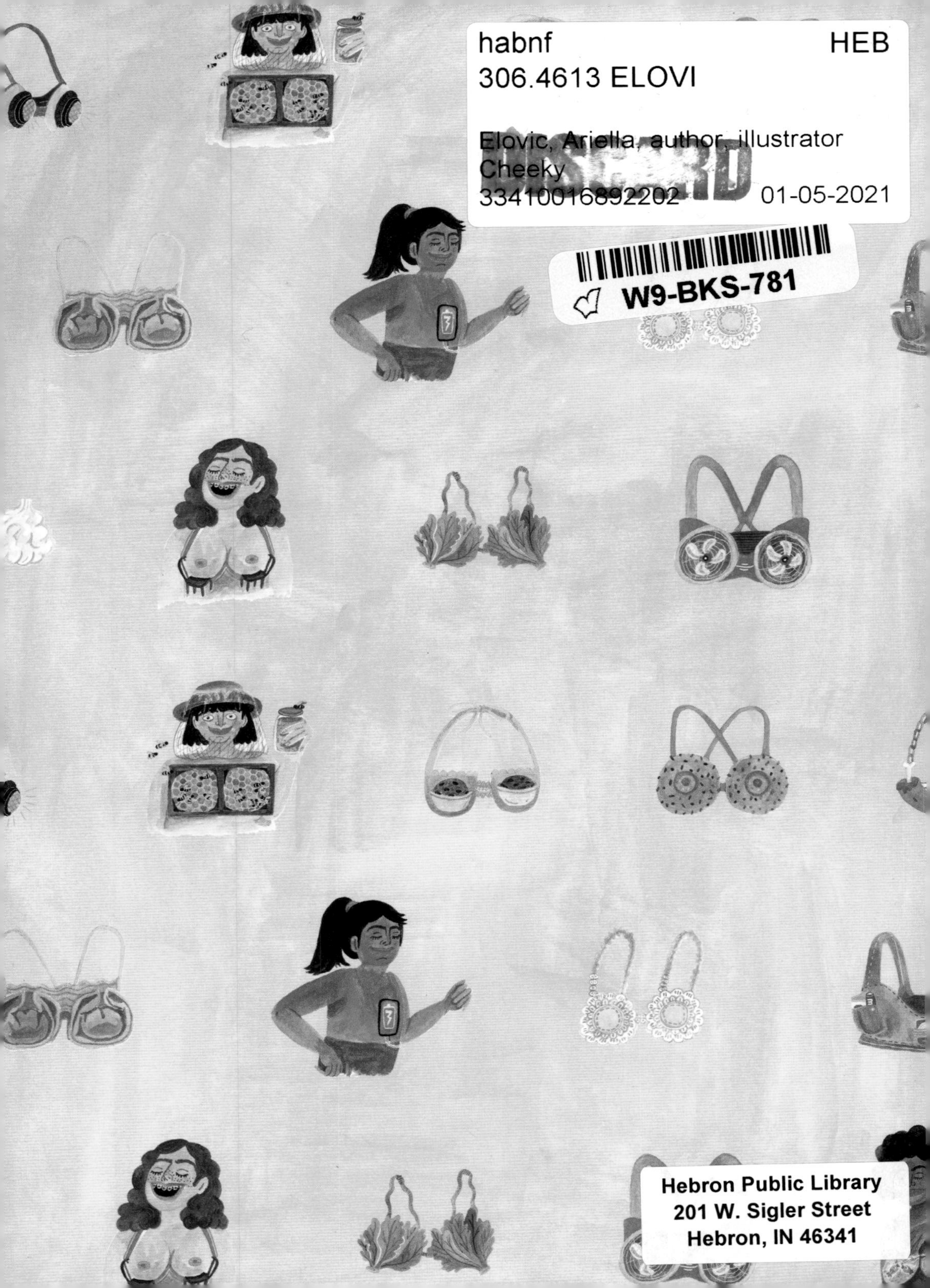

CHEEKY

CHEEKY

A Head-to-Toe
Memoir

ARIELLA ELOVIC

BLOOMSBURY PUBLISHING
NEW YORK · LONDON · OXFORD · NEW DELHI · SYDNEY

BLOOMSBURY PUBLISHING
Bloomsbury Publishing Inc.
1385 Broadway, New York, NY 10018, USA

BLOOMSBURY, BLOOMSBURY PUBLISHING,
and the Diana logo are trademarks of
Bloomsbury Publishing Plc

First published in the United States 2020

ISBN: HB: 978-1-63557-452-4; eBook: 978-1-63557-453-1

Library of Congress Cataloging-in-Publication Data is available

2 4 6 8 10 9 7 5 3 1

Designed and typeset by Katya Mezhibovskaya
Printed and bound in Printed and bound by C&C Offset Printing Co Ltd, China
To find out more about our authors and books
visit www.bloomsbury.com and sign up for our newsletters.

FOR ALL THE WOMEN
IN MY LIFE

CONTENTS

HELLO!

hey there, i'm ariella

I'm an illustrator living and working in New York City.

I HAVE A FULL-TIME JOB IN AN OFFICE AND COMING HOME TO PAINT IS THE DESSERT OF MY DAY. I CHANGE INTO PAJAMAS, THROW ON A TV SHOW, AND GET TO IT.

SNACKS IN TINY BOWLS ARE ESSENTIAL TO MY CREATIVE PROCESS.

This past year, I've been invested in a pretty big project: to accept and love my body and myself more wholly. I think six was my peak self-love year, and I've been on a mission to reclaim at least some of that confidence, feistiness, and joy.

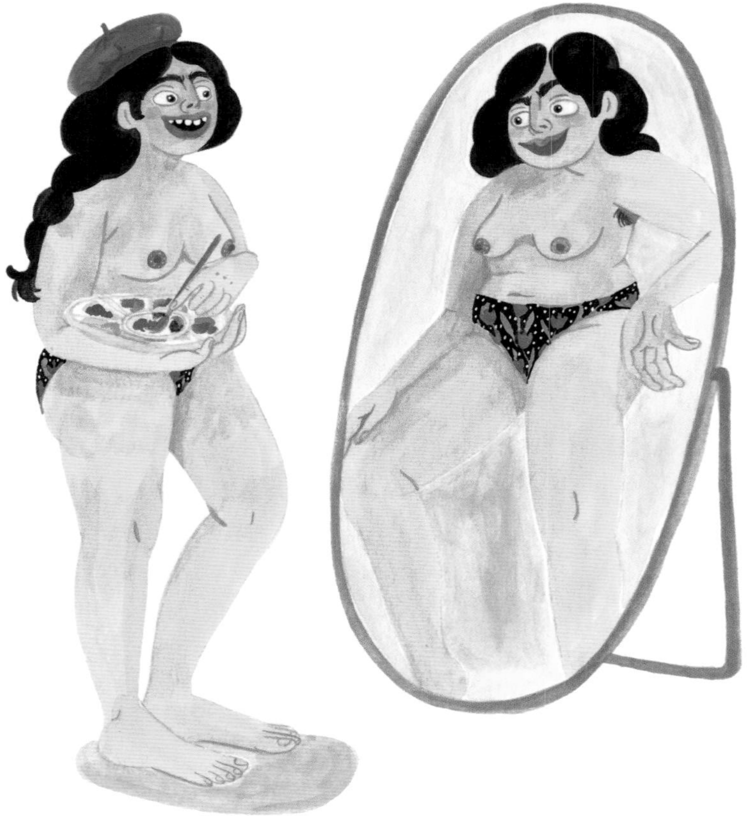

A really effective way for me to do this has been to paint my body naked, noting each tummy roll and unexpected hair that sprouts from my body. To see my body as matter-of-factly as little Ariella would have—rather than as a never-ending project with countless areas to wax, shrink, tone, or hide.

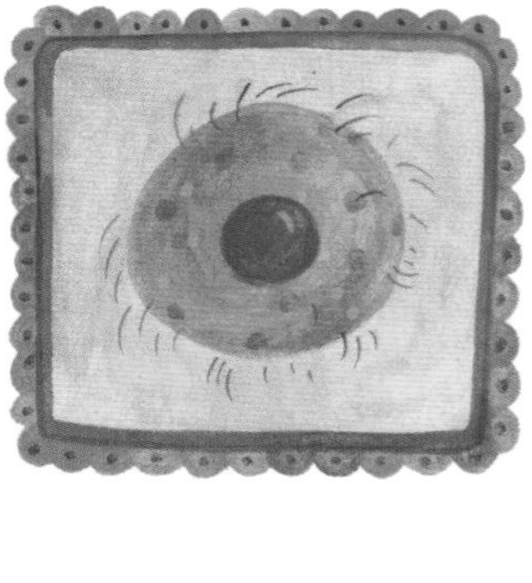

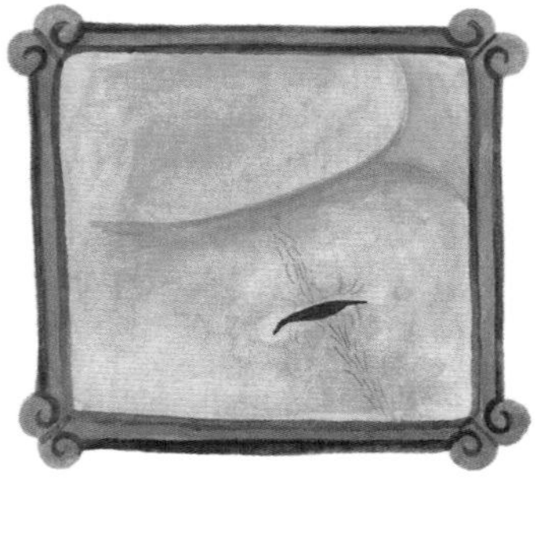

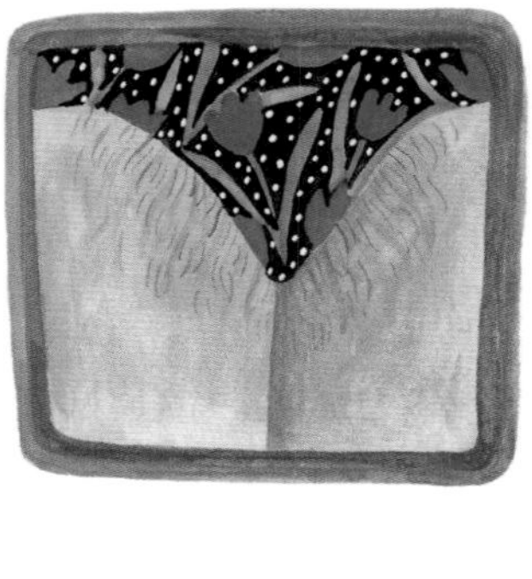

As women grow up, we're expected to reject our own bodies. Rather than celebrating all our bodies can do (or simply acknowledging their humanness), we are inundated with messaging that our natural bodies are simply a starting point and there is always work to be done. We are expected to do this work—and to *want* to do this work.

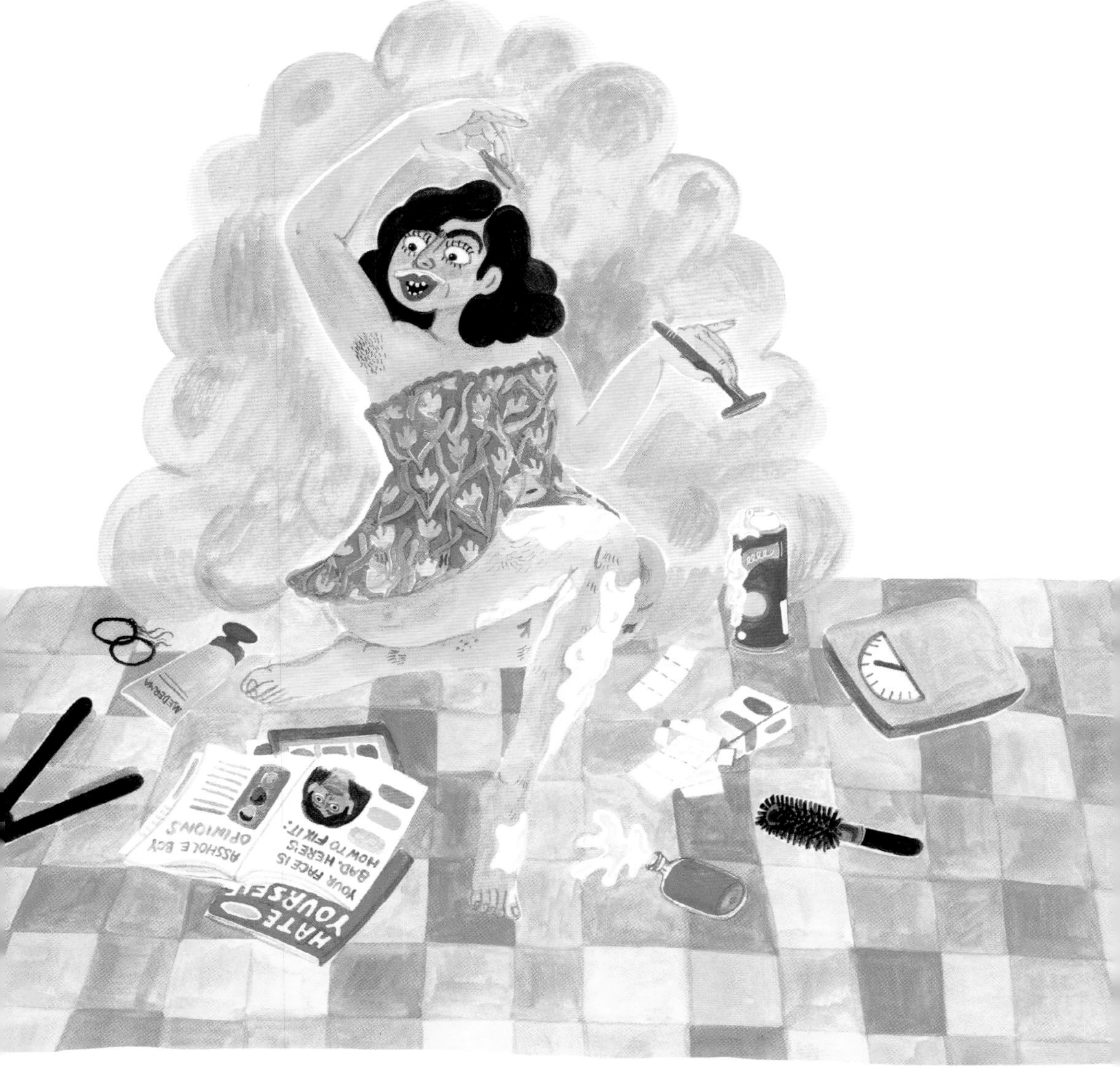
YOUR FACE IS BAD, HERE'S HOW TO FIX IT:
ASSHOLE BOY OPINIONS
HATE
MEDERMA

We're encouraged over and over to surrender power. We are taught to be polite, to be agreeable, to put others before ourselves. To not take up space, emotionally or physically. To instead distance ourselves from our own bodies, and also from those bodies' needs and limitations and desires.

I'm lucky to have grown up with parents who never commented on my looks. They instead put emphasis on striving to be the best me I could be, and I had the power to define who that was. Despite this support, there was still a point at which I surrendered my sense of self to outside opinion.

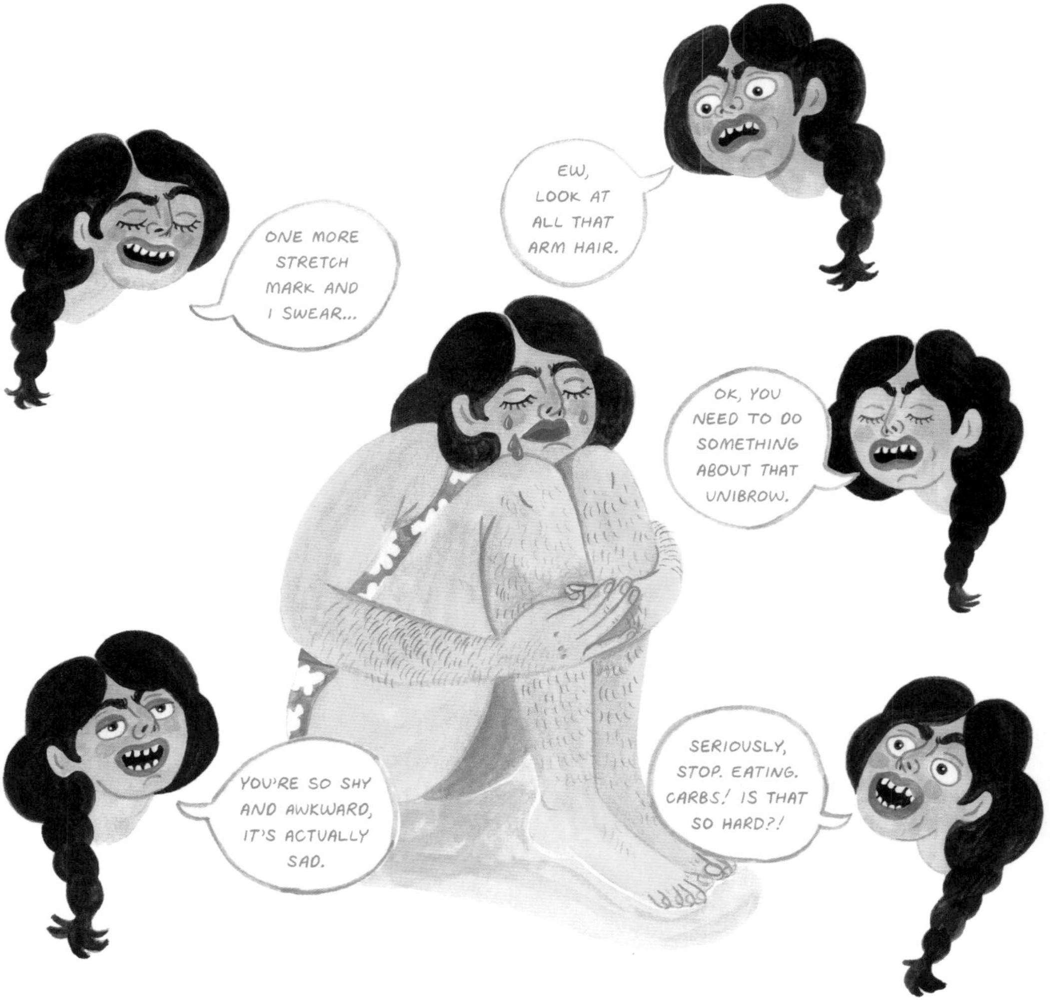
EW, LOOK AT ALL THAT ARM HAIR.
ONE MORE STRETCH MARK AND I SWEAR...
OK, YOU NEED TO DO SOMETHING ABOUT THAT UNIBROW.
YOU'RE SO SHY AND AWKWARD, IT'S ACTUALLY SAD.
SERIOUSLY, STOP. EATING. CARBS! IS THAT SO HARD?!

My body slowly morphed from simply being who I was to this wild and unpredictable being that sucked all my energy as it brought out my harshest inner critic who encouraged me to compare myself to others.

I let my box of Sally Hansen eyebrow wax determine how thin my eyebrows should be—which resulted in a pair of catastrophic brow fragments.

I feared sitting near boys during lunch at school because I felt I would be judged for eating more than a piece of fruit in front of them.

At fifteen, I found a pair of Spanx in my mom's underwear drawer and made them a signature part of my wardrobe. I wore them under jeans so I didn't have to confront the reality of my tummy rolls: truly the most uncomfortable combination.

TO BE FAIR, THIS WAS IN THE TIME OF LOW-RISE JEANS WHEN ONE UNCALCULATED MOVE WOULD EXPOSE YOUR ENTIRE BUTT CRACK. I WAS DESPERATE FOR MORE COVERAGE.

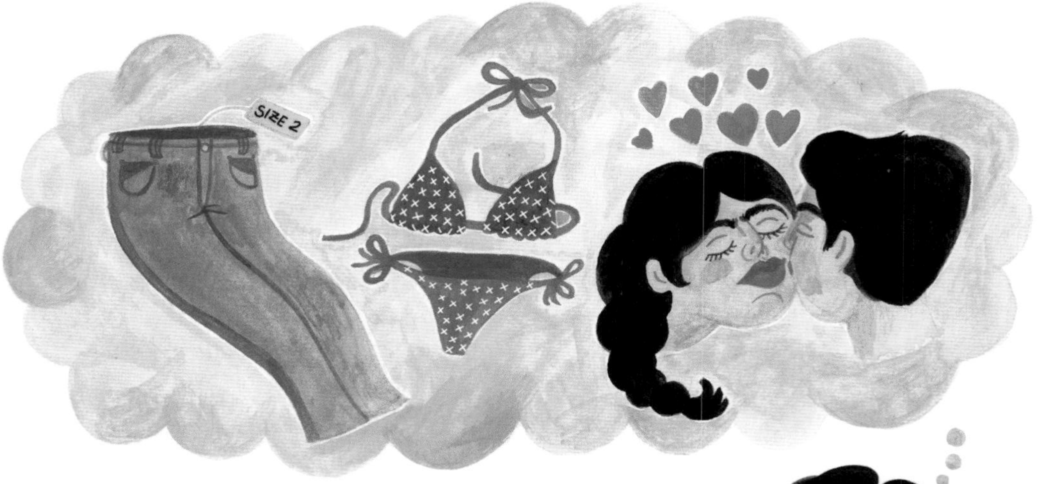
SIZE 2

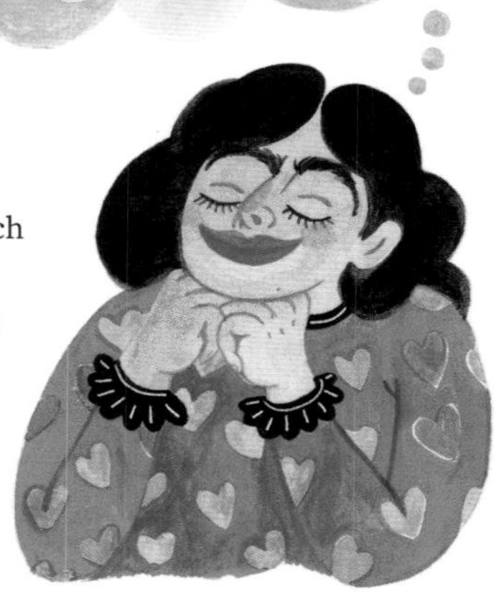

I calculated my BMI incessantly, comparing it to the BMIs of actresses close to my height as a way to determine how much weight I had to lose to look good. I was hesitant to buy new jeans because I was always hoping to lose another five pounds (in contrast, I had chosen to go up a size in third grade because I decided I liked the feeling of a loose waistband more than one that fit). I daydreamed about how fantastic my life would be once I hit those goal numbers. I'd be pretty enough to wear bikinis and have a boyfriend!

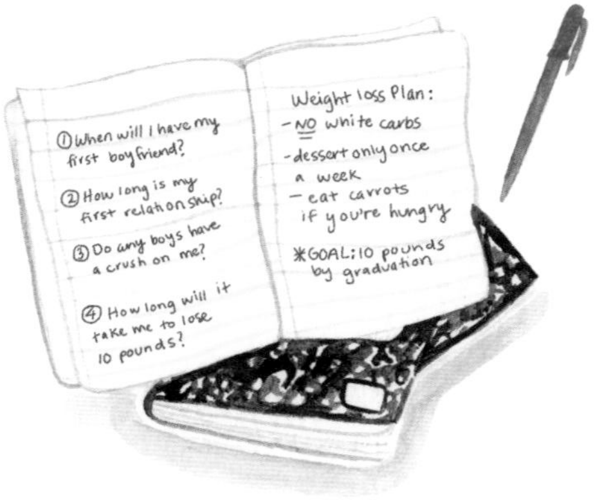
① When will I have my first boyfriend?
② How long is my first relationship?
③ Do any boys have a crush on me?
④ How long will it take me to lose 10 pounds?
Weight loss Plan:
- NO white carbs
- dessert only once a week
- eat carrots if you're hungry
*GOAL: 10 pounds by graduation

I spoke up less often in school for fear of coming off as too abrasive, and instead filled journals with wishes and goals for my future self.

I wasn't interested in pursuing a romantic life at that point, but I fantasized about my first kiss and love finally happening because I felt those milestones were hallmarks of being a valuable girl. Shout-out to the Disney classics!

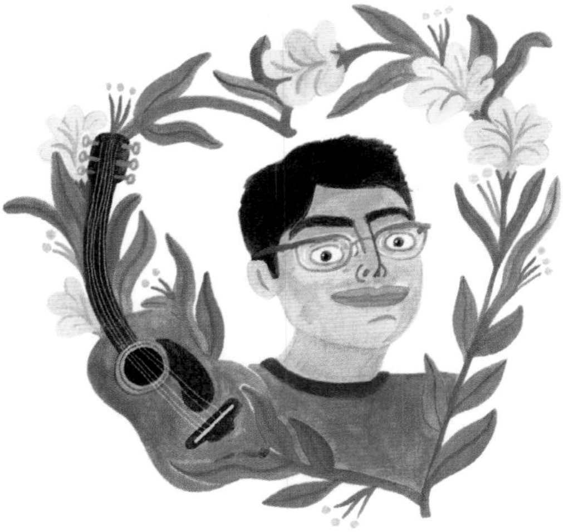

In high school, my biggest crush was the president of the environmental club, who played Bob Dylan songs on his guitar in the hall. (Are you drooling? Because, honestly, I still kind of am.)

When I heard rumblings that he was going to ask me to prom, I literally fled the scene. I ran out of the school, got into my car, and drove home.

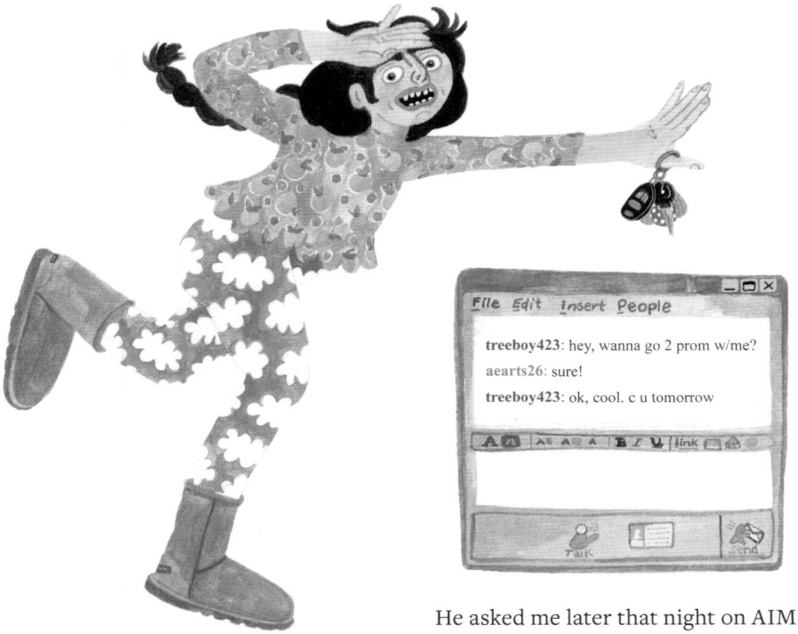
File Edit Insert People
treeboy423: hey, wanna go 2 prom w/me?
aearts26: sure!
treeboy423: ok, cool. c u tomorrow
Talk
Send

He asked me later that night on AIM.

Leading up to prom, I avoided him at all costs and on the night of, I did not make eye contact with him once. I am proud of myself for dealing with that situation in the only way that felt comfortable for me at the time—no matter how socially awkward that solution was. But I think a date, let alone a first kiss, with my crush felt impossible at that point because I was certain that I didn't yet look the part.

I spent my college years fixated on the need to fit the particular mold of what I thought it meant to be a pretty, desirable girl. Lots of rules to follow, and lots of guilt anytime I would stray from those rules.

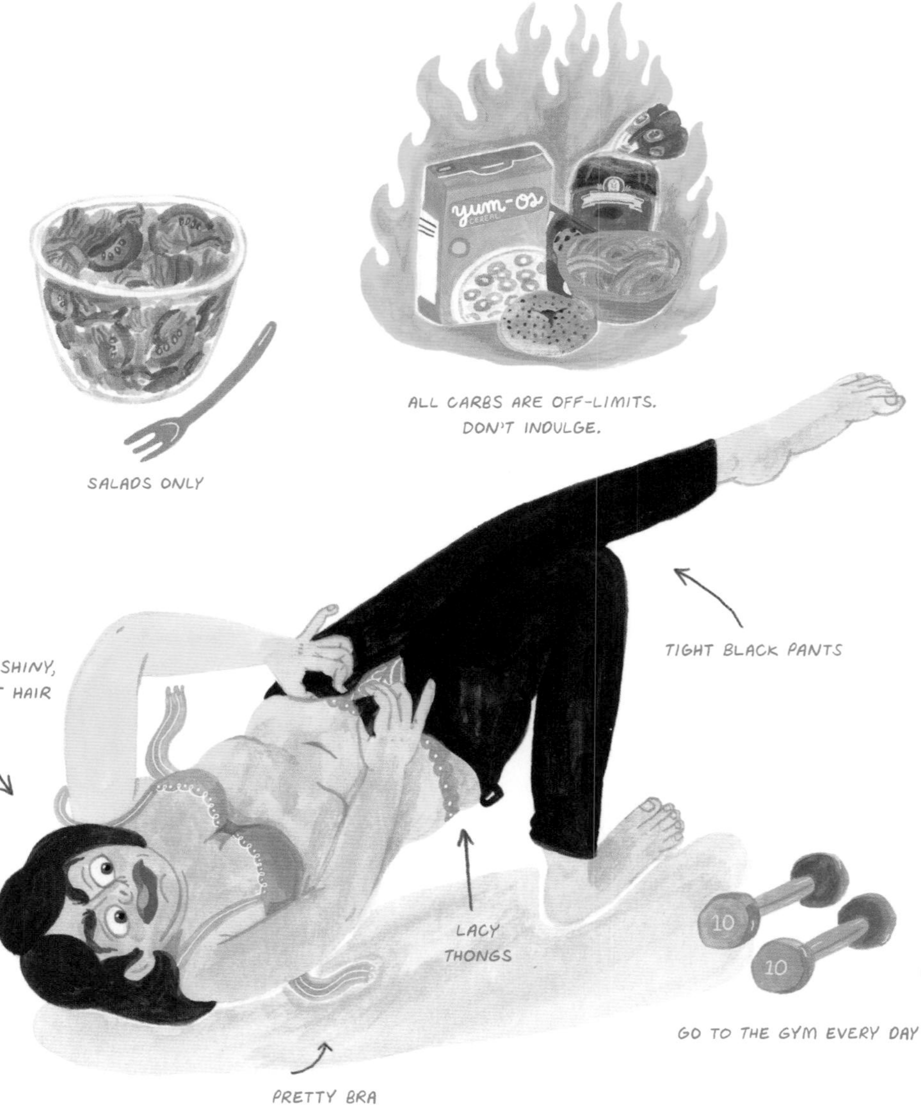
yum-os
CEREAL
ALL CARBS ARE OFF-LIMITS.
DON'T INDULGE.
SALADS ONLY
TIGHT BLACK PANTS
SMOOTH, SHINY,
STRAIGHT HAIR
LACY
THONGS
10
10
GO TO THE GYM EVERY DAY
PRETTY BRA

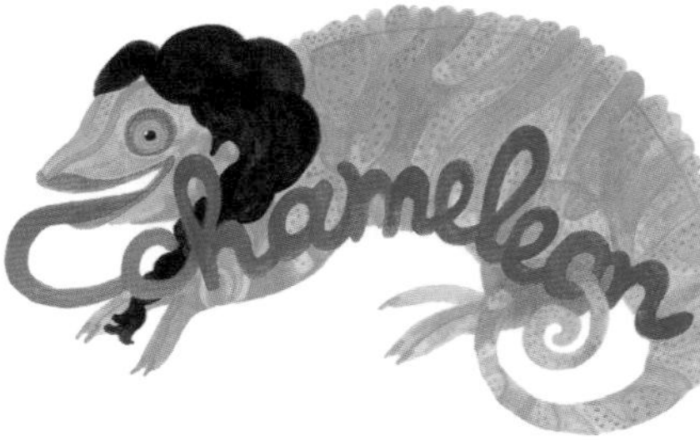
Chameleon

When I moved to New York and took the leap into online dating, I was overwhelmed by the idea of the different types of young woman I could be. A date would always throw me into a shopping spiral as I was suddenly convinced that a specific shoe or shirt could make or break the night.

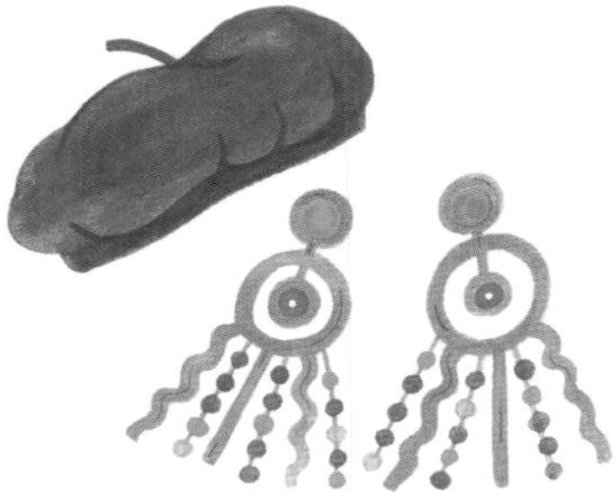

SPUNKY ARIELLA:
Mature and eclectic.

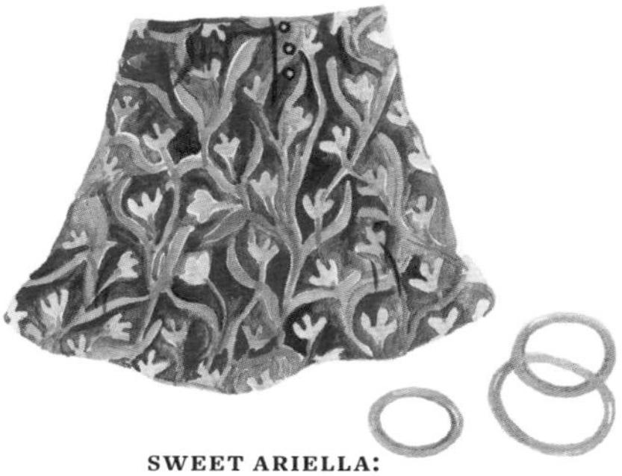

SWEET ARIELLA:
Gentle and feminine;
won't scare the preppy boys away!

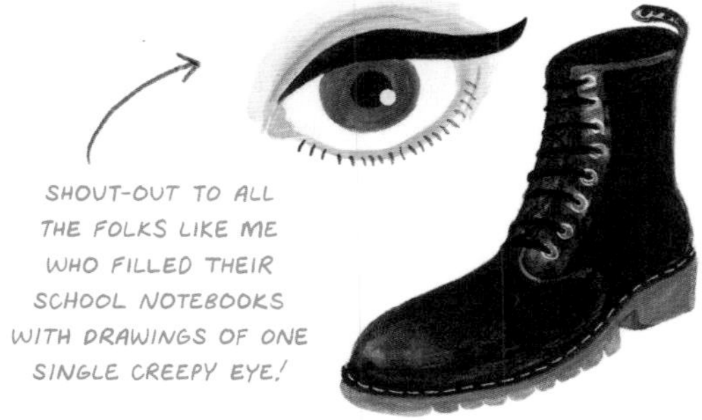
SHOUT-OUT TO ALL THE FOLKS LIKE ME WHO FILLED THEIR SCHOOL NOTEBOOKS WITH DRAWINGS OF ONE SINGLE CREEPY EYE!

EDGY ARIELLA:
Cool girl in art class all grown up.

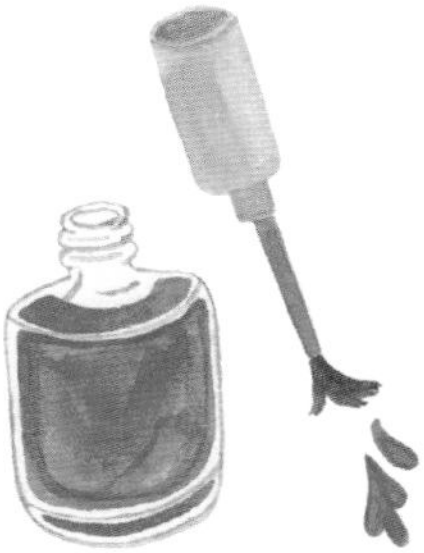

NO MATTER WHAT:
Red nail polish always,
the ultimate seduction tool.

Rather than hoping I liked my date, I focused on making sure my date liked me. What type of music would this person's kind of person listen to? What shoes or nail polish color would this person like? These versions of me—even the parts as small as my fingernails—weren't me, nor were they for me. I was devoted to a never-ending process of making myself more suitable for others, and each obsession moved me further away from recognizing the pretty awesome human that was getting lost in all of it.

But here I am now in my late twenties, finally getting back in touch with that fabulous lady.

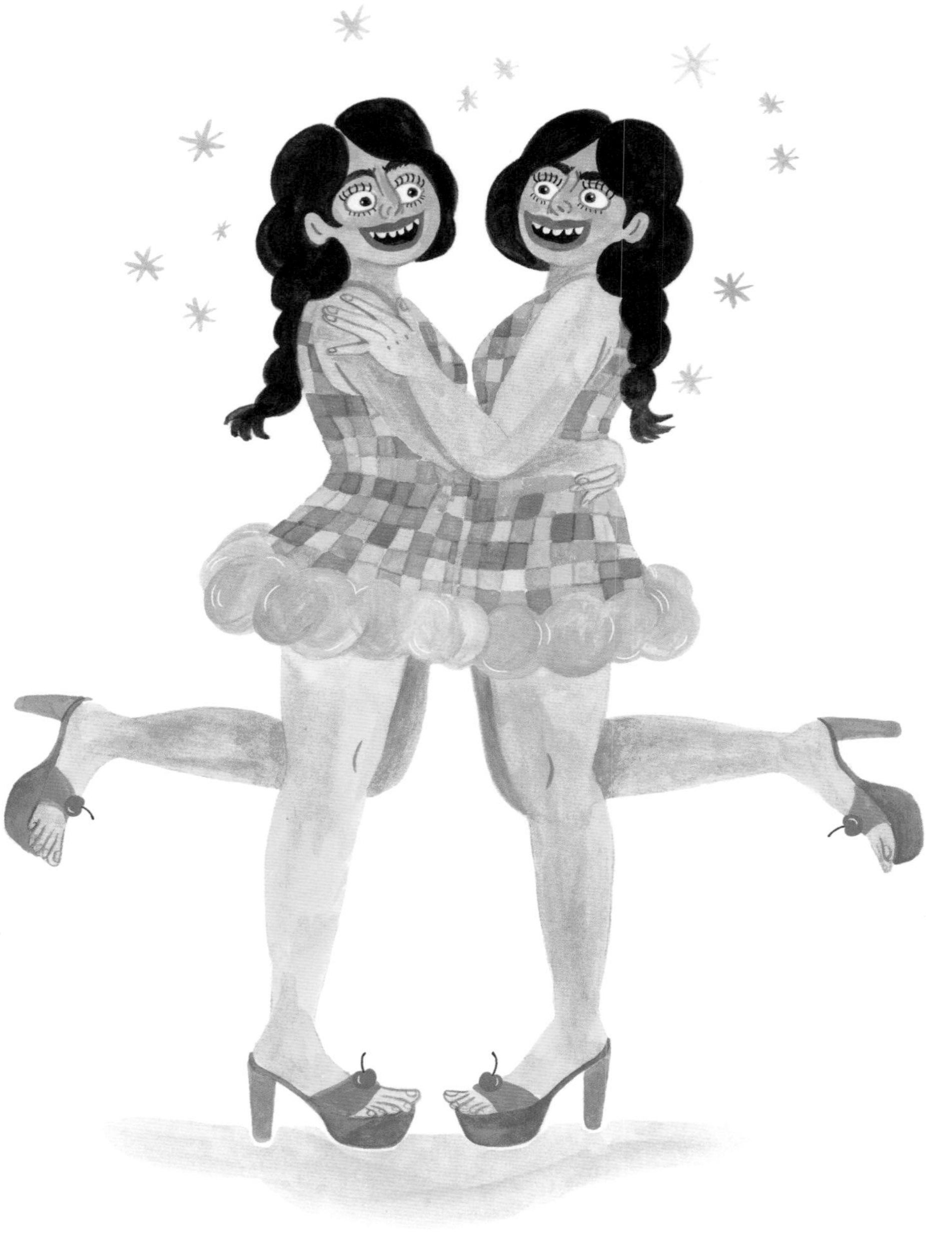

how did i get here?

I could never have snapped out of my critical spiral without my close group of female friends. When it comes to combating years of negative self-talk (plus years of ads showcasing silky smooth skin and messaging that fat is evil), reinforcements are vital.

the yentas

JESSE

LEILA

MAYA

NOA

ADI

ELLIE

I met these women—The Yentas, as we now call ourselves—seventeen years ago at the Jewish sleepaway camp where I had spent my summers when I was growing up. This group quickly became the best friends I had ever had, but I eventually lost touch with them when I went off to college and my school year was no longer bookended by summers together. Five years ago, I went to an alumni weekend at the camp and was so happy to reconnect with them. Being back together for those three days was a confidence reboot and it reminded me just how important it is to have The Yentas in my life.

Growing up, The Yentas had always encouraged me to take joy in moments that would normally cause anxiety or shame. At a time when periods felt taboo, The Yentas turned them into a superpower:

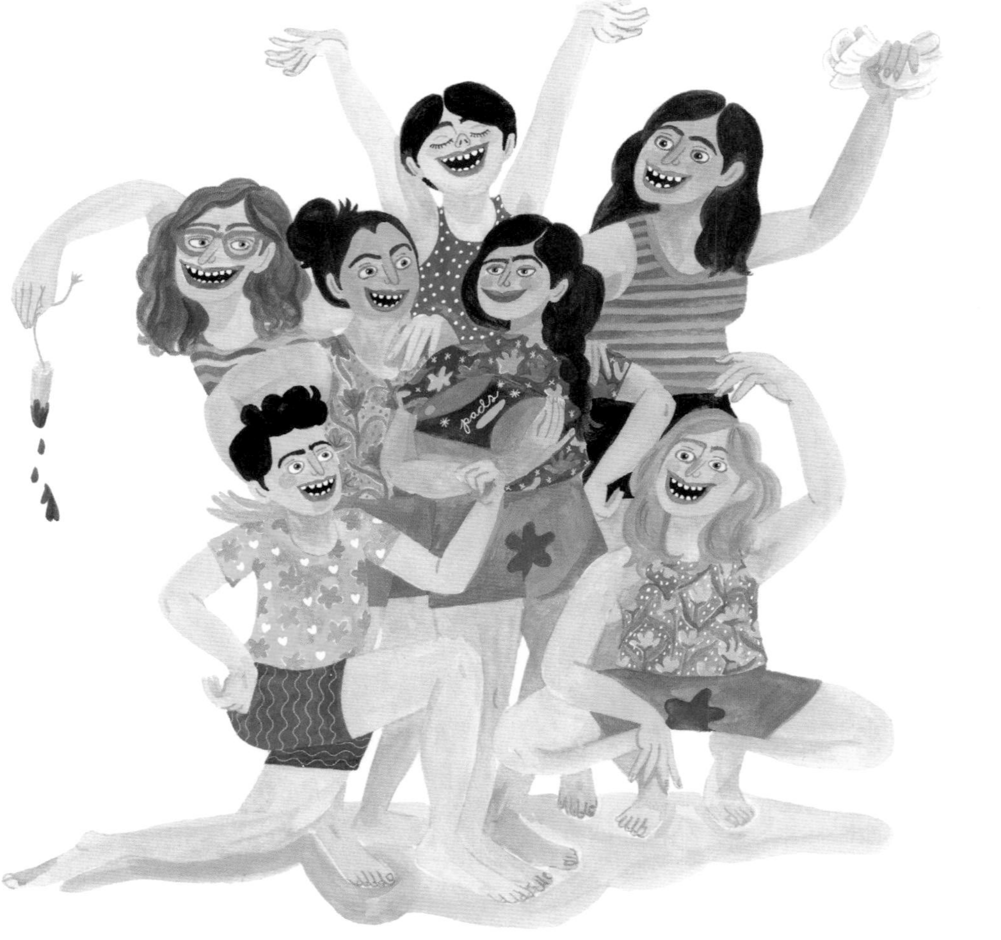

pads

To get out of our weekly capsizing drills in boating class, we would band together and declare it was our "time of the month" and we simply couldn't get wet from the waist down. We took such a thrill in seeing our male counselors leave us be at the mere mention of our periods, knowing they wouldn't dare question their abnormal frequency.

Together we were **VERY GROSS & VERY POWERFUL.**

We have built a community by sharing, laughing about, and taking pride in the grossest, stickiest, funniest, most mysterious, most frustrating, and most human aspects of ourselves.

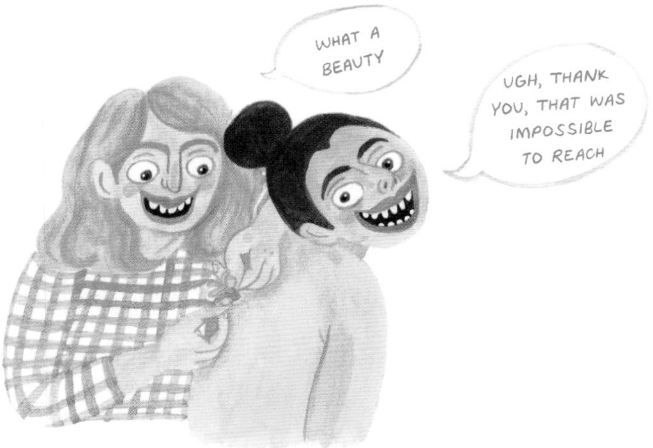
WHAT A BEAUTY
UGH, THANK YOU, THAT WAS IMPOSSIBLE TO REACH

The fact is some of us are tall, some of us are round, some nipples are large, and most butt cracks are hairy. We all have moments of self-doubt, times when we feel everything we do or say is judged (by others and ourselves), and sometimes we feel alone in those experiences. The Yentas have taught me the joy that springs from connecting around those tough moments.

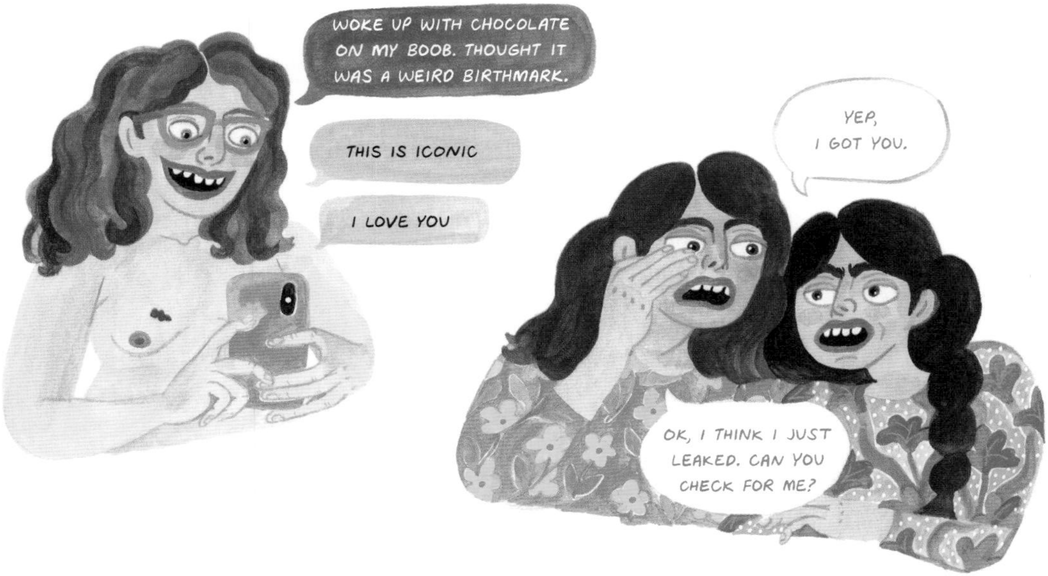
WOKE UP WITH CHOCOLATE ON MY BOOB. THOUGHT IT WAS A WEIRD BIRTHMARK.
THIS IS ICONIC
I LOVE YOU
OK, I THINK I JUST LEAKED. CAN YOU CHECK FOR ME?
YEP, I GOT YOU.

This book is a memoir about a very personal topic: learning to joyously embrace one's body more completely. To embody this sentiment in the most authentic way possible, I'm bringing you through my own journey—my head-to-toe reboot.

I make this note to call out that *Cheeky* is limited in some ways to my own experience as a white Jewish woman. My story, and the stories of my friends, does not represent all bodies. Given that fact, you very well might not see yourself physically all of the time in this book. What I do hope, though, is that my story helps you find your own way to recalibrate and reconnect with your body. To celebrate yourself, inside and out. My hope is that *Cheeky* is just the beginning of the conversation!

Getting cheeky is about relishing the powerful feeling of reclaiming and redefining how we relate to our bodies. Writing this book and taking the time to paint and pay tribute to the parts of my body I've hidden from myself and others has been my way of learning to love myself just as I am. I hope you find your own way too. I hope I might help you find it.

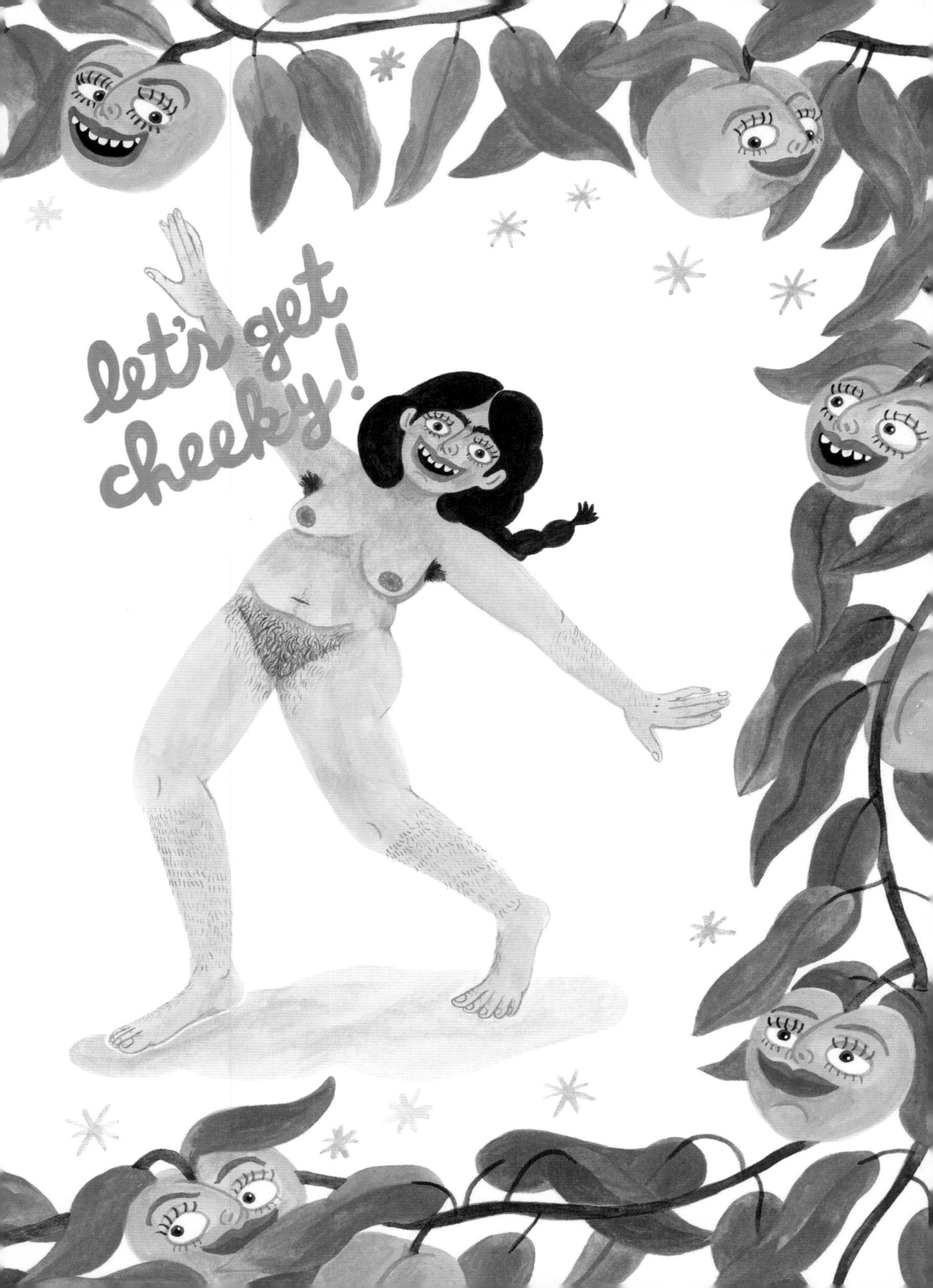
let's get cheeky!

FACE

Mirrors.
We've got a love-hate relationship.

a magical PLACE TO PLAY

As a kid, my relationship to my reflection was simple and fun. I spent a significant amount of time making faces at myself in the mirror, becoming different characters as I sat contorting, twisting, and stretching my cheeks and making up voices or strange cackling sounds. Sometimes I'd actually scare myself and would have to stop.

I USED TO THINK THAT THIS PARTICULAR
SQUISHING OF MY FACE WAS A PREVIEW FOR
WHAT I'D LOOK LIKE AS AN OLD WOMAN.

My friends and I loved choreographing dances to the *Spiceworld* album, performing in front of mirrors, blank TV screens, or large windows—anything reflective. We were both the show and the audience. I was always Posh Spice.

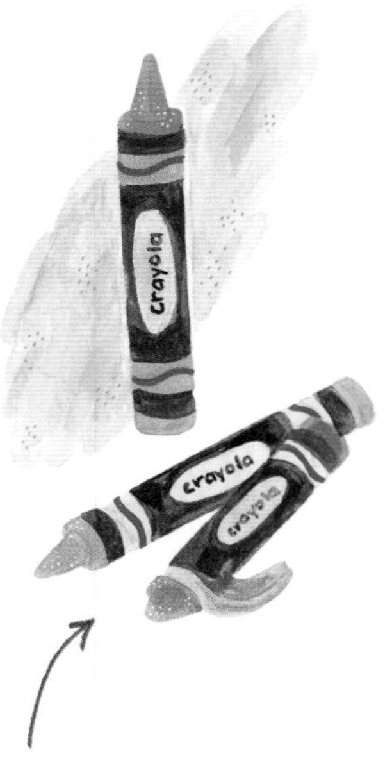
crayola
crayola
crayola

TO COMPLETE THE LOOK, WE WOULD DIP INTO MY CRAYOLA GLITTER CRAYON COLLECTION AND DRAG THOSE WAXY STICKS ACROSS OUR CHEEKS, EYES, AND LIPS UNTIL WE HAD ACHIEVED SOME SEMBLANCE OF BLUSH, EYESHADOW, AND LIPSTICK.

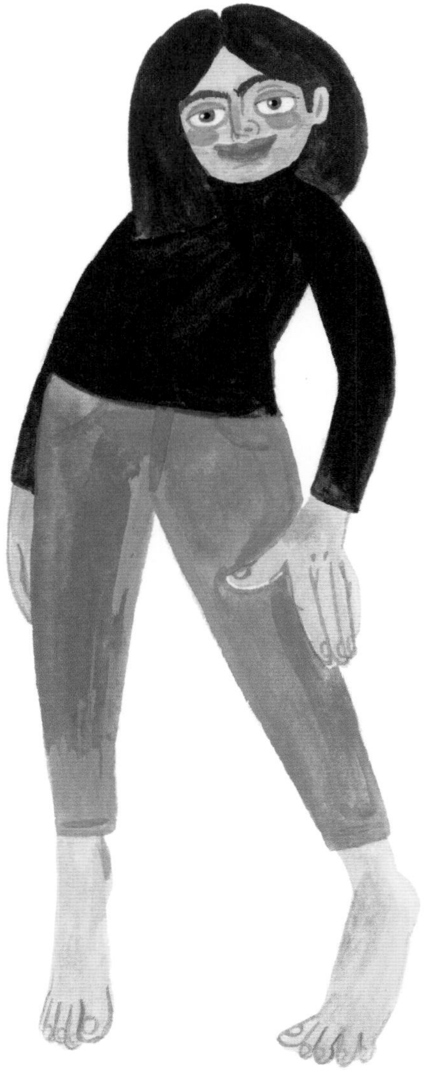

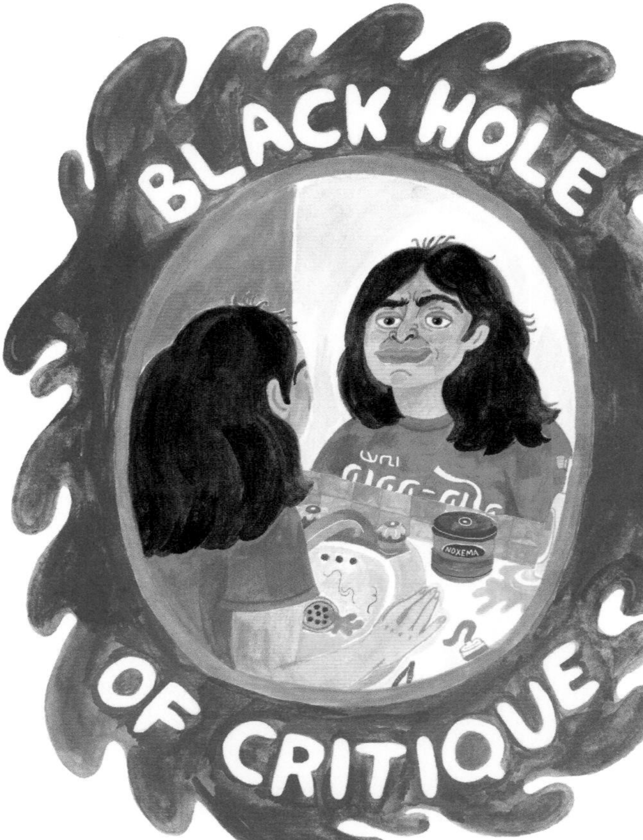
BLACK HOLE
OF CRITIQUE
NOXEMA

As I got older, my relationship to mirrors changed.

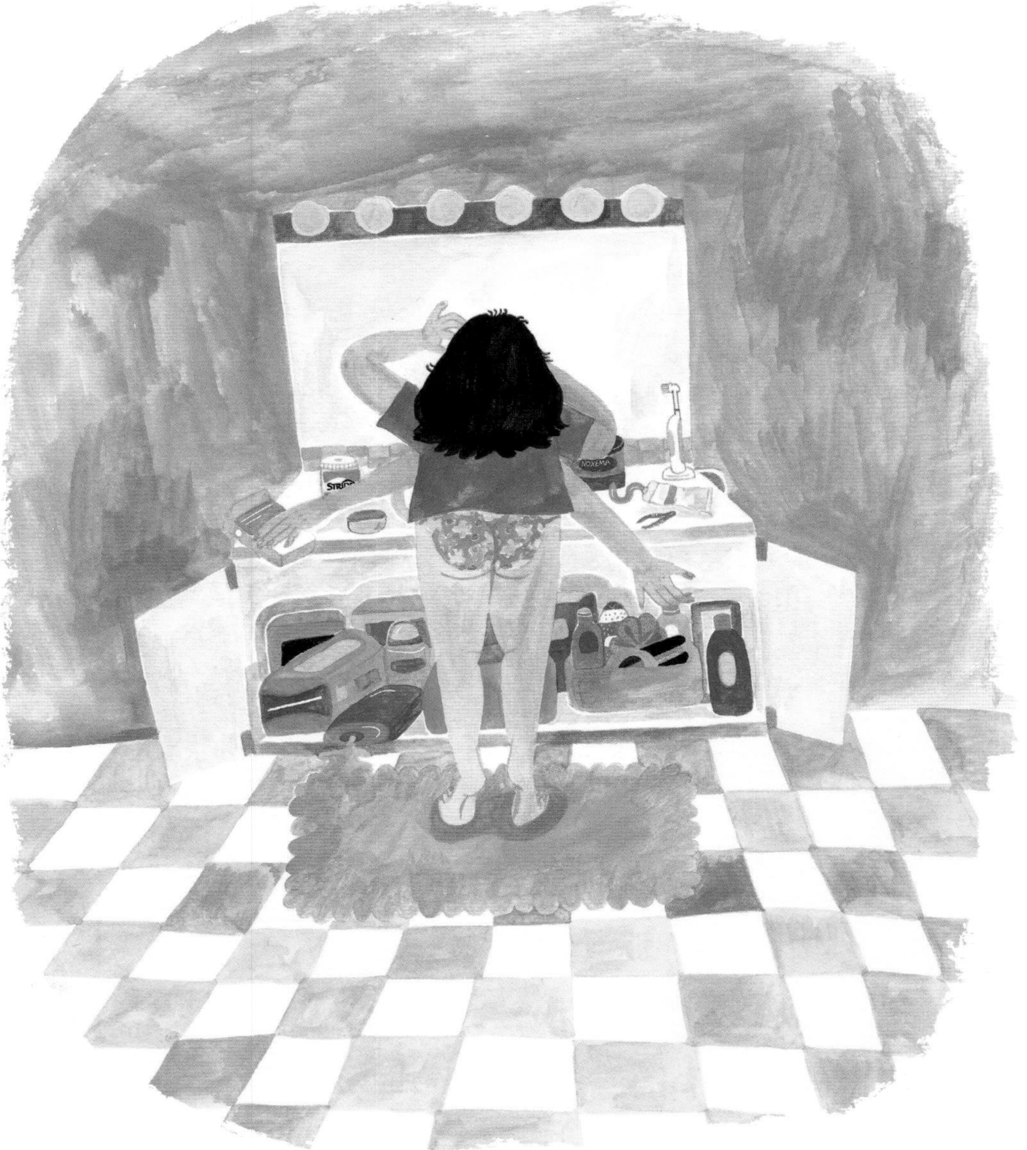
NOXEMA

Mirrors became the meeting place for myself and my inner critic;
the bathroom a secret lair in which to edit and perfect.

I hated my round face and how squishy my cheeks were. A friend's mom once told me that she couldn't tell if I had high cheekbones or not because my cheeks were "so filled out."

I always did a closed-mouth smile for pictures because I thought a toothy one made my cheeks look too big.

I walked around sucking in my cheeks to make them look thinner. I thought this was subtle.

I avoided being seen from the side because I thought my sideburns were ugly. Not to mention the mole that lives beneath the left one.

My too-round face became a minefield: pimples erupting in every corner, blackheads emerging all over my nose, and swaths of shiny oil spreading across my forehead. I spent hours in the mirror trying to control and camouflage the chaos.

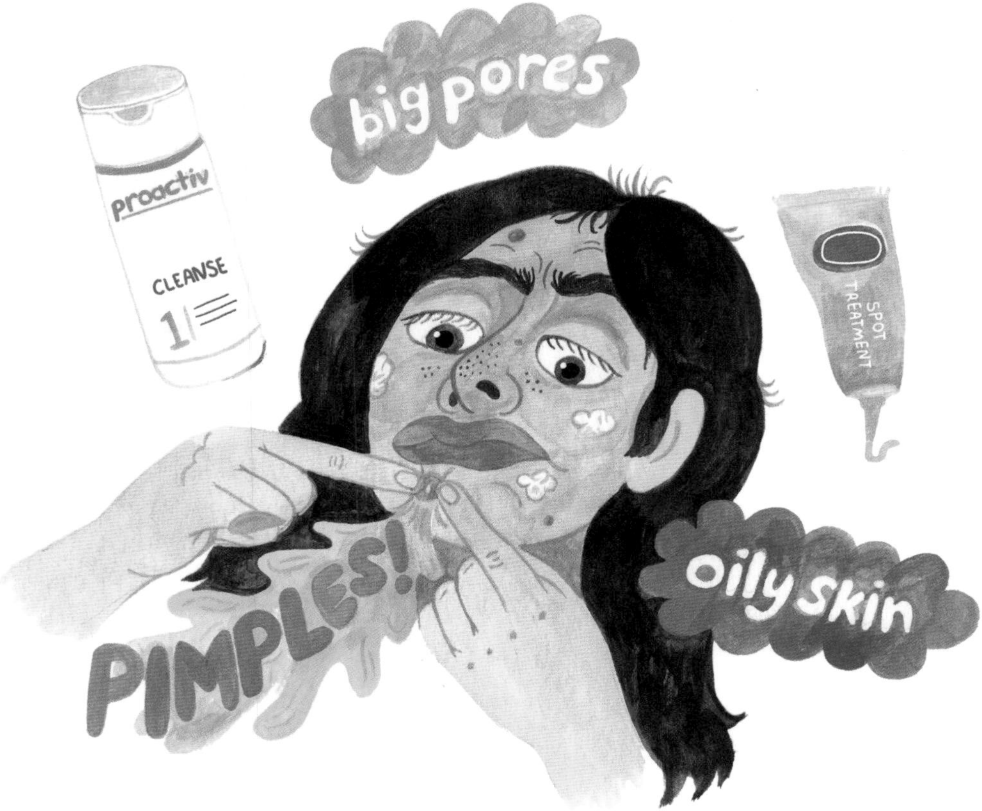
big pores
proactiv
CLEANSE
1
SPOT TREATMENT
PIMPLES!
oily skin

orthodontia

My cheeks felt even bigger with all that metal pushing up against my lips.

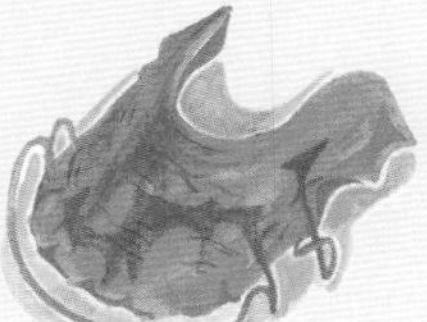

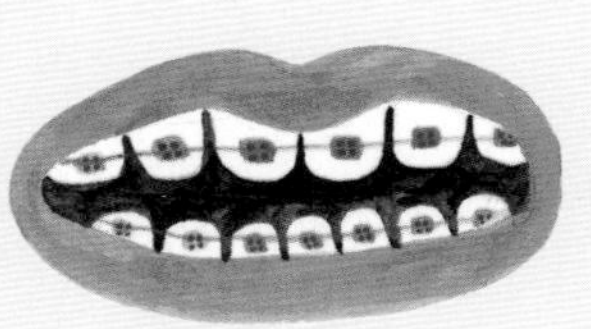

My retainer: the most vile object known to mankind. Soggy, old, smelly food tucked in every corner.

My orthodontist called braces "teeth jewelry"—because I'm a girl and of course the idea of jewelry will distract from the sharp metal squares glued to my teeth.

UGH, AND <u>SO</u> MUCH FACIAL HAIR

HEBREW FOR GRANDMA

My Savta Chava gave me a book of Frida Kahlo art for Hanukkah when I was ten, adding that she thought we looked alike. Now I would take that as a true compliment, but back then I was absolutely horrified by the comparison.

Facial hair was at the top of my list of things to change about myself, and I was determined to make my hairless dream a reality with the help of countless boxes of at-home waxing kits. Around once a month, I'd spend an evening ripping the hair off my face. This ritual always had to take place at night because I'd be mortified if anyone saw me covered in the red splotches this activity left on my face. As much as it was important for me to be hairless, it was necessary to give the impression that I was naturally this smooth, naturally this normal.

WAXING TO-DO LIST

POTENTIALLY ALL THIS (DARK) PEACH FUZZ TOO?

1. **EYEBROWS**

TWEEZE. IT'S WAY TOO EASY TO FUCK THIS UP WITH WAX.

USE A SLIVER OF A STRIP SO YOU DON'T TAKE OFF TOO MUCH LIKE LAST TIME!

✳ GENERAL NOTE: WAX AGAINST THE GRAIN.

2. **UPPER LIP**

QUICK, LIKE A BAND-AID.

✳ JUST ONE BEAD OF SWEAT WILL RUIN EVERTHING. MAKE SURE YOUR LIP IS TOTALLY DRY FIRST.

3. **SIDEBURNS**

I KNOW THIS IS A WILD IDEA, BUT JUST GO FOR IT.

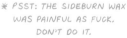

✳ PSST: THE SIDEBURN WAX WAS PAINFUL AS FUCK. DON'T DO IT.

if i could, i would

I spent many a school assembly looking at the backs of girls' necks with fascination and envy. How were their necks that hairless while mine was—as I felt at the time—simply beast-like?

the UPPER LIP LICK

Waxing became a part of my routine. Having even the slightest unibrow or peach fuzz was unacceptable. I closely monitored my upper lip hair situation by licking my upper lip every so often so I'd be sure to nip even the faintest of baby hairs in the bud.

bathroom lip wax

*BAR MITZVAH BOY MUSTACHE STATUS

One afternoon at work—on a day that I had a third date with a guy I was really starting to like—I realized I had forgotten to wax my upper lip. I had walked out of the house and been in public with full lip bangs! How badass!

Not being quite badass enough to take my mustache out on the date, however, I decided I would counter with what I thought to be a fairly equal act of rebellion (and a great story to tell The Yentas).

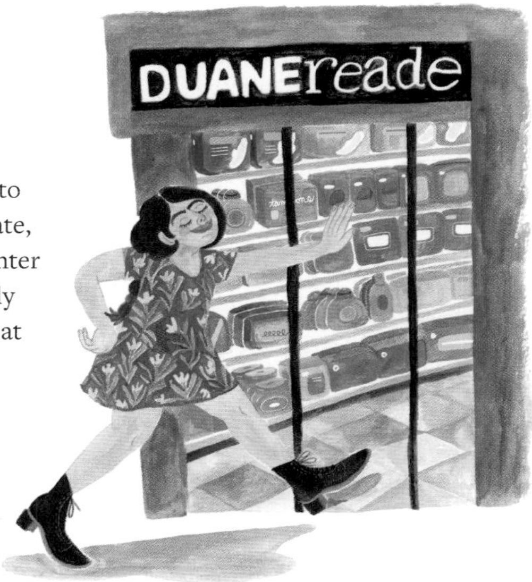
DUANEreade
I WILL FOREVER APPRECIATE HOW MANY DUANE READES THERE ARE IN NEW YORK CITY.

Instead of panicking and rushing home to take care of the matter in the privacy of my own bathroom, I picked up an at-home waxing kit (the strips that you can heat by rubbing them between your hands), and set up shop in one of the stalls at work.

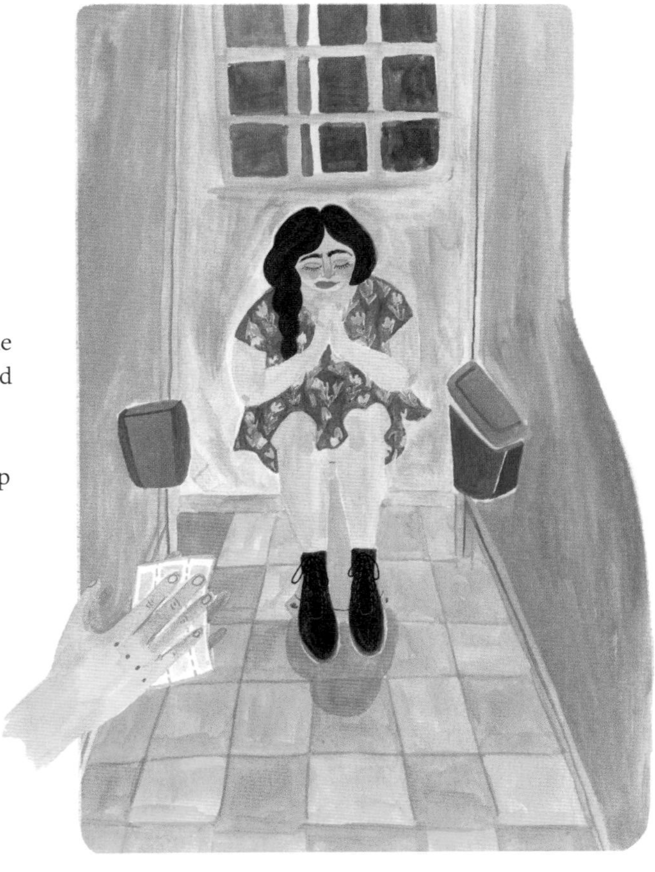

I gleefully texted The Yentas, bragging about how resourceful I had been and how shamelessly I intended to sport my raw and red upper lip for my coworkers to see.

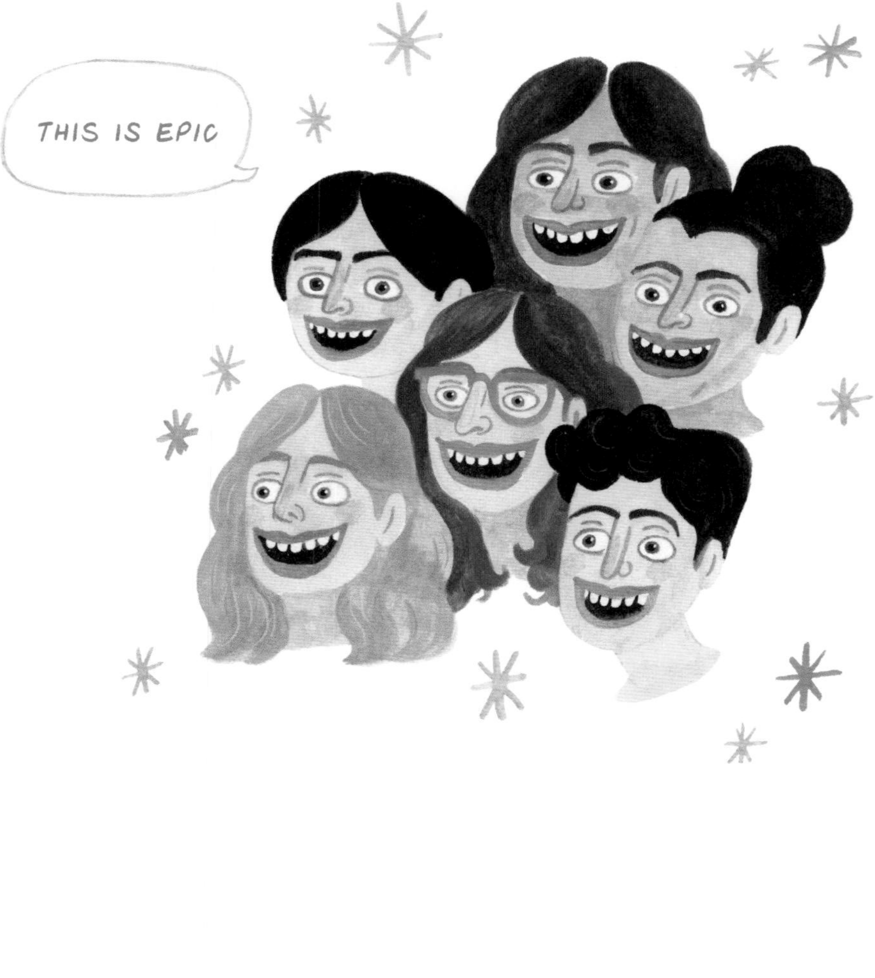
THIS IS EPIC

IMPERFECTIONS ARE FUN

As silly as this might sound, that semi public waxing was a big milestone for me. It was thrilling to experience my mustache as a fun, badass adventure rather than as a stressful effort to hide my flaws. In sharing that moment with The Yentas, I was able to break away from my inner world of critical pressure. Connecting with each other on some of the bizarre or "unsightly" things our bodies produce can be really fun.

FULLY FORMED
SEBUM IS A GIFT.

The Yentas have unanimously decided that extracting blackheads—your own or others—
is one of the greatest joys in life. It's really a blessing that they exist in the first place.

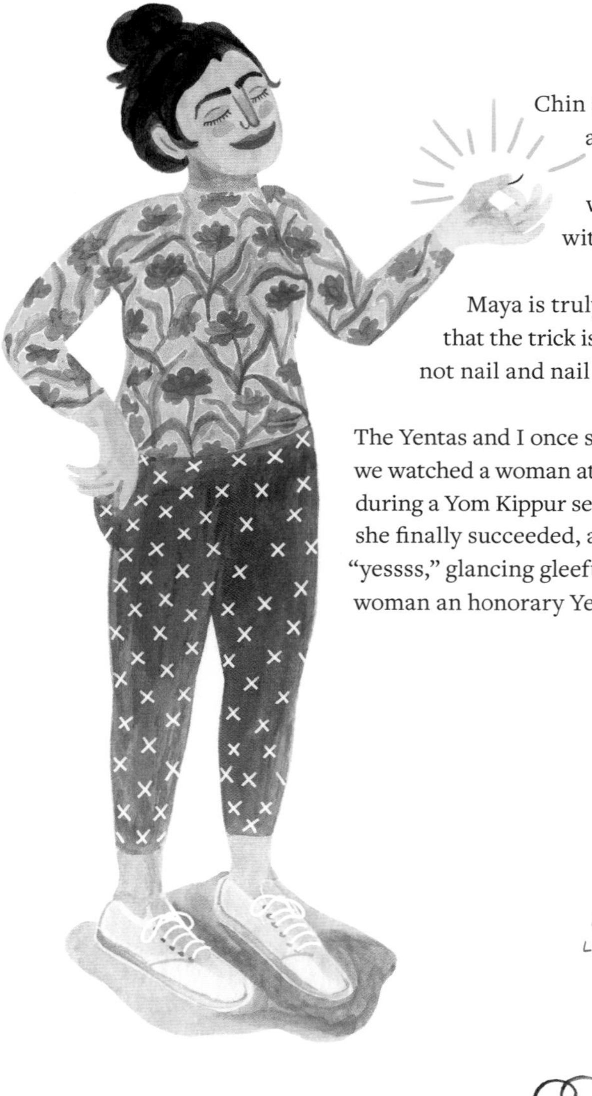

Chin and mole hair are so much thicker than all other hairs and they're so much fun to pluck. It's even more satisfying when you're able to pluck one out with just your fingers.

Maya is truly a human tweezer. She has explained that the trick is to trap the hair between skin and nail—not nail and nail as one might think.

The Yentas and I once sat on the edge of our seats in rapture as we watched a woman attempt a tweezer-less chin hair pluck during a Yom Kippur service. We had to hold our applause when she finally succeeded, and instead ecstatically whispered "yessss," glancing gleefully at one another and declaring the woman an honorary Yenta.

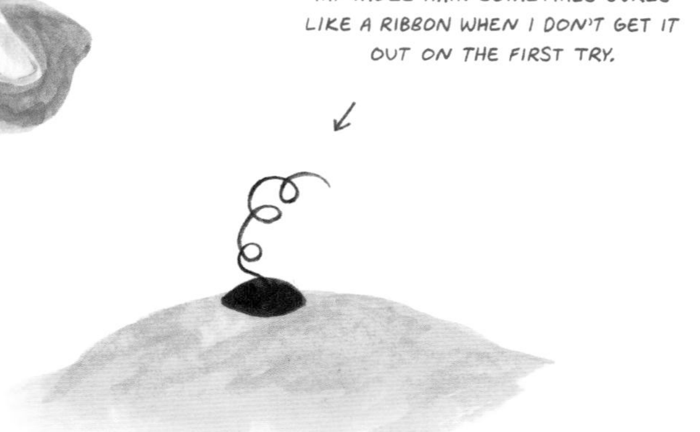
MY MOLE HAIR SOMETMES CURLS
LIKE A RIBBON WHEN I DON'T GET IT
OUT ON THE FIRST TRY.

an ode to MOLES

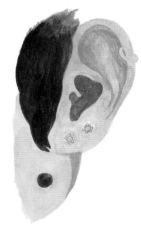

Growing up, the mole below my left ear was always something I kept covered and was embarrassed by. When I was younger, my Savta Illana told me to never get that mole removed. Savta Illana was an elegant, striking woman and had a wisdom about her that made me feel like I should listen to this piece of advice. She told me that she'd gotten one of her moles removed and regretted it. She told me my mole was a beauty mark, and made me special.

My sister Alex and I both have had fleeting (and sometimes not-so-fleeting) thoughts about getting rid of our moles. Now we are decidedly on board. Moles are iconic. Call us Robert De Niro!

this is my face

It sometimes looks smooth from far away, but it's not.

I used to pluck my eyebrows down to half their size,
but now I'm really loving how unruly and thick they are.

*FUN PARTY TRICK: I BRUSH 'EM UP
AGAINST THE GRAIN TO CREATE
THIS THEATRICAL LOOK:

the brow boa

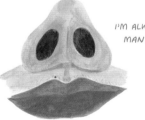

Gross earring smell. There's really
nothing like it, and I'm obsessed with it.

I'M ALWAYS SURPRISED BY HOW
MANY NOSE HAIRS I HAVE.

I have a lovely field of chin hair that
looks like a faint peach fuzz in some lights
and like a full-blown beard in others.

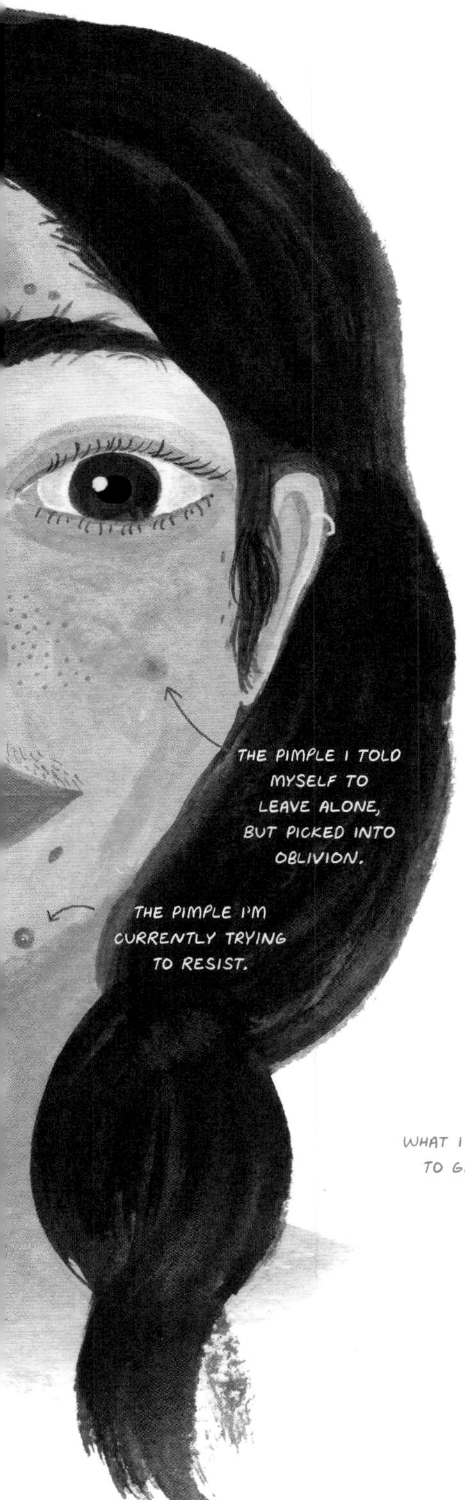
THE PIMPLE I TOLD MYSELF TO LEAVE ALONE, BUT PICKED INTO OBLIVION.
THE PIMPLE I'M CURRENTLY TRYING TO RESIST.

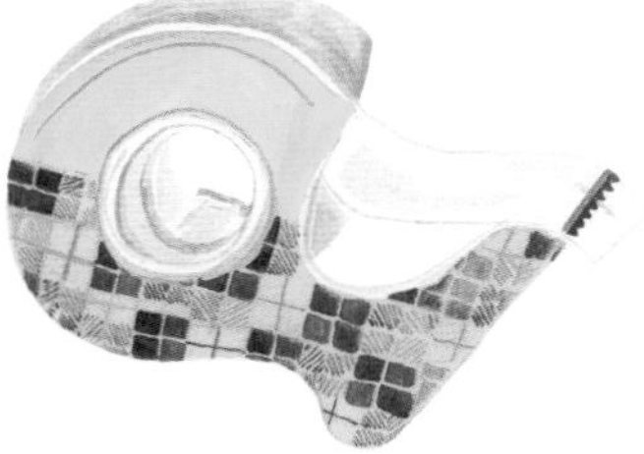

I once tried waxing my upper lip with double-sided Scotch tape. It didn't work. Lately I've been letting my upper lip hair run wild and taking it out on the town. Once in a while I catch someone making eye contact with my mustache and in my head I think, "Yes, I am aware, and yes, it is allowed."

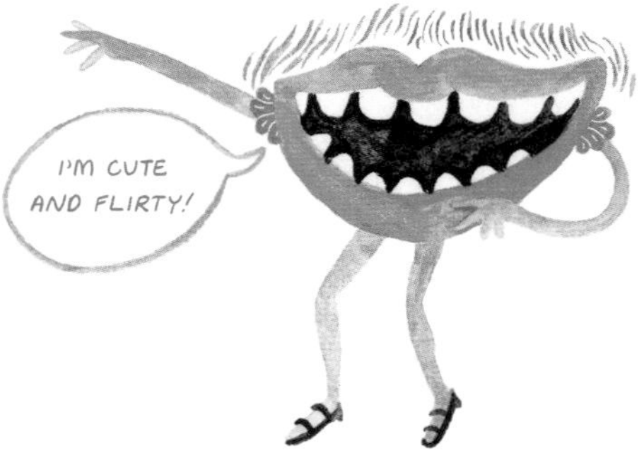
I'M CUTE AND FLIRTY!

Each time I successfully pop a pimple, I imagine that my other, trickier pimples are screaming, "Don't encourage her!!!"

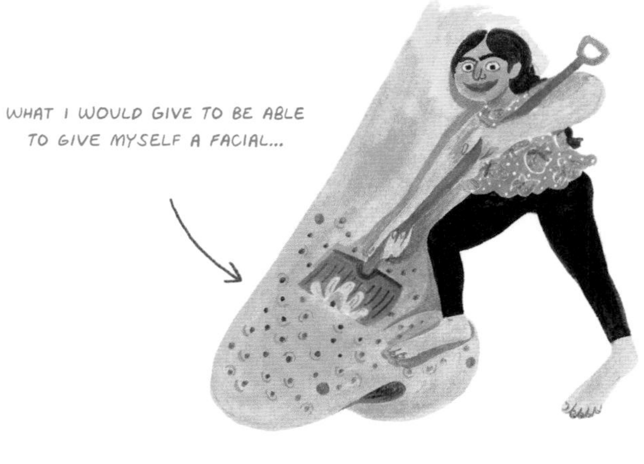
WHAT I WOULD GIVE TO BE ABLE TO GIVE MYSELF A FACIAL...

who's that girl?

OK...WE'RE STUNNING

These days, mirrors carry less baggage and seeing myself is a lot less stressful. Looking at my own reflection used to be an exercise in comparing myself to others and considering how others might see me. Now I know I look exactly how I should: I look like me!

call me frida

My unibrow and mini mustache are actually kind of cute.

HAIR

IF NOT YET CLEAR, I HAVE HAIR EVERYWHERE. THIS SECTION DEALS WITH THE HAIR ATOP MY HEAD SPECIFICALLY.

I was born on March 21, 1991, at 8 pounds, 6 ounces, and with a full head of hair.

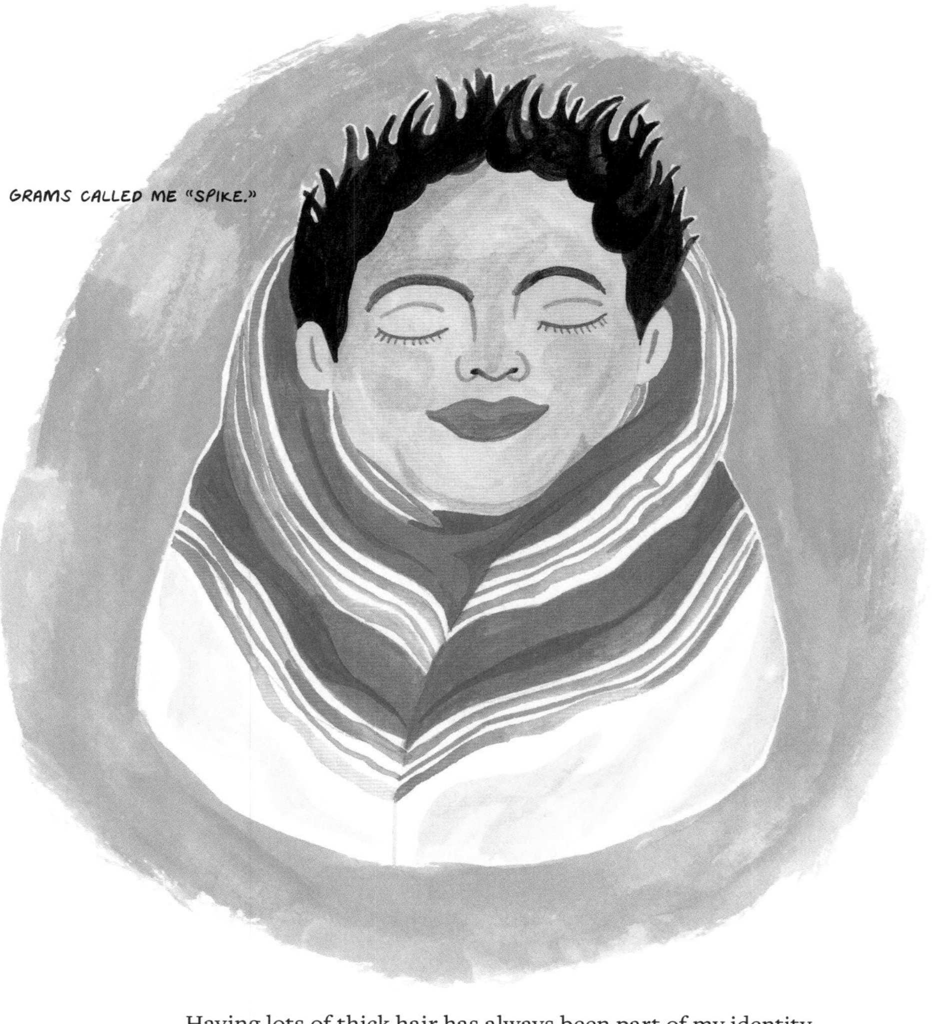
GRAMS CALLED ME "SPIKE."

Having lots of thick hair has always been part of my identity.
Not a good or bad thing, just a fact.

As a little kid, my hair was the perfect laboratory for experimentation.
It was exciting to see all the different shapes it could take.

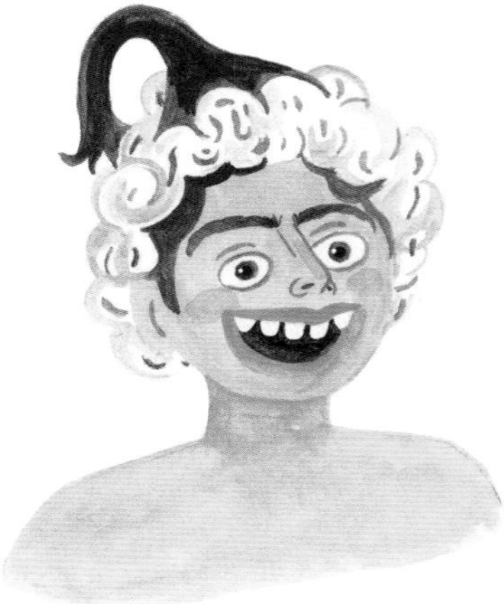

A BATHTIME FAVORITE. MY SISTER ELISHA AND I WOULD OFTEN PRETEND WE WERE WITCHES, CONCOCTING POTIONS WITH AS MANY DIFFERENT COMBINATIONS OF SHAMPOOS AND SOAPS AS WE COULD FIND. THE SUDSY MIXTURES WERE PERFECT FOR CONSTRUCTING WILD UPDOS.

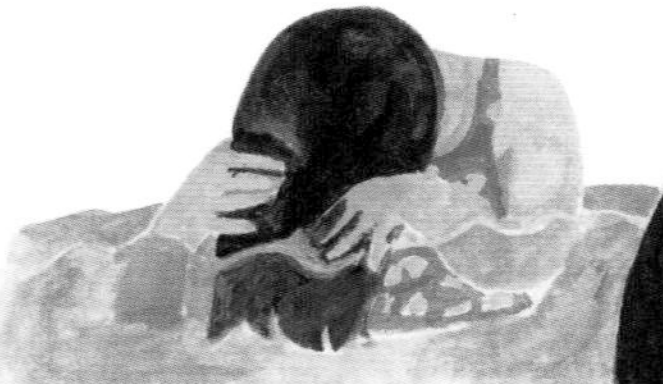

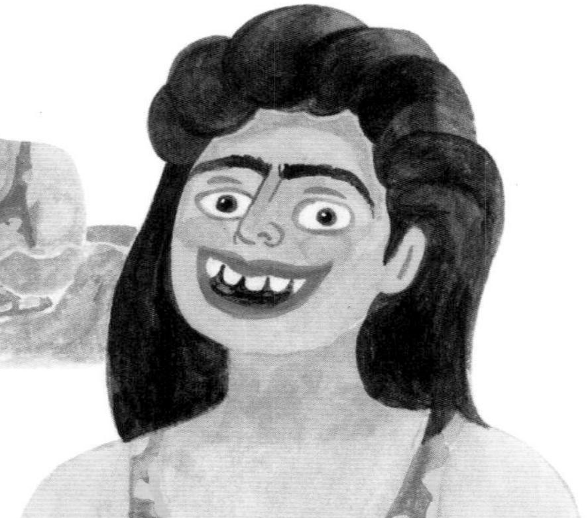

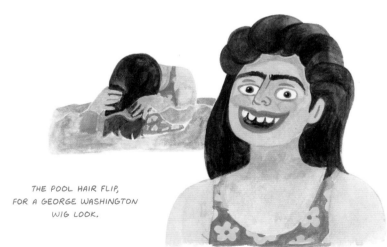

THE POOL HAIR FLIP, FOR A GEORGE WASHINGTON WIG LOOK.

After closely observing my hairdresser's work at the age of eight, I felt qualified to trim hair myself. I was eager to share my newfound talent with dolls and sisters alike. One afternoon, I found a pair of scissors that were for some reason in the back of our family car. Elisha's curls were too tempting to resist. My deed went undetected for almost an entire day. When my mom discovered that a not-so-insignificant chunk of hair was missing from Elisha's head, she assumed that Elisha was the one who had given herself a (in my opinion) pretty edgy makeover. I humbly let my work go uncredited and only confessed to the now infamous backseat haircut a few years ago.

HAIR accessories

WHEN I WAS YOUNG, MY HAIR WAS JUST A VEHICLE FOR SPARKLES AND COLOR.

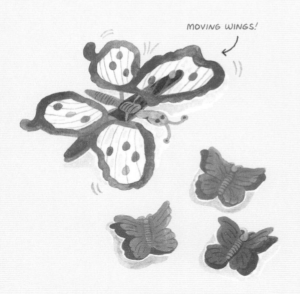

Couldn't get enough of these. So many sizes, shapes, colors, and patterns!

MOVING WINGS!

Butterfly clips: the stars of the show. Hands down.

The commercials for Hairagami blew my mind. I watched in awe as models twisted their hair in formations I never imagined possible.

I WAS SPECIFICALLY INTERESTED IN THIS SHAPE: THE SAME AS MY FAVORITE ITALIAN COOKIE.

VERY FUN, BUT ALSO GUARANTEED TO GET DEEPLY TANGLED IN YOUR HAIR

I LOVED TO GET A GLIMPSE INTO A WORLD WHERE I WAS A REDHEAD OR A BLONDE (OR BOTH AT THE SAME TIME!).

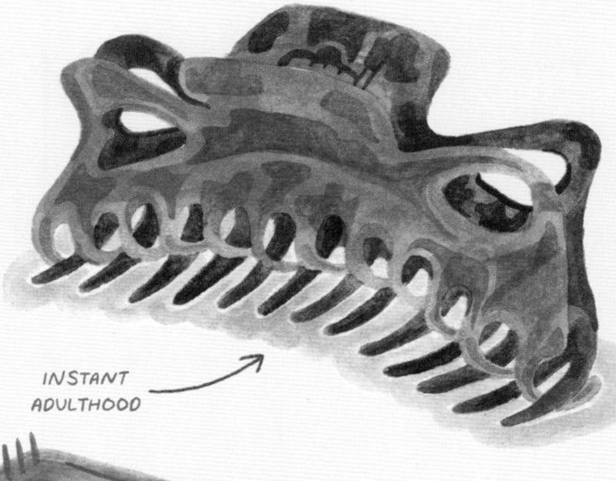

INSTANT ADULTHOOD

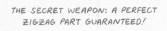

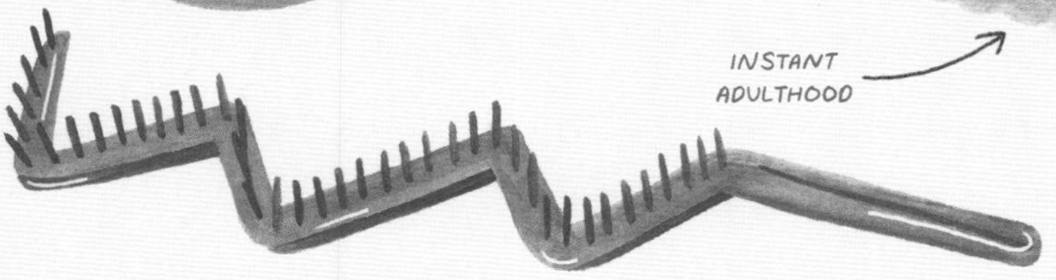

THE SECRET WEAPON: A PERFECT ZIGZAG PART GUARANTEED!

EXPECTATION

I so looked forward to blossoming into a cool teenager—when I would magically have an edgy, sleek look (in my mind, like Debbie from *The Wild Thornberrys*).

REALITY

I had a theory that I could work my way to a more polished head of hair simply by finding and plucking out each frizzy strand. Very practical.

✳ COULD NOT CHEW GUM BECAUSE OF THE BRACES.

The most popular girl in my grade always had the smoothest ponytails, and I tried desperately to recreate her bumpless updo with layers of bobby pins and clips.

Girls in my sixth grade class started using Sun In to make their hair lighter. Blonde was a decidedly cooler color hair. I heard that lemon juice could essentially do the same thing, so I started hoarding wedges in hopes that the juice would accent my very dark hair with gorgeous highlights. Shocker: this absolutely did not work.

My braided hair looked like a loaf of challah. I always admired how daintily other girls' braids would hang across their shoulders or down their back.

THE ERA OF
STRAIGHT HAIR

By seventh grade, it became clear that I would never tackle the frizz monster on my own, and I needed help. Not wanting to ever risk a bad hair day, I begged my mom endlessly for a hair straightener, and she eventually allowed me to get one in eighth grade. From that point on, I became a straight-hair fiend.

I eventually switched over to a blow-dryer, hoping that more volume would distract from my chubby cheeks. I went on to perfect the art of the blowout and it became a nonnegotiable (and incredibly time-consuming) part of my daily routine.

MY EARS DID NOT
SEE THE LIGHT OF DAY
FROM HIGH SCHOOL
THROUGH COLLEGE.

In high school, I woke up as early as five in the morning to make sure I could have freshly washed and dried hair. A touch of grease would make me feel simply unpresentable. To hide the roundness of my cheeks, I stopped wearing my hair in ponytails or tucking my hair behind my ears. I figured that the more hair was in and around my face, the slimmer it would seem.

I thought this was a subtle face-slimming method, but a boy in my high school class had somehow seen through it all and asked if I wore my hair down so far in front of my cheeks to hide my circle of a face.

MORTIFYING

LICE

Lice. I've had the true honor of having this lovely infestation about six times in my life. Yes, six. Six happens to be my lucky number, so I consider my numerous run-ins with these pests a good omen.

My grown-up understanding of lice is that they prefer a good, squeaky-clean scalp. This piece of intel of course never circulated through any of my classrooms. An early dismissal after a lice check meant two things: a) you had lice and b) you were vile.

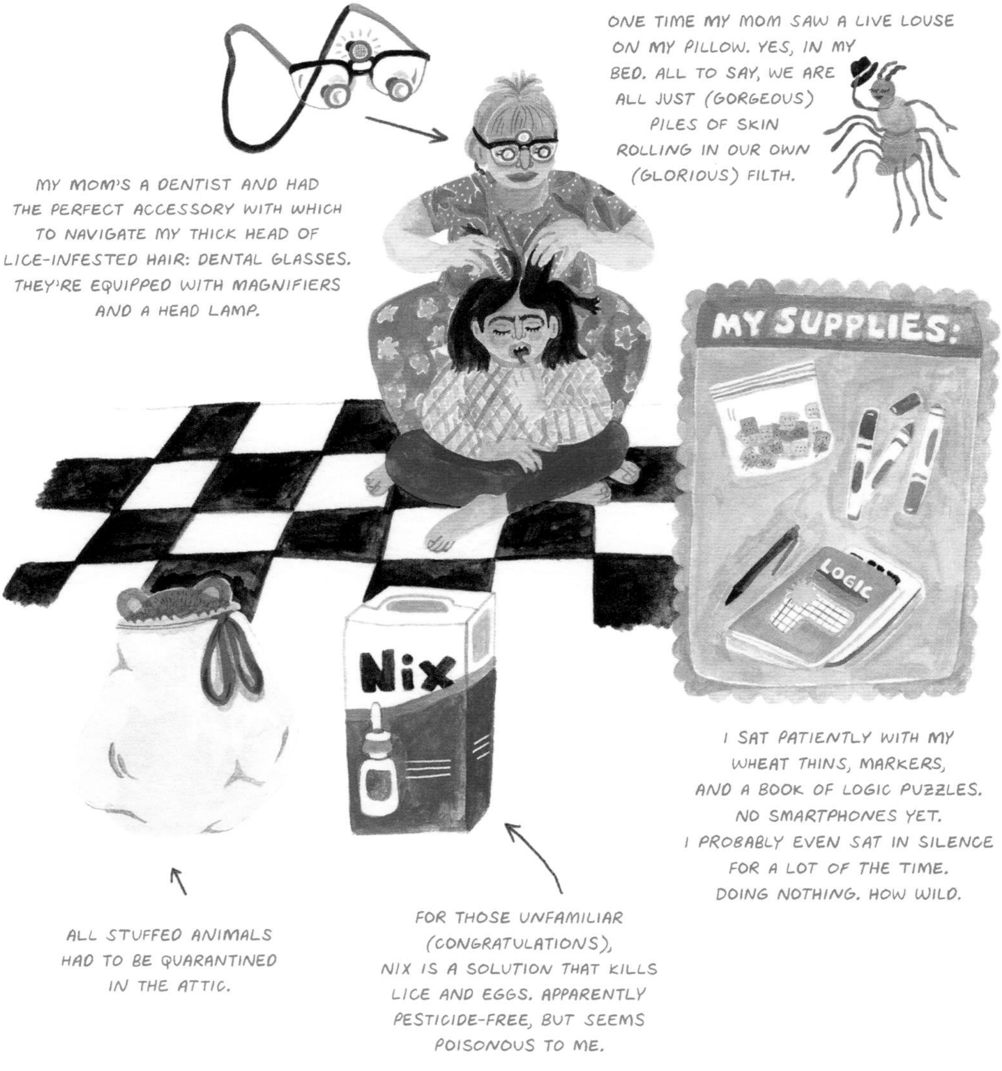
ONE TIME MY MOM SAW A LIVE LOUSE ON MY PILLOW. YES, IN MY BED. ALL TO SAY, WE ARE ALL JUST (GORGEOUS) PILES OF SKIN ROLLING IN OUR OWN (GLORIOUS) FILTH.
MY MOM'S A DENTIST AND HAD THE PERFECT ACCESSORY WITH WHICH TO NAVIGATE MY THICK HEAD OF LICE-INFESTED HAIR: DENTAL GLASSES. THEY'RE EQUIPPED WITH MAGNIFIERS AND A HEAD LAMP.
MY SUPPLIES:
LOGIC
Nix
I SAT PATIENTLY WITH MY WHEAT THINS, MARKERS, AND A BOOK OF LOGIC PUZZLES. NO SMARTPHONES YET. I PROBABLY EVEN SAT IN SILENCE FOR A LOT OF THE TIME. DOING NOTHING. HOW WILD.
ALL STUFFED ANIMALS HAD TO BE QUARANTINED IN THE ATTIC.
FOR THOSE UNFAMILIAR (CONGRATULATIONS), NIX IS A SOLUTION THAT KILLS LICE AND EGGS. APPARENTLY PESTICIDE-FREE, BUT SEEMS POISONOUS TO ME.

I had my last (to date) run-in with lice at sixteen when I spent three months studying abroad in Israel—a tradition for juniors at my Jewish high school. That experience with lice was different than before because I had it with my two roommates.

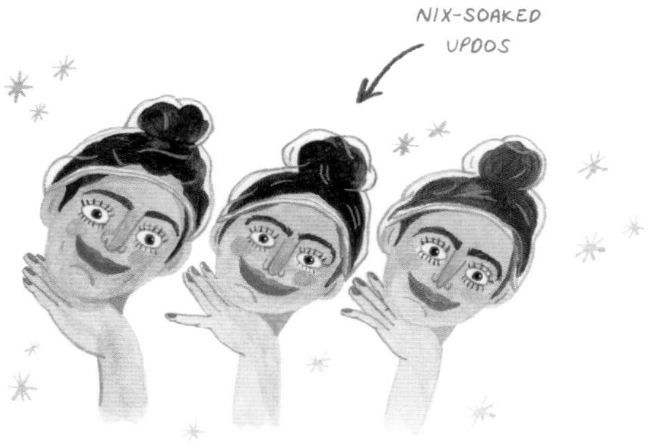
NIX-SOAKED UPDOS

There was no school nurse conducting lice checks, and no exiles to our respective homes. Instead, when we felt that all-too-familiar, terrible itch, the three of us supported each other as our suspicions were confirmed.

Together, we combed through the aisles of the corner drugstore to gather supplies, trekked back home sharing past lice stories, and converted our bedroom into a nitpicking den.

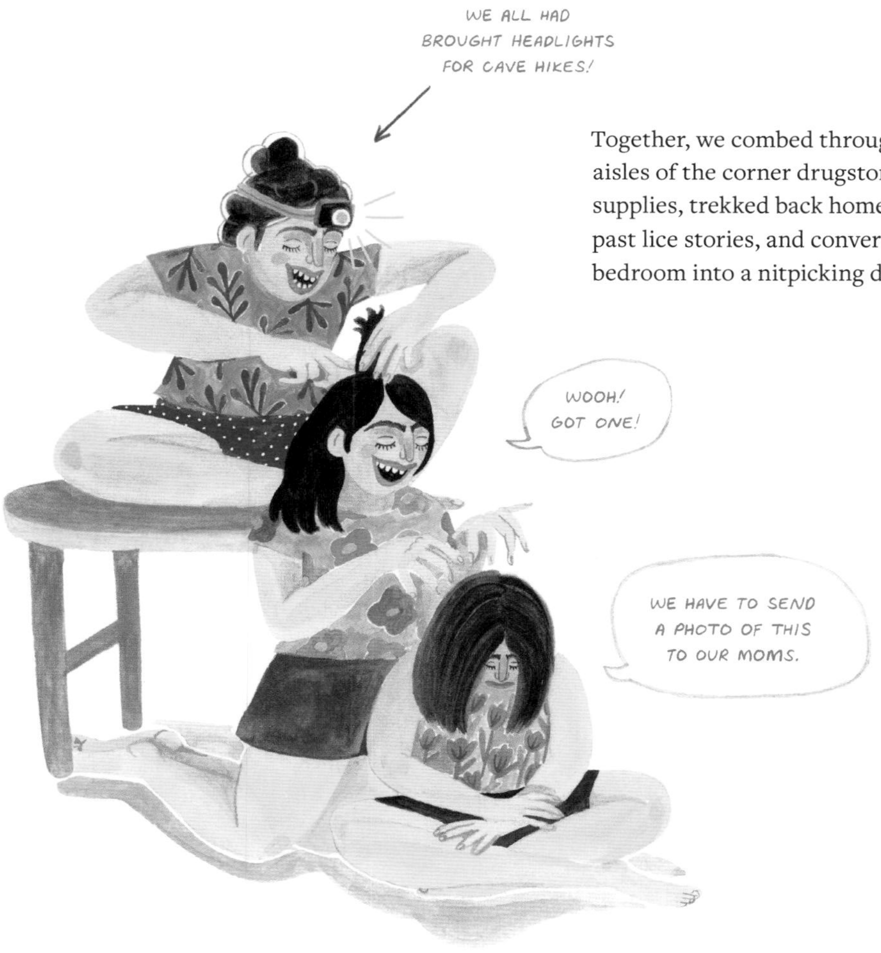
WE ALL HAD BROUGHT HEADLIGHTS FOR CAVE HIKES!
WOOH! GOT ONE!
WE HAVE TO SEND A PHOTO OF THIS TO OUR MOMS.

HAIRSTYLES
through the years

1992–1994

Bowl Cut. A (small) part of me is curious to know if I can still pull off this look. I was attached to my pacifier until age six.

1995

Preschool updo.

1999

I amassed quite a large collection of butterfly clips.

1997

My mom insisted on giving me a trim. It didn't go great. Refusing to let her try and "even it out," I wore a hair clip on one side to make the shorter half look intentional.

1998

I didn't watch *Friends* at the time, but "The Rachel" somehow permeated my nine-year-old world. One day on the bus ride home a friend recommended I get angles and layers, so I did.

2000

I felt my best in pigtails (of course inspired by Baby Spice).

2000

Mixing things up and channeling Scary Spice.

2000

To create a crimped effect, I slept with my whole head in small braids. One night, I got sick and threw up all over my DIY hack. I had to undo each braid, meticulously washing chunks of vomit from each and every crevice.

2002

A major sequin headband trend.

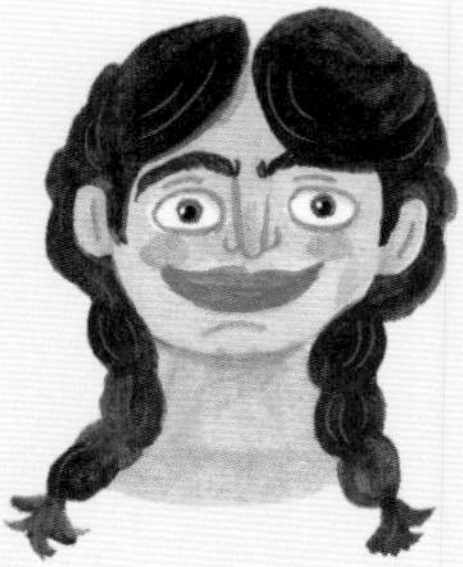

2003

French braids at camp. We had a counselor who would braid each girl's hair every night. We formed a line at her bed.

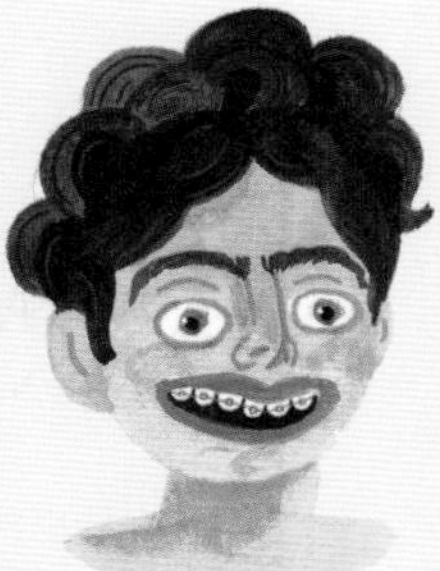

2003

Bat Mitzvah updo. The perfect complement to a mouth full of braces!

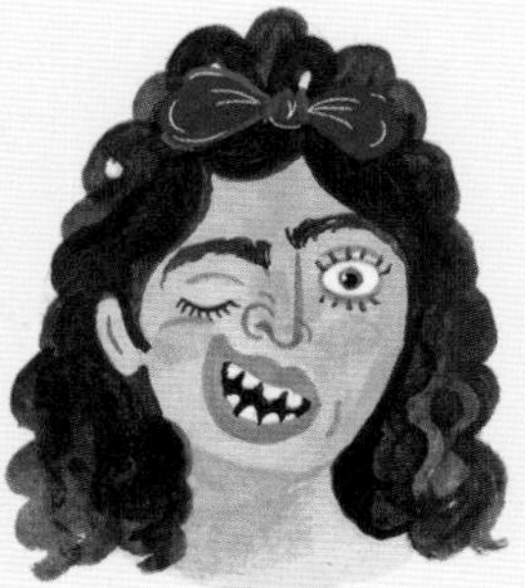

2004

I was a competitive cheerleader. Shocking even to myself. At the time, I felt like Peyton from *One Tree Hill*: an emotionally intelligent cheerleader who liked to draw.

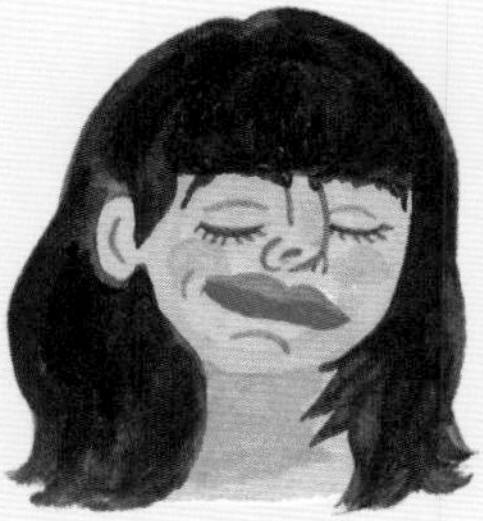

2004

I got bangs again and regretted it immediately. I hated how thick they were.

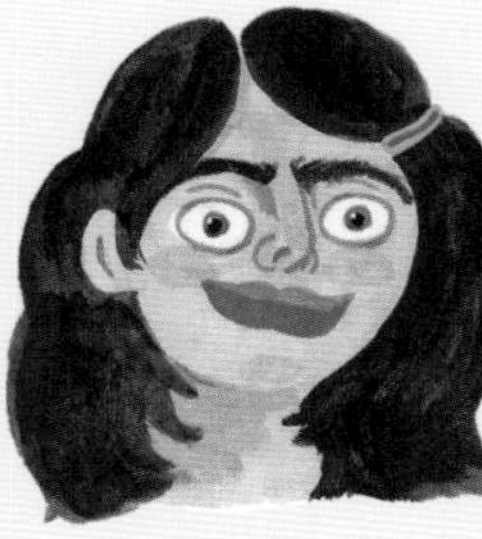

A clip to hide said catastrophic bangs as I grew them out.

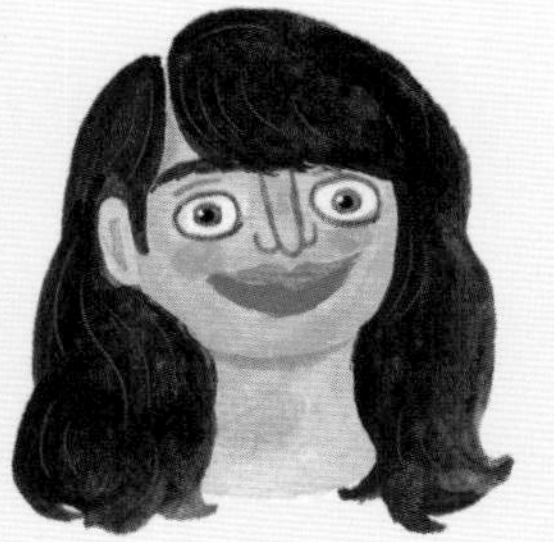

2006

I took one final pass at bangs, but this time sideswept.

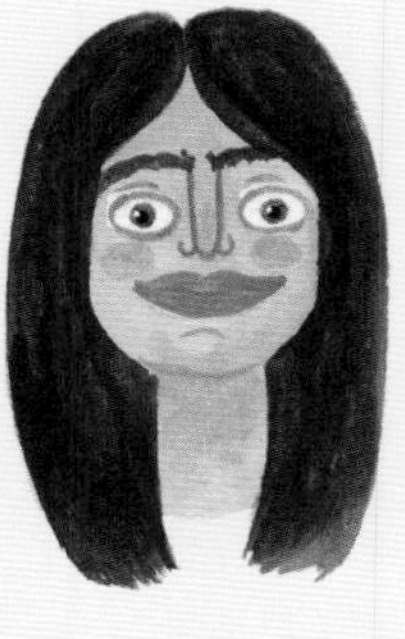

SPRING 2006–2013

I devoted hours of my day to achieving this pin-straight look. I loved picking at my burnt split ends.

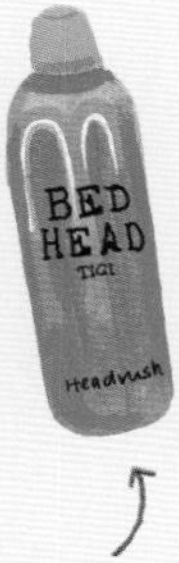
BED HEAD
Headrush

THIS HEAT TOOL SPRAY IS THE MOST NOSTALGIC SMELL IN MY LIFE. INSTANT TEEN SADNESS AND ANGST.

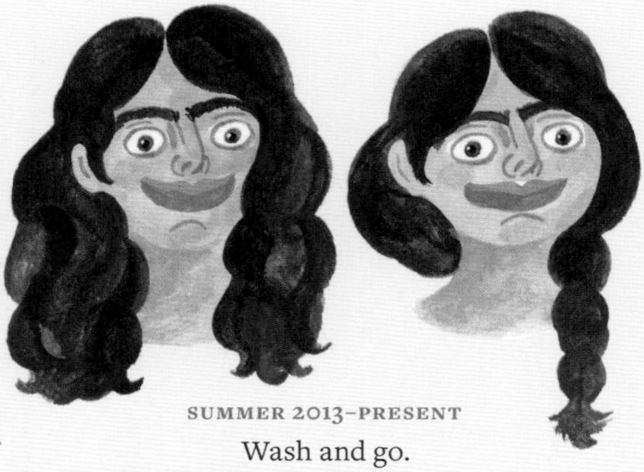

SUMMER 2013–PRESENT

Wash and go. A braid fixes any bad hair day.

At first, my embrace of my natural hair was somewhat accidental. I moved to New York City the summer after college in August (aka the inner ring of humidity hell) and I didn't have air conditioning in my room. I instead opted for a "strong fan" and sweat through my sheets each night. Using a blow-dryer in that space would have simply been psychotic. Any additional heat would quickly qualify my bedroom as steamroom adjacent, and my agressive neck and scalp and face sweat would reverse any trace of a blowout I was able to achieve in that hostile environment anyway.

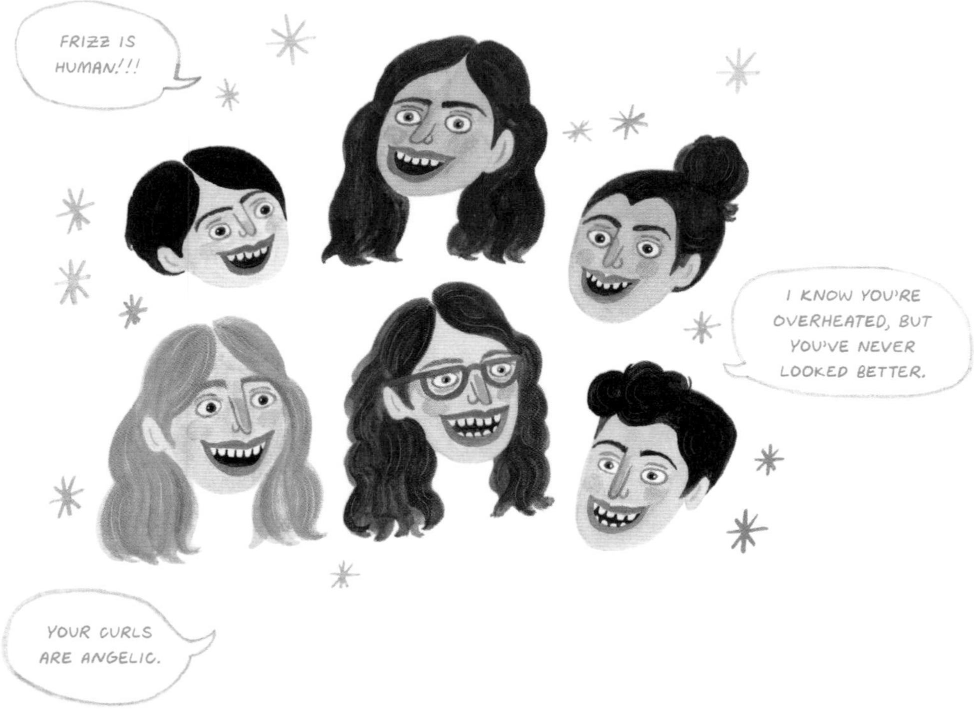
FRIZZ IS HUMAN!!!
I KNOW YOU'RE OVERHEATED, BUT YOU'VE NEVER LOOKED BETTER.
YOUR CURLS ARE ANGELIC.

And so began the era of natural hair.

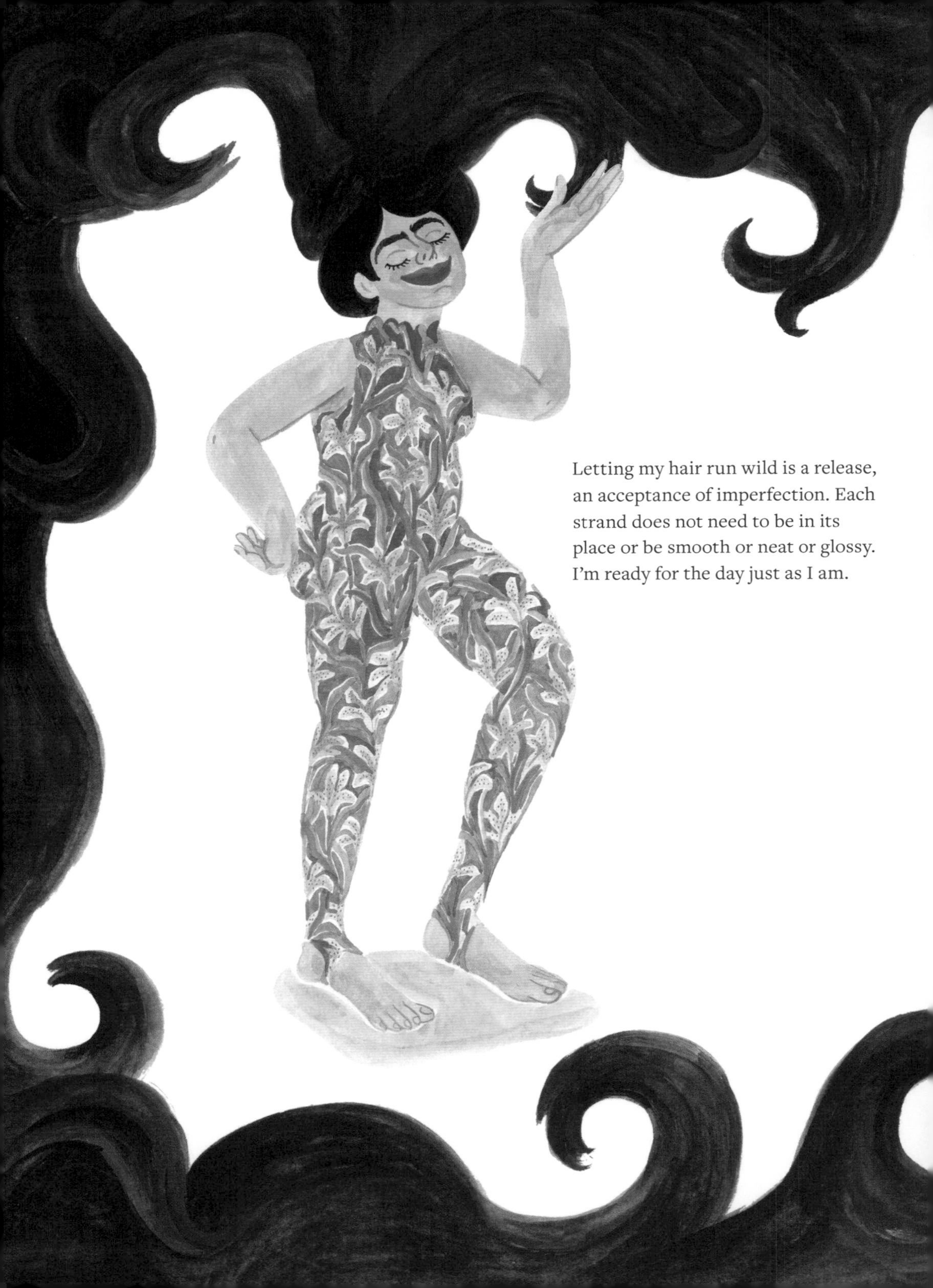

Letting my hair run wild is a release, an acceptance of imperfection. Each strand does not need to be in its place or be smooth or neat or glossy. I'm ready for the day just as I am.

When I stopped
straightening my
hair it felt like
I was coming
home to myself,
the real Ariella.

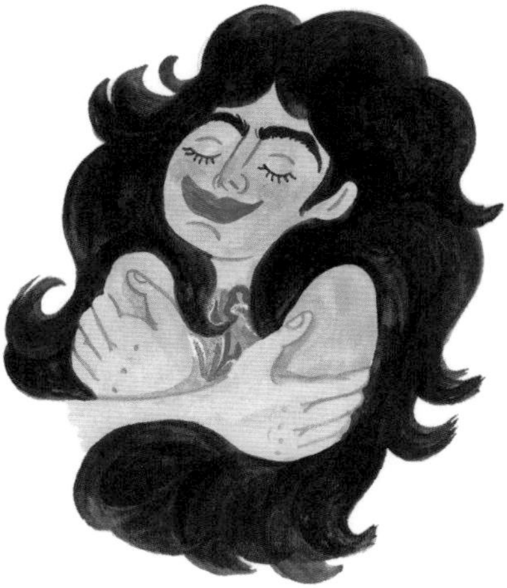

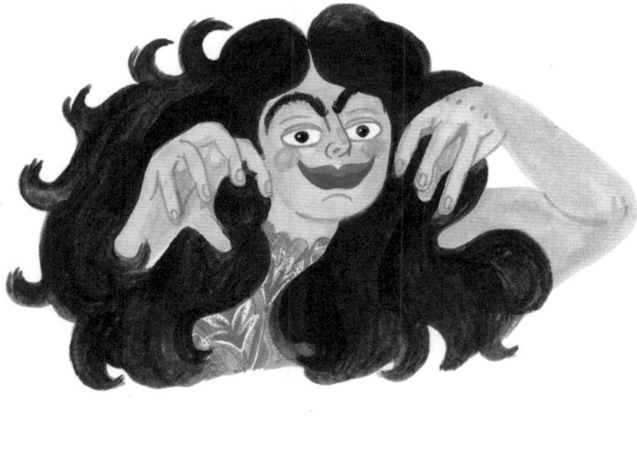

Blow-drying my hair was
a way to feel in control and
"normal." The unexpected
curls and waves and frizz
that once made me feel
insecure and ugly now
feel like an extension of
my personality. They're
unique and feisty.

BOOBS

These are my boobs. Soulful and knowing.

I've never named them (and do not wish to)
but they definitely have personality.

My boobs started making themselves known when I was in fourth grade. I know the exact year because there is clear photographic evidence.

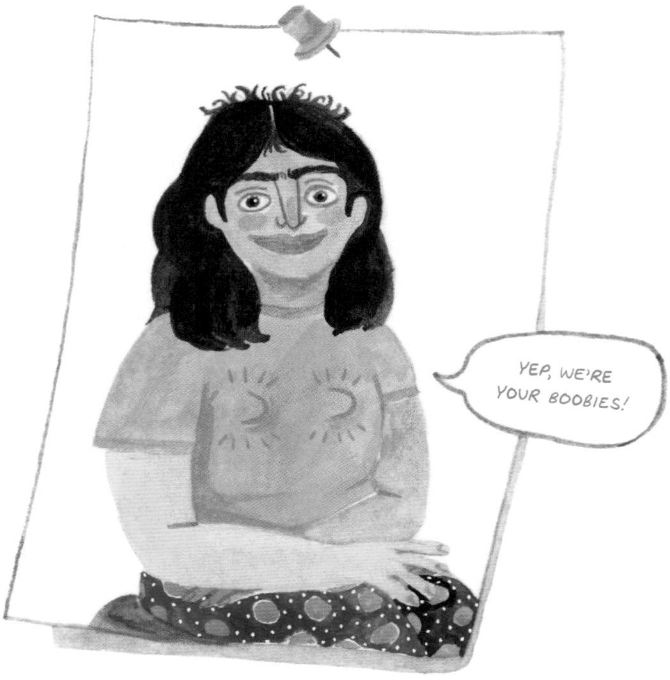
YEP, WE'RE YOUR BOOBIES!

CLASS PICTURE DAY WAS PEAK HUMILIATION. I HAVE A RUNNING THEORY THAT WE'RE SUBJECTED TO IT YOUNG SO WE BUILD A THICK SKIN.

Fourth grade was the year of the anthill boobies. A special window of time when boobs don't quite warrant the support of a bra, but are definitely a thing—poking their heads out to alert everyone that some changes are on the horizon.

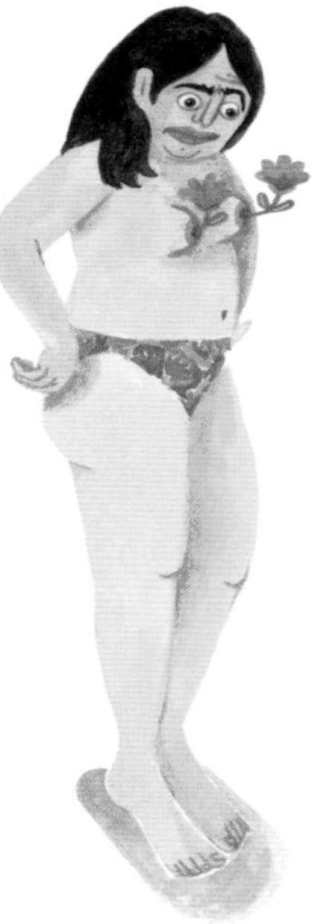

At first, my growing boobs didn't really feel like part of me. They were these strange and swollen globs of fat that were tender and sore. If I wanted to, I was able to give them a squeeze and pinch the bud of my boobs between my fingers. The origin point. I actually think "bulb" is the more appropriate term: a round, bulbous thing taking root. Feeling the bulbs really freaked me out. If I dig around enough, I can still feel them. They still freak me out.

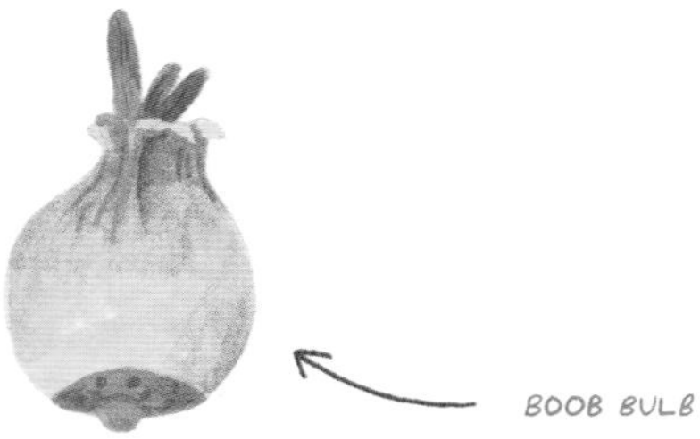
BOOB BULB

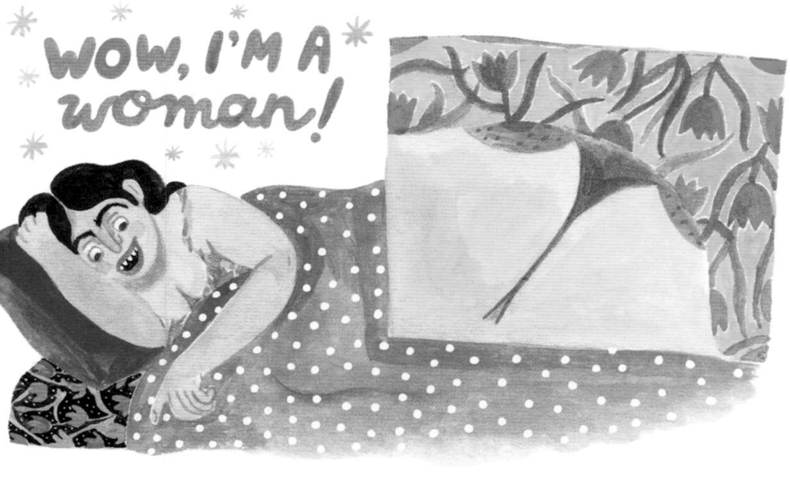
WOW, I'M A woman!

When I laid on my side in bed at night, I could look down at my squished chest and get a sneak peek at what I'd look like with cleavage. It was both a thrilling and shocking glimpse into my life as an adult. Cleavage was mature.

BRA SHOPPING

That thrilling sense of womanhood didn't carry over to when my boobs eventually grew in and it was—as I was told—time to get a bra. A real one with cups and underwire, the works!

My mom and I blocked off an afternoon to go hunting for the perfect bra at the outlet stores. The task was daunting and nearly impossible.

Bra shopping is not fun. You inevitably end up tangled in straps and sweating, all while a stranger is coming straight at your face with measuring tape. I was a bit shocked to learn how un-fucking-comfortable bras are.

OK, SO YOU'RE TELLING ME EVERYONE IS WEARING ONE OF THESE? AND IS HAPPY ABOUT IT? YOU'VE GOT TO BE KIDDING.

THE BRA MONSTER: ATTACKS WHEN MORE THAN THREE BRAS ARE IN THE DRESSING ROOM AT ONE TIME.

I HATE BRAS

Sure, they come in some fun colors and lace is nice sometimes, I guess, but I hated bras from the get-go. I wore them because it's what I—as a woman—was "supposed to do." Bras were going to make me more of a woman.

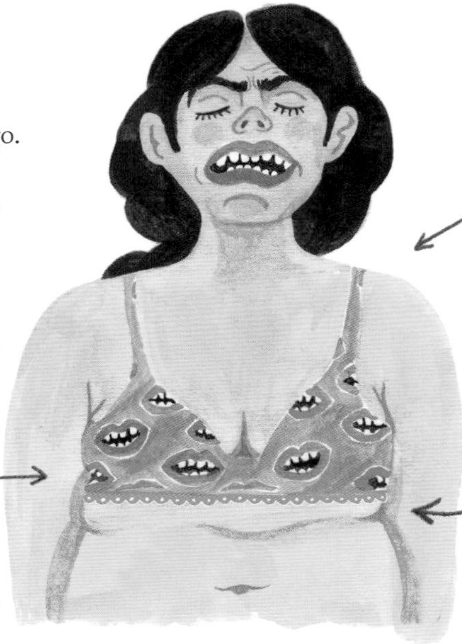
I ALWAYS WORE MY STRAPS AS LOOSE AS POSSIBLE.
THE TWO-PRONGED FAT BUBBLE: THE UNDERWIRE SQUISHES INTO MY SIDE AND DIVIDES MY FAT INTO TWO DISTINCT SECTIONS. ONE SITS ABOVE THE BRA LINE, AND ONE SITS BELOW.
IN HIGH SCHOOL, MY CUP SIZE FELT LIKE A SIGNIFICANT PART OF MY IDENTITY.

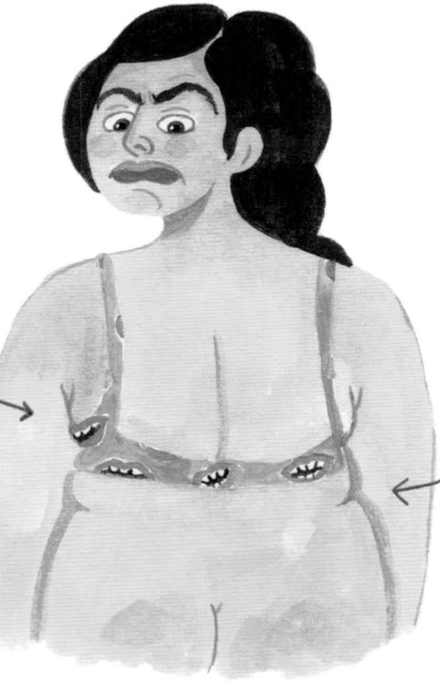
TO KEEP MY FAT IN ONE PIECE, I'D OFTEN PULL MY BRA DOWN UNTIL THE UNDERWIRE SAT HAPPILY BELOW THAT FIRST TUMMY ROLL. AND WHEN I WAS SITTING, I'D GO ROGUE AND JUST PULL MY BRA DOWN UNTIL ITS BOTTOM BAND OVERLAPPED THE WAISTBAND OF MY PANTS. I CANNOT WAIT FOR THE FUTURE WHEN WE ALL WEAR SEAMLESS BODY SUITS.
AT THE RISK OF COMING OFF A TOUCH DRAMATIC: PEOPLE WHO WEAR THEIR BRAS ON THE TIGHTEST NOTCH ARE SOCIOPATHS.
THE.BACK.SQUEEZING. JUST THINKING ABOUT IT MAKES ME IRRITABLE.

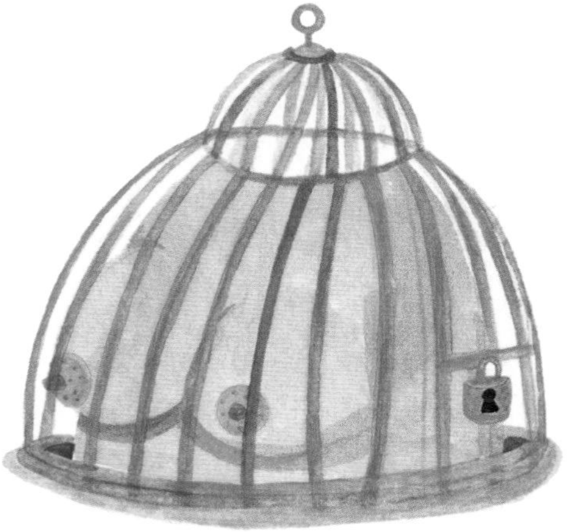

Even when I thought I had found a semi-tolerable bra, the moment I put it on at home and prepared to wear it in real life, it turned on me. It made me feel restricted and trapped. Certain sitting positions were uncomfortable because the wires would dig into my stomach.

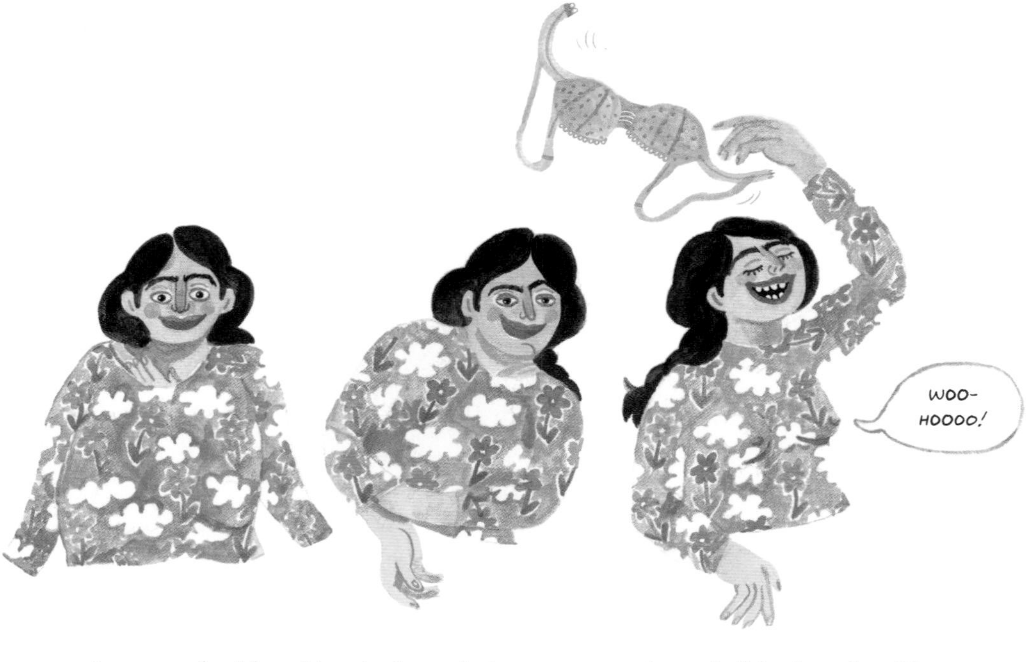
WOO-
HOOOO!

I grew to cherish and longingly await the moment at the end of the day when I'd, with a great big exhale, release my bra clasp and set my boobs free.

THE WIERDEST PLACES I'VE FOUND MY BRA

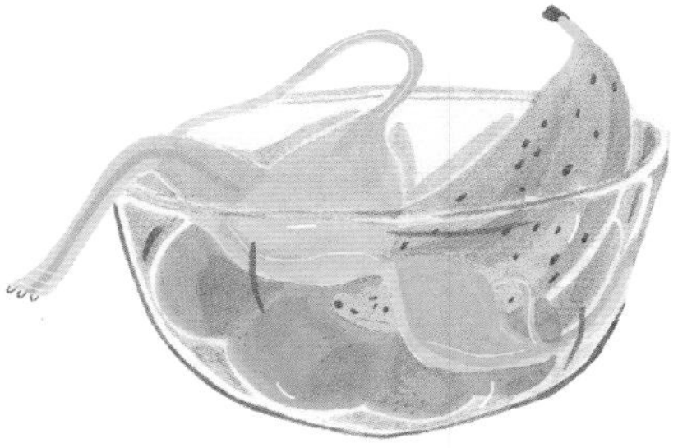

fruit bowl

In high school, I was so eager to get rid of my bra I rarely made it upstairs to my room to do so. I needed a snack the minute I got home, so the bra always came off somewhere between the front door and the fridge.

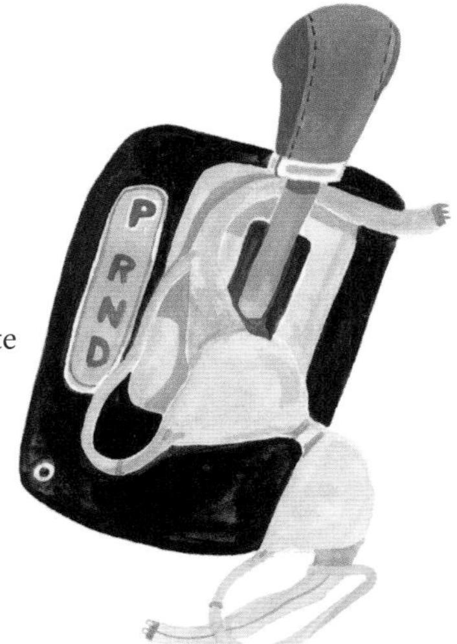
P
R
N
D

gear shift

When I started driving to school at seventeen, my bra hardly even made it in to the house. I had a forty-five-minute commute home each day, and my car was a relaxation zone. To prep for the drive, I'd find the perfect song on the radio and let my boobs roam free.

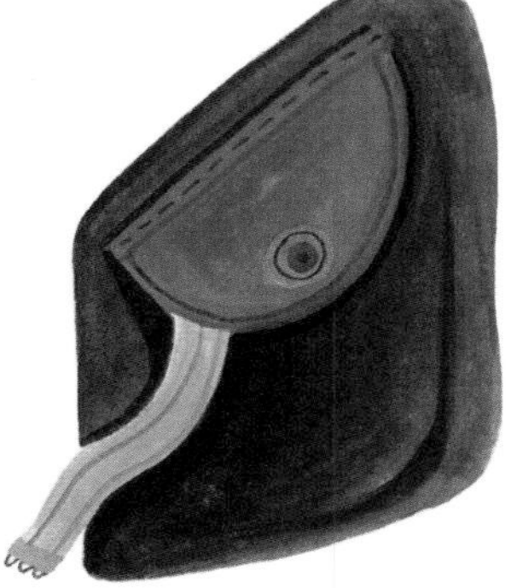

coat pocket

I was the rare teen taking my bra off at the movie theater not for makeout purposes, but for comfort. I'd stow my discarded bra in my coat pocket and inevitably forget it was in there until it revealed itself—usually at inopportune moments, like at the cash register in the grocery store.

TIMES I'VE ACCIDENTALLY FLASHED my BOOBS

As much as I hated keeping my boobs caged in, I was embarrassed when one or both of them got loose in public . . .

SWIM CLASS

At fourteen, I was finally forced to do a real standing dive off the dock at camp. I'd been putting off this moment for as long as possible, opting for knee dives instead. The day of the dive came as a surprise, and I hadn't come to swim class prepared. I was wearing a cute tube top tankini. Upon entering the water, I knew something had gone terribly wrong. Water rushed up my nose (note: dirty, green lake water laced with small, moldy lake creatures who are probably still alive and thriving in my nasal canals) and my boobs felt good. Too good. My top had slid down my torso and I was giving the notorious leeches an afternoon show. I fortunately caught the spill early enough and was able to pull the suit up as I frantically swam to the surface to breathe and relieve my stinging, flooded nose.

A NOTE ON TANKINIS:

I always wore tankinis because I felt a full suit was too prudish and screamed, "I'm hiding my tummy rolls in here." The tankini was still a two-piece, and therefore cool and for skinny girls. Only now as I write this do I understand the true charm of the tankini: full coverage without the nightmare of fully undressing in a public bathroom, inviting poop-germ air into every pore and crevice of your body. Or worse: the tricky side pull that inevitably ends in urine-soaked hands and/or inner thighs.

BOOGIE BOARDING

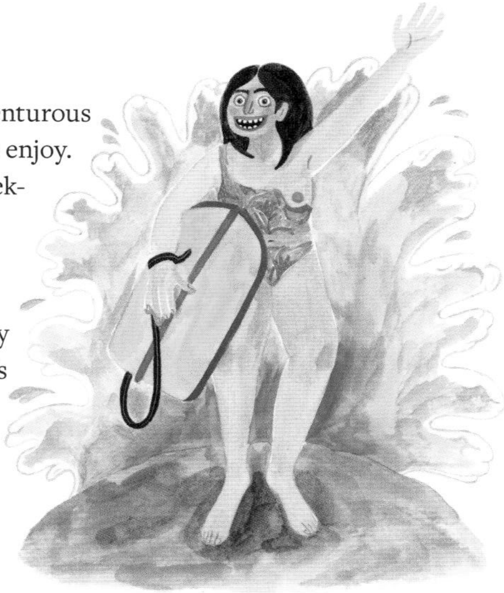

My childhood friend Lizzie got me into a lot more adventurous activities than I would have been naturally inclined to enjoy. The list includes riding a bike downhill, going to a week-long intensive basketball camp, and water sports.

One weekend I went with her family to Cape Cod for a day at the beach. I had just caught a great wave on my boogie board and as I made my way to shore to Lizzie's entire family—including grandparents—I realized that my full left boob was out. This was my first public wardrobe malfunction. I was completely alone in that moment. Exposed. Just me and my fairly new boob.

AT SCHOOL

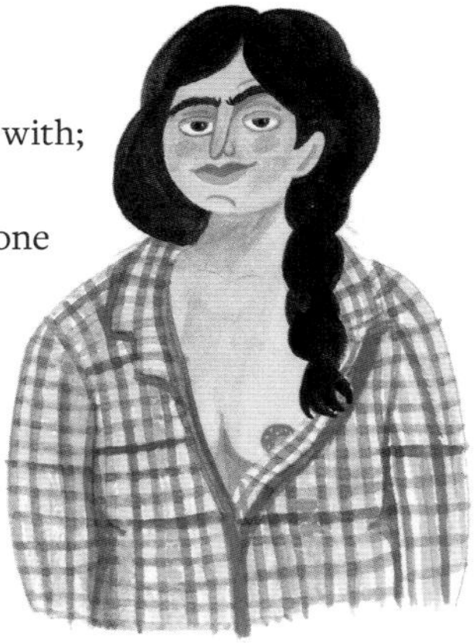

I had a favorite flannel in college that I never felt I had to wear a bra with; the thick fabric and dense pattern could conceal any level of nipple protrusion. One day as I was walking back to my desk, it came undone just enough for my areola to peer out. It was a bit embarassing, but I decided in that moment that little Ariella would probably have thought I was a total artsy badass.

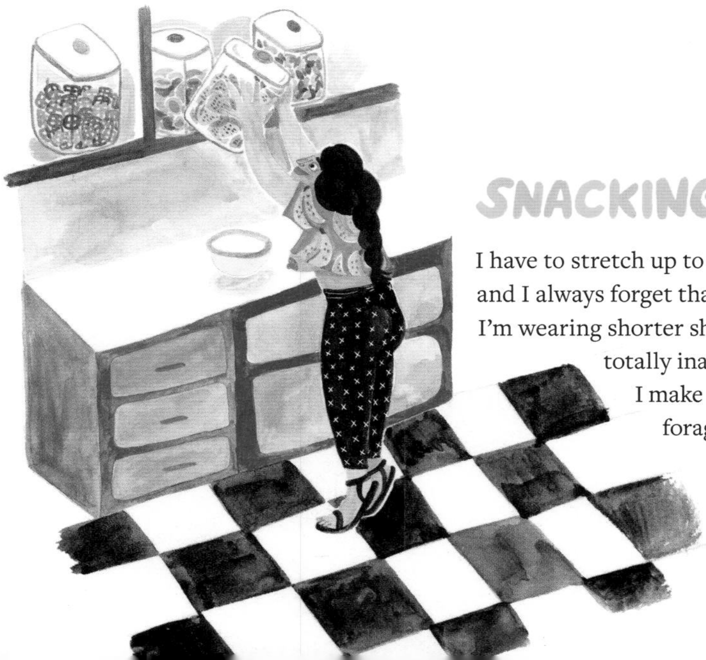

SNACKING AT WORK

I have to stretch up to reach the snacks in my office, and I always forget that my boobs easily peek out when I'm wearing shorter shirts. This peekaboo moment is totally inappropriate, but also thrilling. Now I make sure the coast is clear before foraging in the cabinets.

BIG BOOBS

I found out that Yentas Maya and Jesse have a very different relationship to bras. They've got big boobs and for them, bras are often equal parts nuisance and necessity. Oh, and are almost impossible to find.

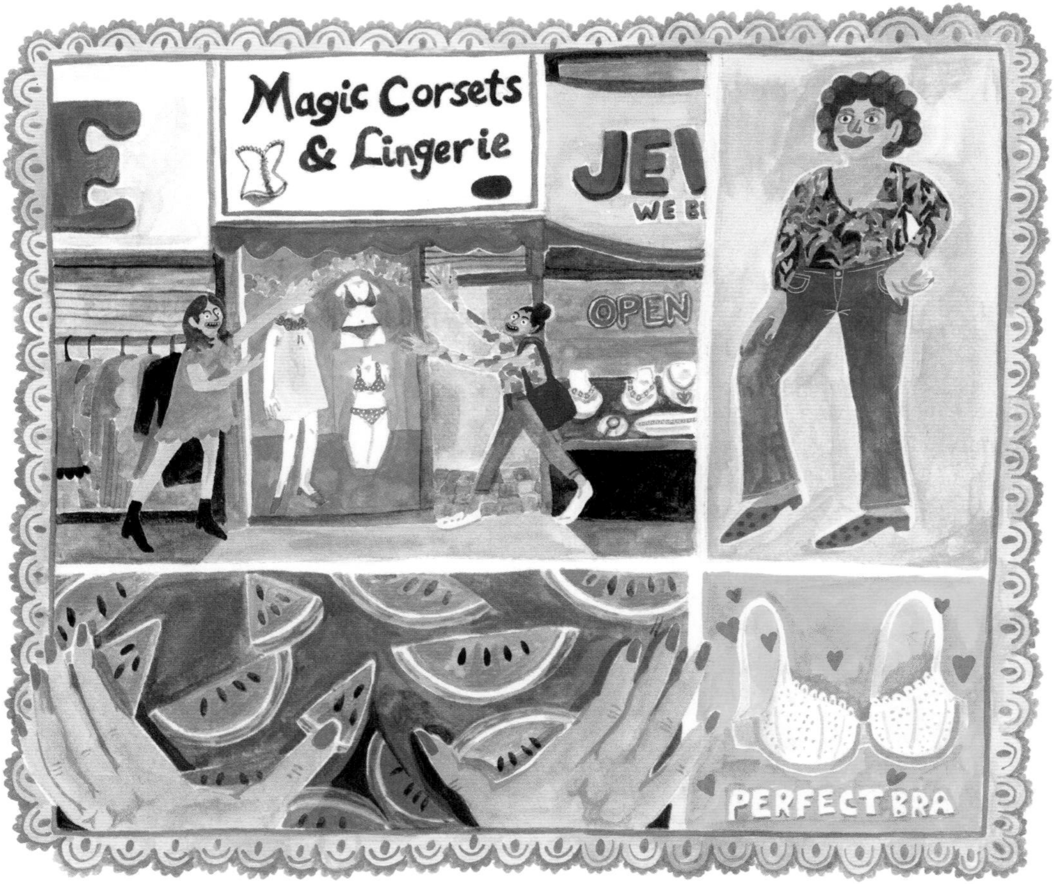

Magic Corsets & Lingerie
JE
WE B
OPEN
PERFECT BRA

They recently discovered a magic lady in Brighton Beach who—with one look and a cupping of your boobs—knows exactly which bra is perfect for you. This place is aptly named Magic Corsets & Lingerie.

FANTASY **REALITY**

Demystifying *Baywatch*: Jesse and Maya set the record straight on what it's really like to run with big boobs. The whole situation is far more dicey than mainstream media portrays. Rather than gently bouncing globes radiating with sexual energy, big boobs on the move look more like a juggling act. One boob will inevitably go rogue and jump right out of its bra cup while the other will slither out of its holding place.

boob smell

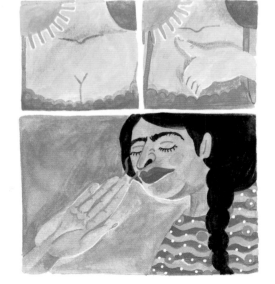

The boob smell phenomenon: Maya and Jesse had been going on and on about their other-worldly boob sweat smell for years. I had never experienced such a thing in my own body. In a demonstration of pure, true, deep friendship I agreed to take a whiff for myself. Jesse dipped her hand into her heat-of-summer cleavage and presented her fingertips to me. I took a smell and was immediately changed. It's a cheesy plus tortilla chip–type situation. Not pleasant, but also not entirely awful. Savory.

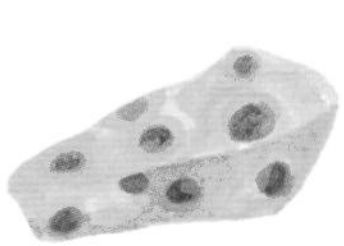

fantasy BRAS

PULL-UP BRA
Headband inspired
by Blair Waldorf.

MENTOS
PEPPER
SPRAY
FLOSS

UTILITY BRA
Always prepared
for anything.

MEDUSA
Ultimate protection against
the male gaze.

THE GOOD SAMARITAN
The perfect accessory for
the subway in summertime.
A gift for both yourself
and your neighbor.

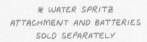
✳ WATER SPRITZ
ATTACHMENT AND BATTERIES
SOLD SEPARATELY

AQUARIUM
Giving a new meaning
to breastfeeding.

TERRARIUM
Free the nipple and make
sure the succulents are
getting enough sun!

COMPOST
Locally grown
and biodegradable!

DEATH GRIP
For the best support—
in this life and beyond!

DOILY
For an antique,
chic granny look.

HEADLIGHTS

Perfect for nighttime bicycle and pedestrian commutes!

BEE KEEPER

Talk about local honey!

THE COOKIE POUCH

Keeps your treats deliciously gooey!

BUBBLE WRAP

The most perfect bra for your most precious cargo.

✳ ALSO . . . KIND OF HOT?

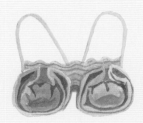

COMFORT FOOD

Your boobs will always feel at home in these tortellini!

BAT MITZVAH

Supporting your boobs with gusto—and Tiffany & Co. gift ribbon.

POWER SOURCE

The perfect accessory for runners or friends who always panic when they realize they forgot to recharge.

✳ POWERED BY YOUR SWEAT!

BAGEL BIDDIE

For the carb lover in all of us.

✳ COMES IN PLAIN, CINNAMON RAISIN, SESAME, AND POPPY SEED. EGG BAGELS AND GLUTEN-FREE OPTIONS AVAILABLE UPON REQUEST.

SHAVING CREAM

A childhood favorite— and the only strapless bra I've ever worn comfortably.

BRA TIMELINE

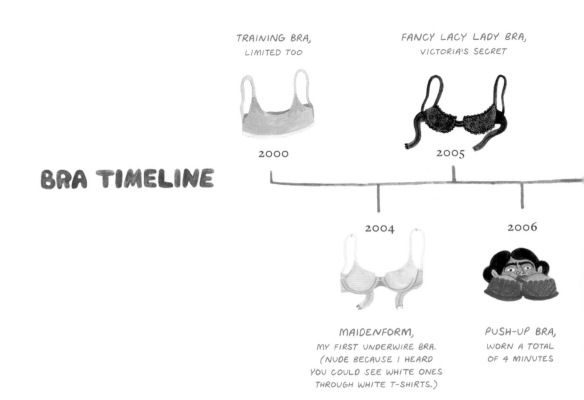

TRAINING BRA,
LIMITED TOO

2000

FANCY LACY LADY BRA,
VICTORIA'S SECRET

2005

2004

MAIDENFORM,
MY FIRST UNDERWIRE BRA.
(NUDE BECAUSE I HEARD
YOU COULD SEE WHITE ONES
THROUGH WHITE T-SHIRTS.)

2006

PUSH-UP BRA,
WORN A TOTAL
OF 4 MINUTES

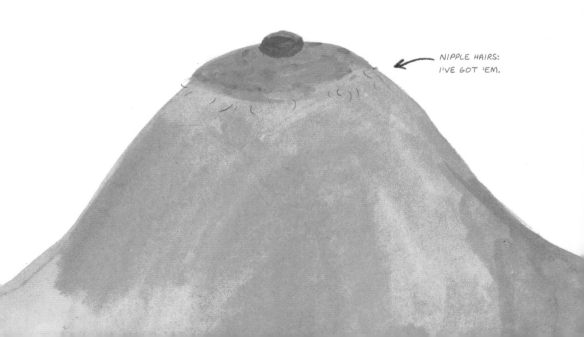

NIPPLE HAIRS:
I'VE GOT 'EM.

CONSTANTLY ADJUSTING MY UNDERWIRE

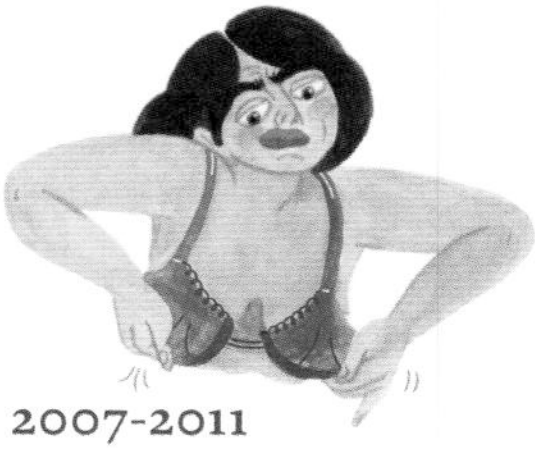

2007-2011

FUCK IT

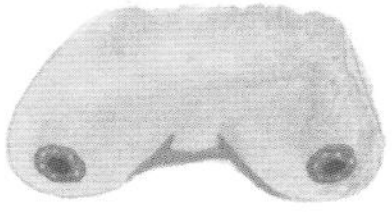

SUMMER 2018–PRESENT

2012

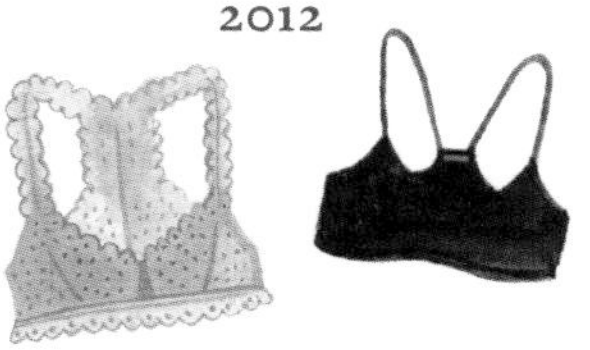

BRALETTES
- FAIR AMOUNT OF SUPPORT
- SOFT, NO DIGGING WIRES
- CAN PULL DOWN OVER THE STRIP OF TUMMY FAT UNDER MY BOOBS

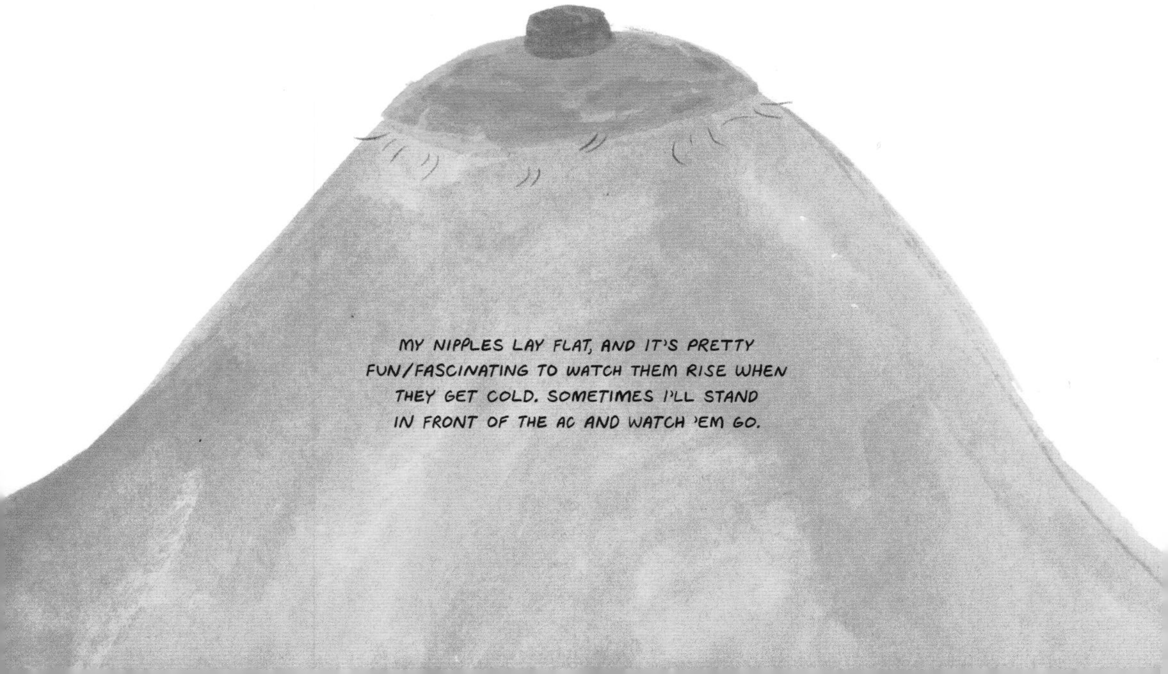
MY NIPPLES LAY FLAT, AND IT'S PRETTY FUN/FASCINATING TO WATCH THEM RISE WHEN THEY GET COLD. SOMETIMES I'LL STAND IN FRONT OF THE AC AND WATCH 'EM GO.

the joy of going BRALESS

Doing away with bras has made my boobs feel more like me.
I don't like restrictive clothing or itchy lace, so why would my boobs?

Whenever I need to run,
I just hold my boobs in my hands.

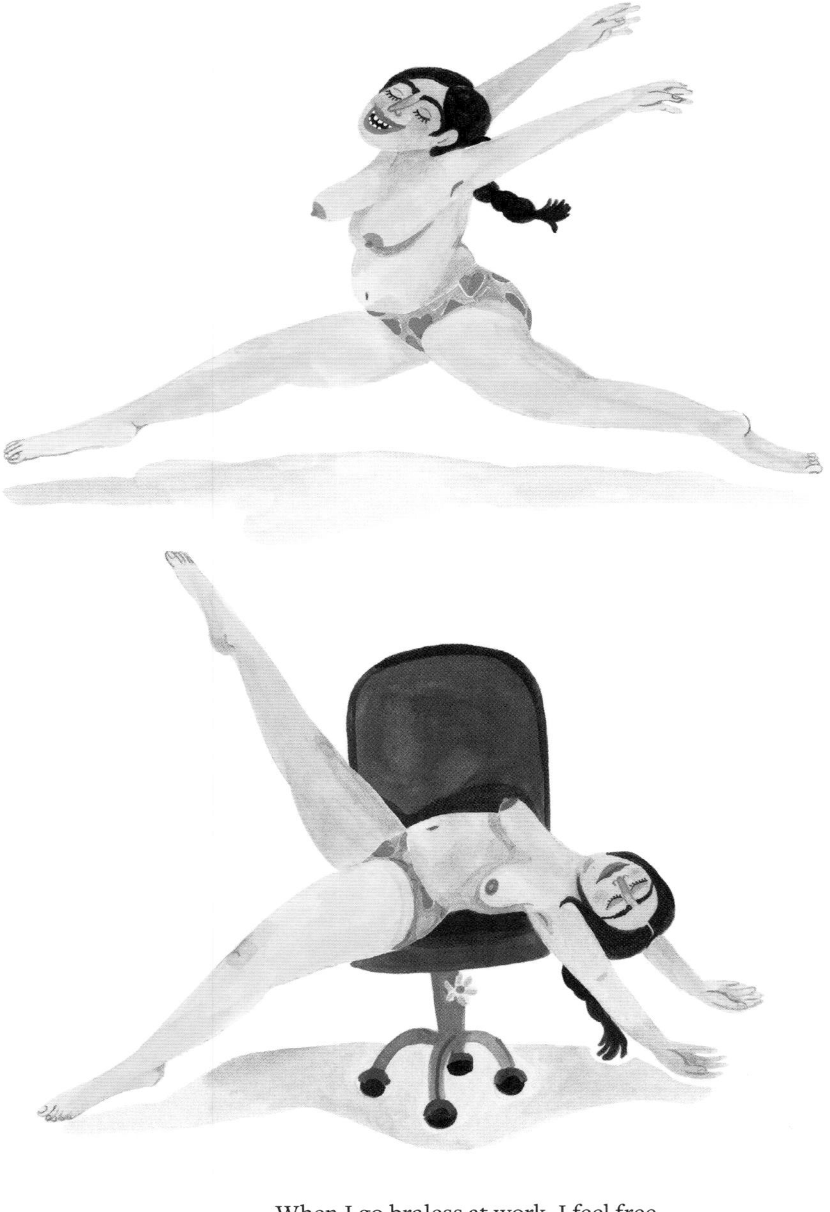

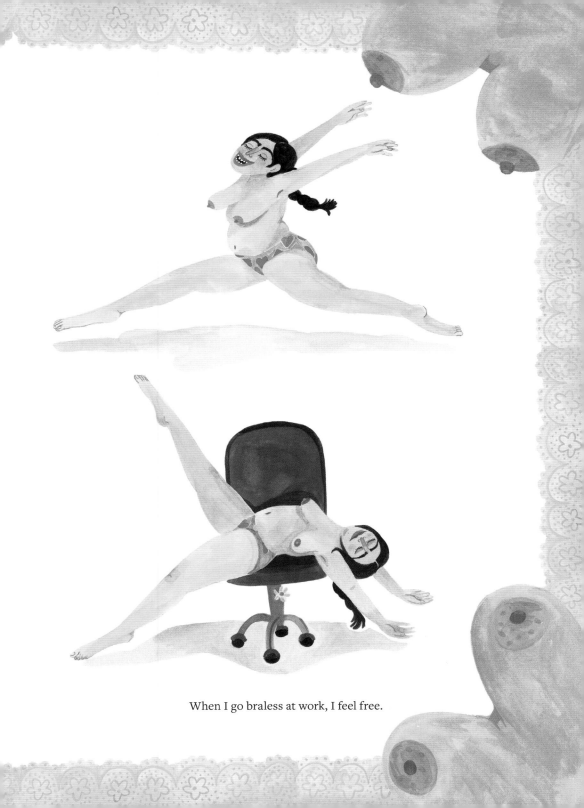

When I go braless at work, I feel free.

ARMS, HANDS & ARMPITS

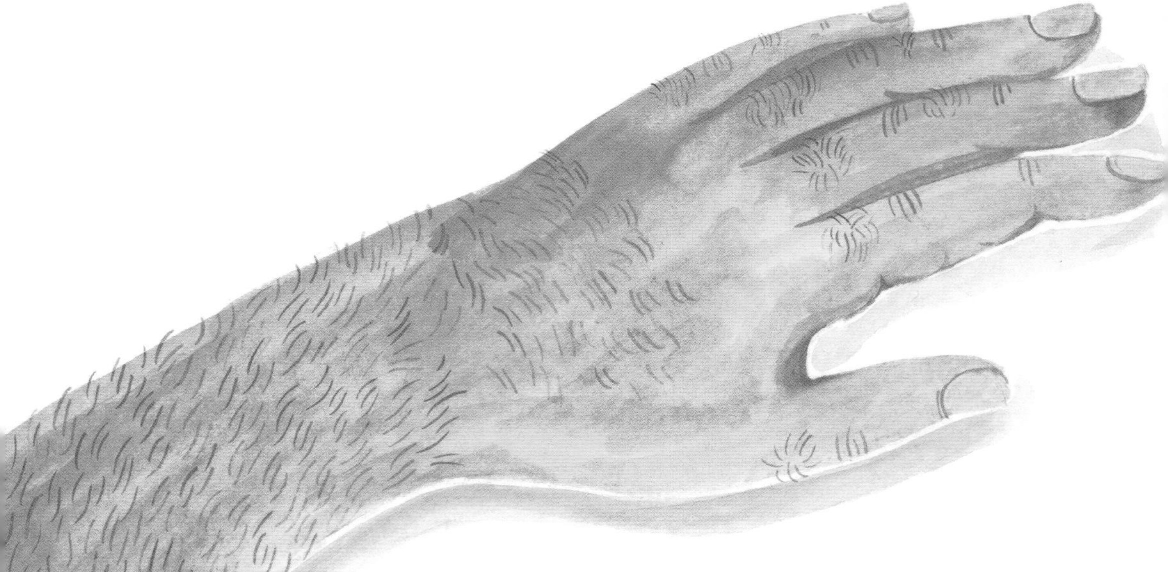

My arms have always been a

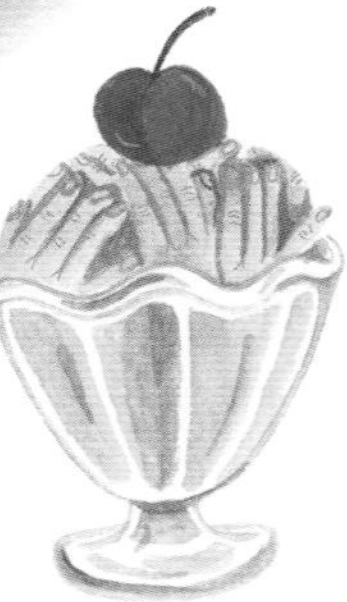

CONFIDENCE MINEFIELD

They're covered in hair, my pits sweat excessively, and, cherry on top: my fingers at one point housed a smattering of warts. So adorable.

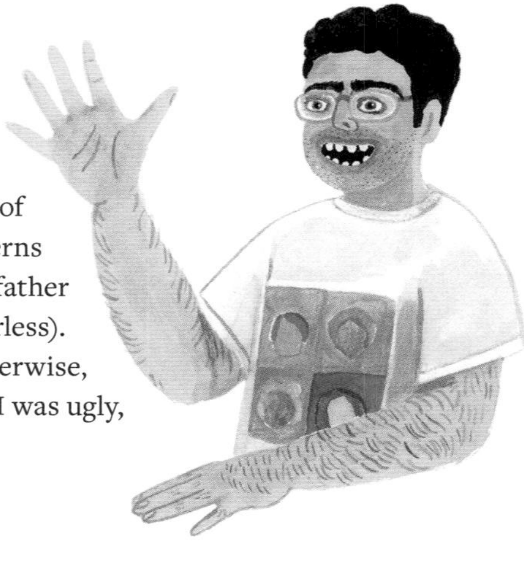

At a young age, I became very aware of the fact that my hair and sweat patterns more closely resembled those of my father (my mom is blonde and virtually hairless). Without any resources to tell me otherwise, I internalized this fact to mean that I was ugly, abnormal, and simply a monster.

In fourth grade, everyone in my class was getting initialed L.L.Bean backpacks. I loved looking through the catalog to see what bag and thread color options were available. This was the perfect birthday gift to ask for and I wanted to be prepared with a detailed request. Unfortunately, my eagerness to art direct my future backpack distracted me from a very simple but totally damning fact: my initials are A.P.E. Walking around with that set of letters on my back would be way too on the nose.

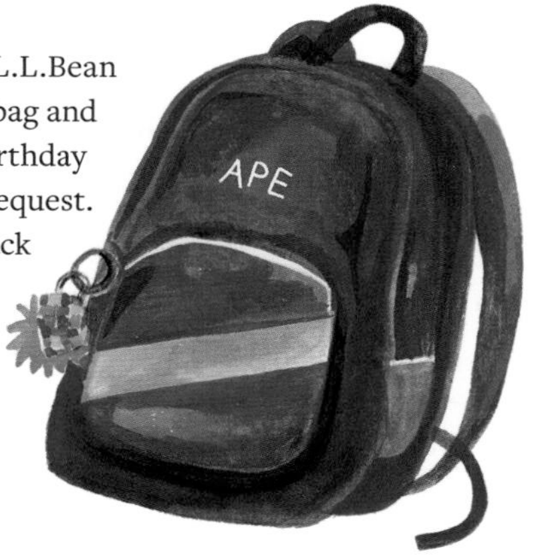
APE

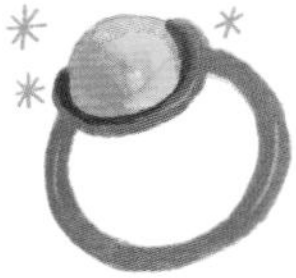

I avoided wearing rings or painting my nails because I felt any accessories would only highlight how unladylike my hands were. Bracelets were essentially neon signs pointing to my hairy arms.

I WENT THROUGH A PHASE OF WAXING MY KNUCKLE HAIRS. SO PAINFUL.

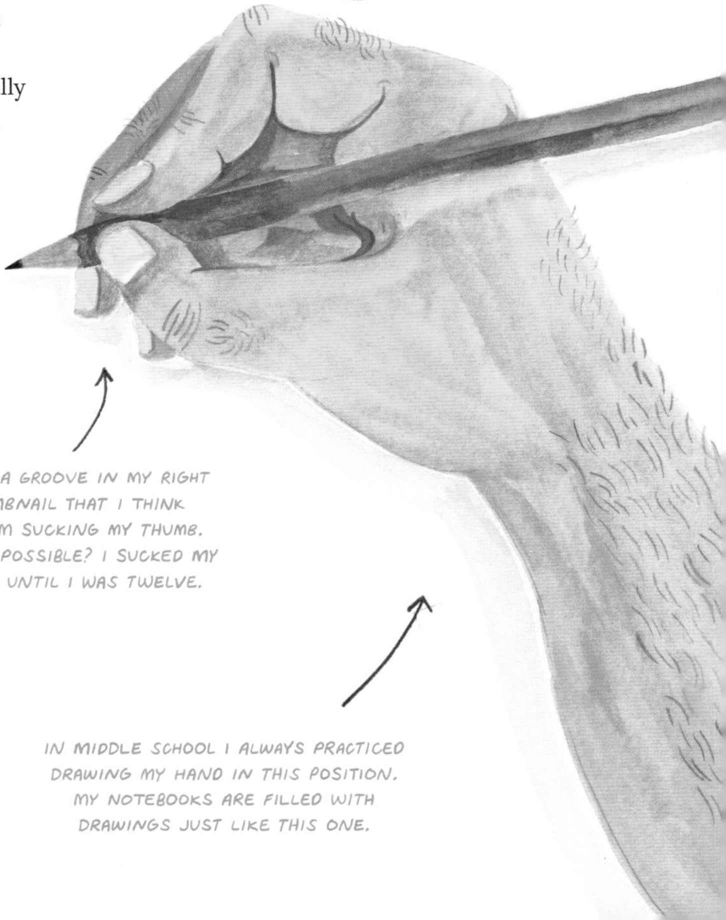

I HAVE A GROOVE IN MY RIGHT THUMBNAIL THAT I THINK IS FROM SUCKING MY THUMB. IS THAT POSSIBLE? I SUCKED MY THUMB UNTIL I WAS TWELVE.

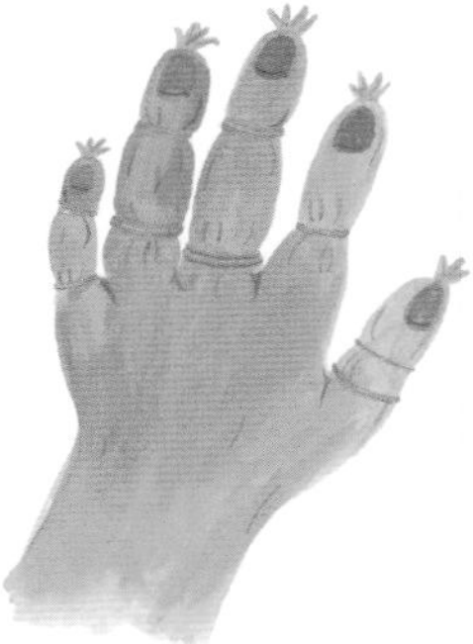

ME TRYING OUT THAT STACKABLE RING TREND.

IN MIDDLE SCHOOL I ALWAYS PRACTICED DRAWING MY HAND IN THIS POSITION. MY NOTEBOOKS ARE FILLED WITH DRAWINGS JUST LIKE THIS ONE.

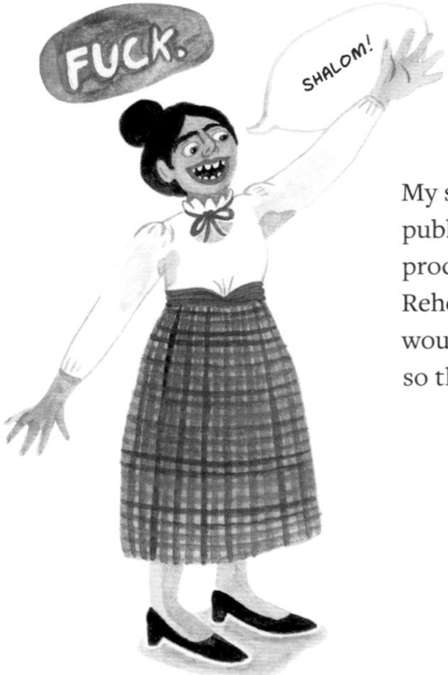
FUCK.
SHALOM!

sweat

MY SOGGY PIT HACKS, AN EVOLUTION.

My sweating became most apparent (and upsettingly public) when I landed the lead role in my middle school's production of *Miri Poppins* (*Mary Poppins*, but in Hebrew). Rehearsals were a sweaty death trap in which my pit stains would be on full view. My crush was at these rehearsals, so the situation had to be handled.

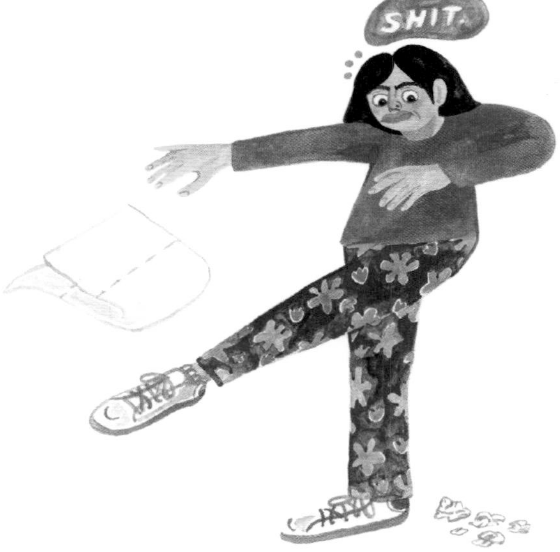
SHIT.

I snuck into my parents' bathroom each morning to take secret swipes of my dad's man deodorant. I was too ashamed to tell my parents about my sweat woes.

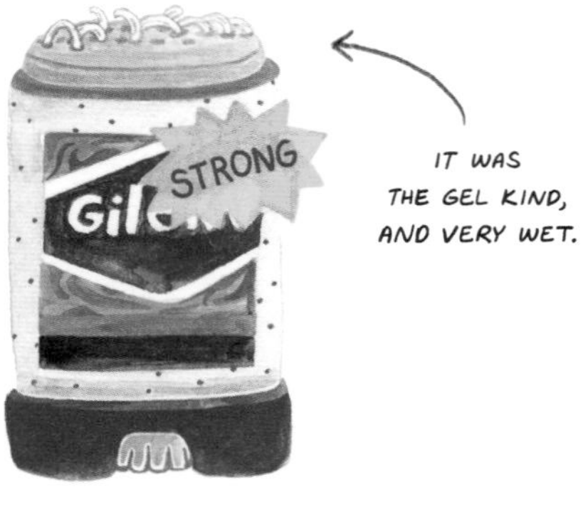
STRONG
Gil
IT WAS
THE GEL KIND,
AND VERY WET.

I soon learned that Gillette was, sadly, no match for my pits.

For added backup, I'd line the armpits of my shirts with toilet paper. I walked around rehearsals smelling of cologne and leaving trails of shriveled toilet paper in my wake, running to the bathroom to refresh my pit linings every chance I got.

Come high school, my fashion choices were directly informed by my sweaty pits. I convinced myself that the Techwick shirts I reserved for family ski trips had a home in my everyday wardrobe. They were the perfect material for my dilemma: they would absorb and wick away any chance of a pit stain! I bought one in almost every color available.

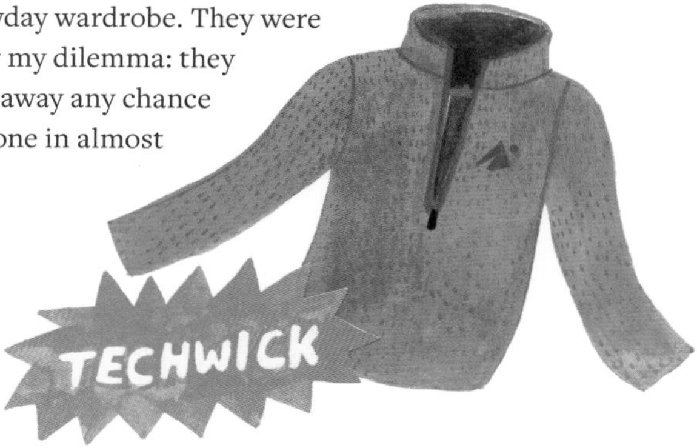
TECHWICK

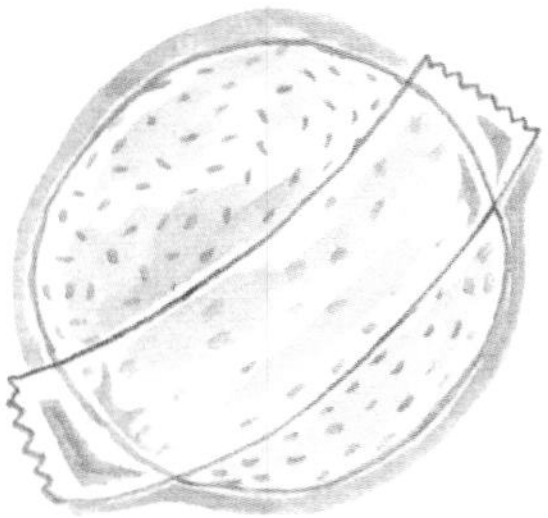

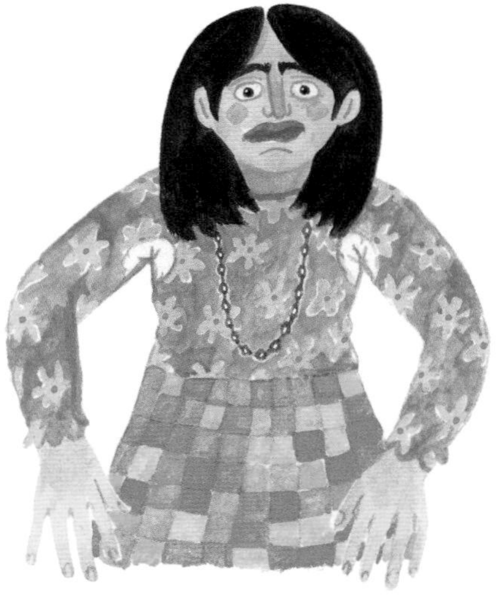

My Jewish high school celebrated Shabbat (the weekly Jewish Sabbath) with a spruced-up dress code every Friday. My Techwick shirts didn't quite fit the festive bill, so I had to get creative with a new soggy pit solution. I taped cotton pads to the inside of my shirts (a step-up from my amateur toilet paper approach in middle school) and—for fear of shifting their position in transit—I tried to walk around without rubbing my armpits against my torso.

DEODORANT ROUNDUP

Once I got my license and started driving to and from school, I had the freedom to go to drugstores on my own and begin the search for the perfect antiperspirant.

ARRID
EXTRA DRY
ANTI-PERSPIRANT & DEODORANT
CREAM

This is the first deodorant I bought on my own. The packaging made it seem intense and strictly business. It's a tub of cream, applied by hand. I once bit a nail that had some hidden underneath. Arrid tastes chalky and awful, FYI.

Secret
CLINICAL
STRENGTH
Clear Gel
ooh-la-la lavender
Dove
clinical
protection

For some reason, all of these clinical protection brands (in particular the lavender scents) make me smell putrid. At one point, I thought it wise to double up and dab this deodorant directly onto the pits of my shirts. Wouldn't recommend.

SINCE 1678
Tom's
OF MAINE
LONG LASTING
wild
lavender

I'm in love with the *idea* of Tom. Natural! Carefree! But even in the winter, he doesn't stand a chance. Using it is a gentle suggestion that I perhaps shouldn't sweat.

Mitchum
ADVANCED
CONTROL
48HR

Lady Mitchum. The hard-ass Jane Austen character of deodorants. This stuff is no-nonsense. It stings my skin, and leaves white rings on my clothing.

72 Hour Protection
CERTAIN
DRI
ANTI-PERSPIRANT
DRY
IDEA
AdvancedDry
UNSCENTED
Roll-On

Love a roll-on. I don't smell *great* when I use these, but they go on smooth and keep me fairly dry! A big win.

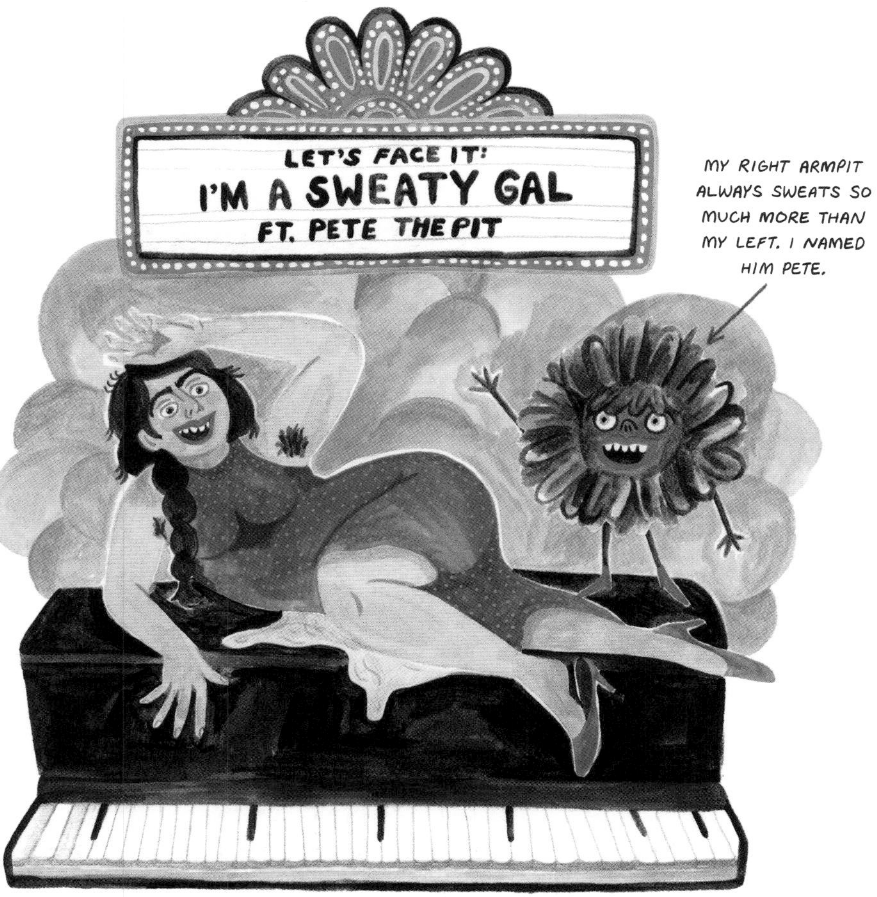
LET'S FACE IT:
I'M A SWEATY GAL
FT. PETE THE PIT
MY RIGHT ARMPIT ALWAYS SWEATS SO MUCH MORE THAN MY LEFT. I NAMED HIM PETE.

And no product that I feel good about putting on my body is ever going to change that fact.

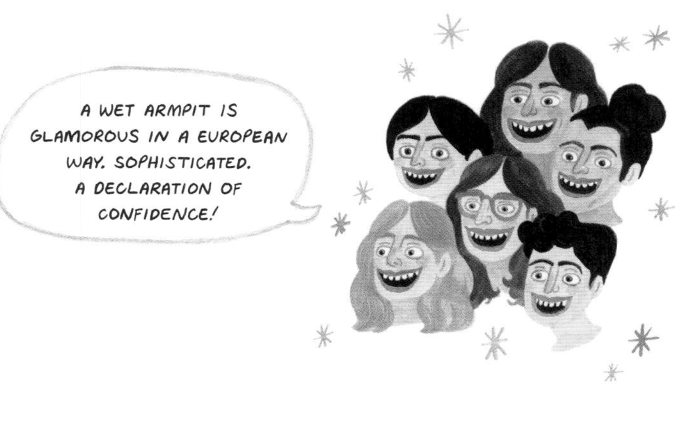
A WET ARMPIT IS GLAMOROUS IN A EUROPEAN WAY. SOPHISTICATED. A DECLARATION OF CONFIDENCE!

armpit hair

I started shaving my armpits in fifth grade after my mom pointed out the fuzz that was slowly growing in. From that moment on, shaving my armpits became a standard part of my routine, always aiming to scrape away even the slightest hint of stubble.

At fourteen, I screamed when I caught a glimpse of my guy friend's fully grown armpit fuzz at camp. We'd known each other since preschool and all of a sudden, he was officially a man.

From what I could tell, boys were encouraged to wear their hair proudly—pits, arms, and elsewhere. Girls, however, were taught that growing up meant growing hair, never speaking of said hair, and getting rid of it immediately.

← SURPRISE! WOMEN ARE ACTUALLY HAIRLESS CATS IN WIGS!

I went on with my life, shaving my armpits without giving it much thought.

That is, until one winter day when Maya sent The Yenta group chat a photo of her grown-out armpit hair. It was an experiment and we all agreed it was gorgeous. French!

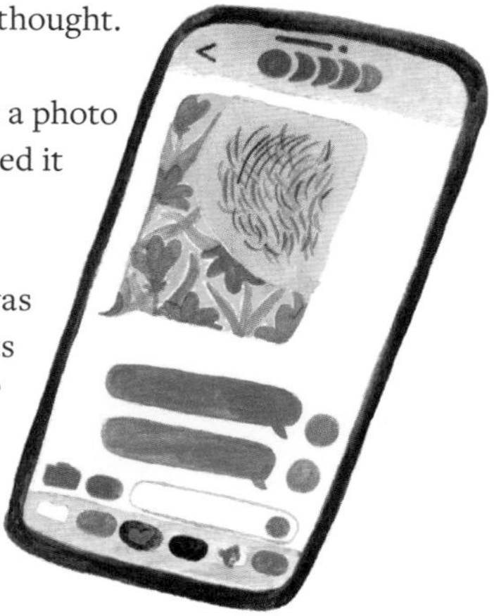

I was officially inspired and decided to grow mine out too. Plus, I was getting a weird rash in my armpits from all the different deodorants and antiperspirants I'd been testing, so maybe the hair would help?

I had no idea what my pit hairs were going to look like and I was excited to find out. It's wild to think that even after twenty-seven years with this body, there was a side of it I'd never seen before.

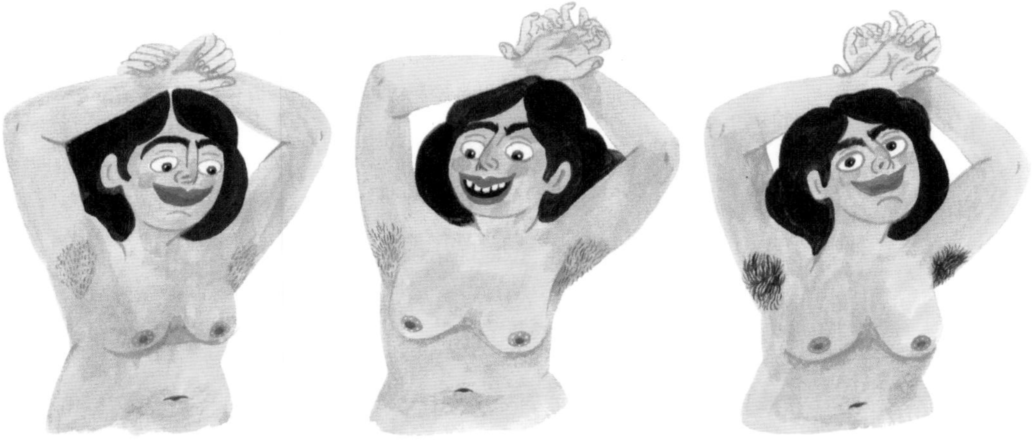

The growing-out process was thrilling. Week by week, I watched as the hairs grew longer and thicker, eager to see what they might look like in their final form. By the end of one month, I was sporting pretty thick pits. My armpit hairs look kind of chaotic. Wiry, energized, and aggressive, creeping out of the crease between my arm and torso.

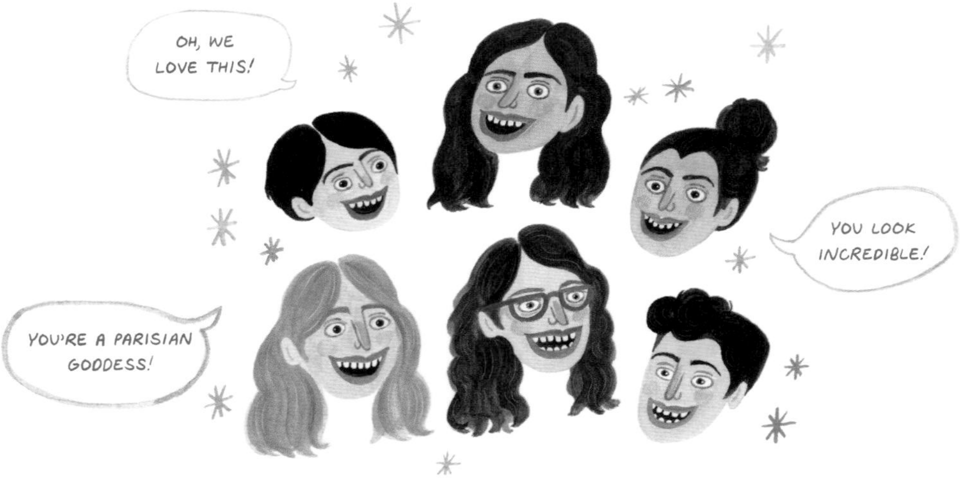
OH, WE LOVE THIS!
YOU LOOK INCREDIBLE!
YOU'RE A PARISIAN GODDESS!

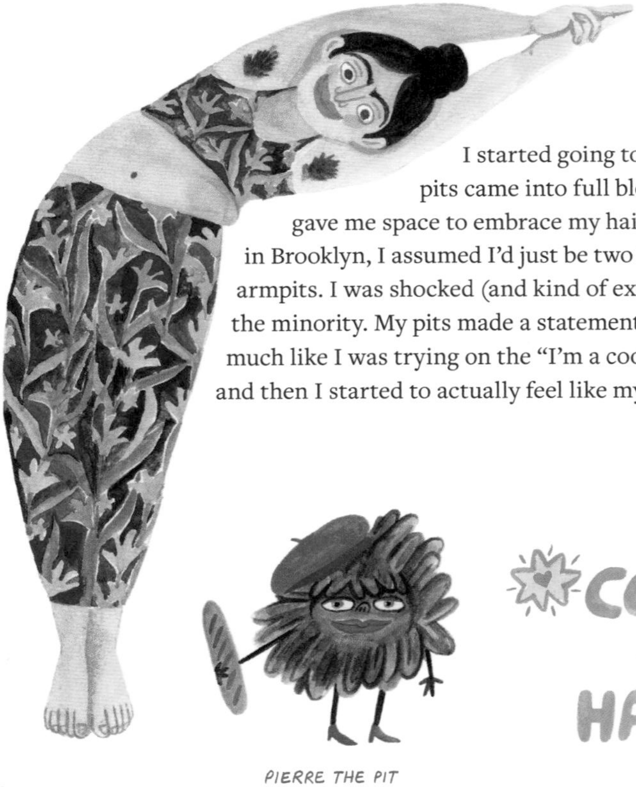

I started going to hot yoga classes shortly after my pits came into full bloom, and this new routine really gave me space to embrace my hair in public. Going to a yoga studio in Brooklyn, I assumed I'd just be two hairy armpits in a sea of many hairy armpits. I was shocked (and kind of excited) to find that I was actually in the minority. My pits made a statement. And I loved it. At first, it felt very much like I was trying on the "I'm a cool girl who doesn't shave" idea, and then I started to actually feel like my armpits were part of my identity.

PIERRE THE PIT

I AM THAT COOL GIRL *with the* HAIRY PITS

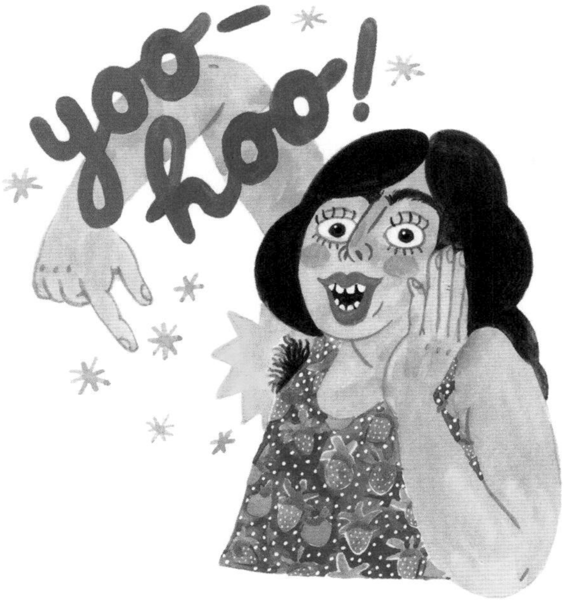
yoo-hoo!

I'm a major rule follower, and my armpits are an invigorating act of rebellion. The first time I went home with my new hairy pits, I took such a thrill in showing them off to my mom and sisters, gleefully flashing them throughout the day.

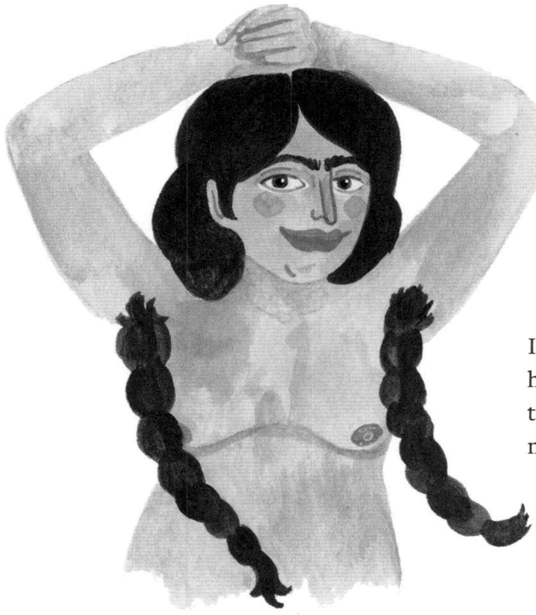

I've always wanted to braid the armpit hair of boys I've dated and no one to this day has let me do it. Now I've got my own to play with!

natural ARMPIT SMELLS

Since growing out my armpit hair, I've found that the flavor profile of my sweat has changed considerably, and it can take on many different forms.

When I come out of yoga class my sweat smells sweet—almost like cotton candy (but also kind of like the 4/5 downtown train in the summer).

I sometimes have a rugged, musty scent—like a bearded Brooklyn boy who drinks whiskey and seems tough but is also a total teddy bear and really listens and makes me laugh.

My pits can really transport me.

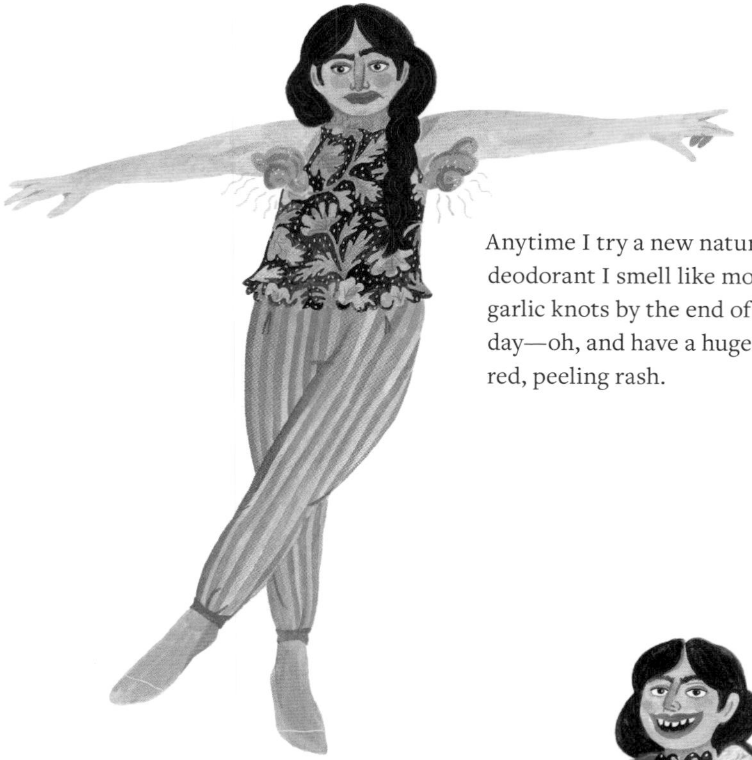

Anytime I try a new natural deodorant I smell like moldy garlic knots by the end of the day—oh, and have a huge, red, peeling rash.

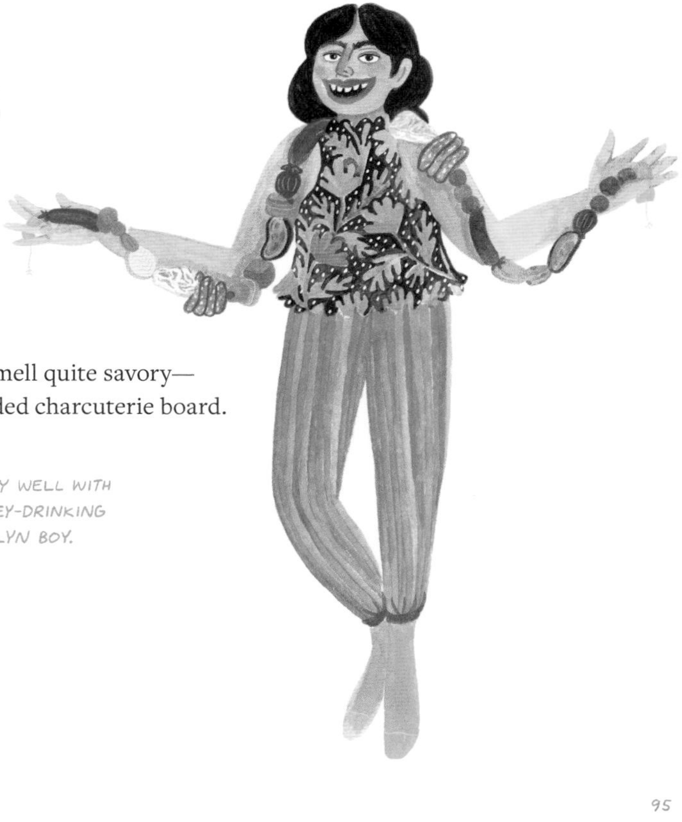

Other times, I smell quite savory—like a well-rounded charcuterie board.

*PAIRS VERY WELL WITH THE WHISKEY-DRINKING BROOKLYN BOY.

arm hair

My arm hair is dark and thick, and growing up, no kid (or adults aside from dads) had arms that looked like mine. I dreaded summer because I usually avoided wearing short-sleeve shirts even on the hottest days (which of course wasn't wonderful for my sweat situation), and when I did go sleeveless I'd always sit with my hands in my lap, using desks and lunch tables to hide my arms.

A GIRL IN MY MIDDLE SCHOOL CLASS SHAVED HER ARM HAIR AND IT GREW BACK REALLY PRICKLY. I KNEW THAT SHAVING WAS PROBABLY THE EASIEST AND QUICKEST FIX, BUT I HATED THE IDEA OF HAVING SHARP LITTLE HAIRS POKING OUT OF MY FOREARMS. SHAVING WAS NOT AN OPTION.

In eighth grade, I started becoming aware of the various hair removal methods that were out there—all thanks to the numerous advertisements that aired during *The O.C.* and *One Tree Hill*. Just as I sat watching these TV shows, admiring the smooth and thin bodies of all the female characters, in came commercials telling me how I could look more like those women in the snap of a finger. How convenient for the patriarchy!

I became determined to find the perfect solution and I, through daily complaining, brought my mom on this journey with me.

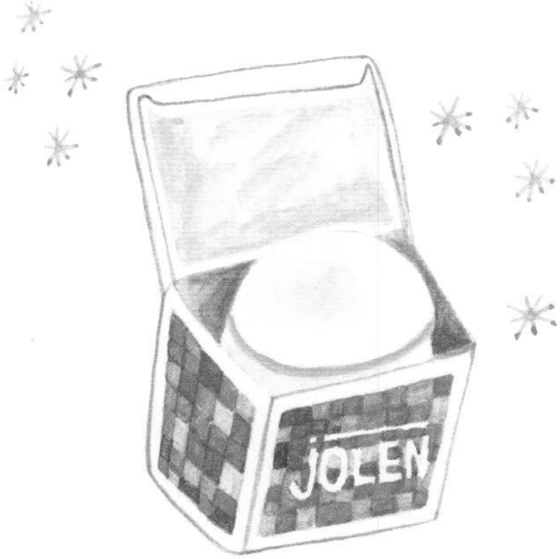
JOLEN

In a joint effort, we found Jolen Creme Bleach. It was a pain-free way to get virtually invisible arm hair. The kit came with a tub of cream and a small tube of powder that would activate the bleach once mixed in. At the start of each summer, I turned my bathroom into a chemical dance party and got to work.

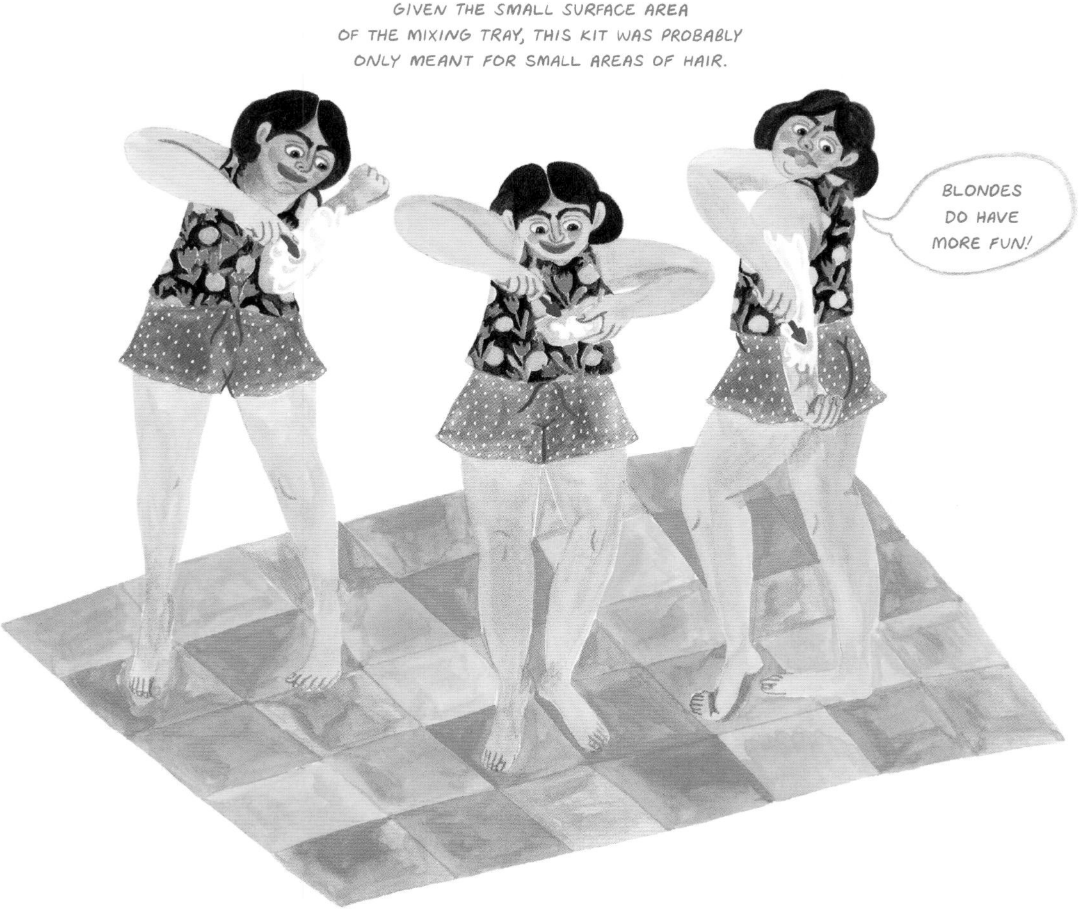
GIVEN THE SMALL SURFACE AREA OF THE MIXING TRAY, THIS KIT WAS PROBABLY ONLY MEANT FOR SMALL AREAS OF HAIR.
BLONDES DO HAVE MORE FUN!

The anxiety crept in when I thought about how my miraculous bleach would never last the full two months at camp. After about two weeks, my darker roots would start to show. I was embarrassed by my hair, but maybe even more embarrassed by the amount of work I had to put in to make it disappear and make me look like everyone else. The idea of having to secretly turn a bathroom stall into my own personal bleaching lab was nightmarish.

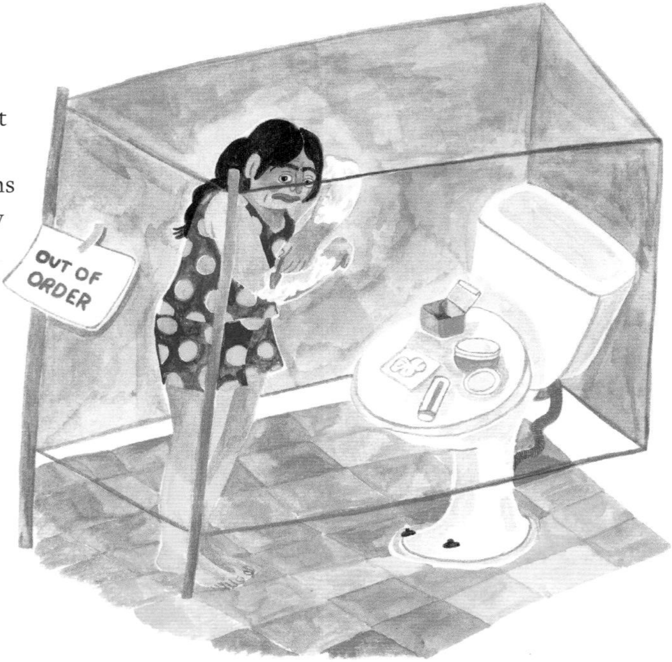
OUT OF ORDER

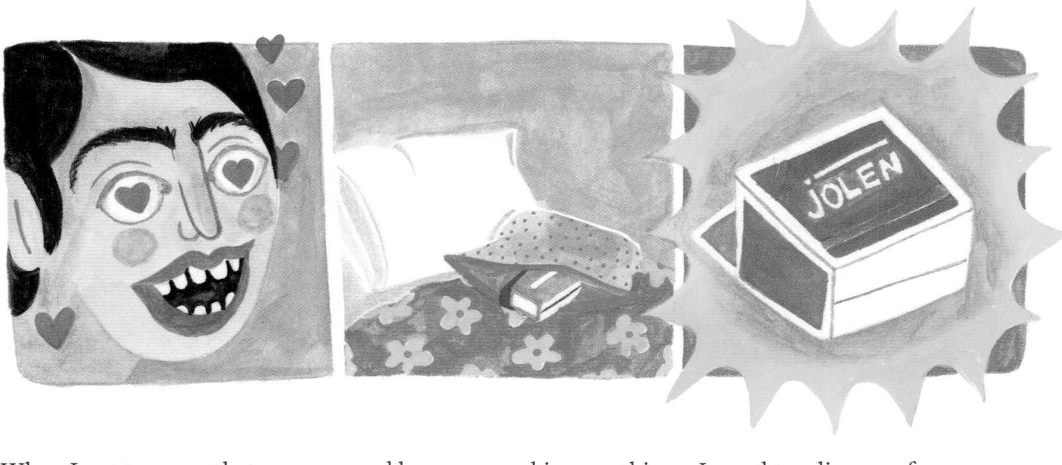
JOLEN

When I got to camp that summer and began unpacking my things, I caught a glimpse of a very familiar shade of turquoise from across the room. Right before my eyes, sitting on a shelf in the bathroom, was a box of Jolen Creme Bleach. Someone else here is hairy too!

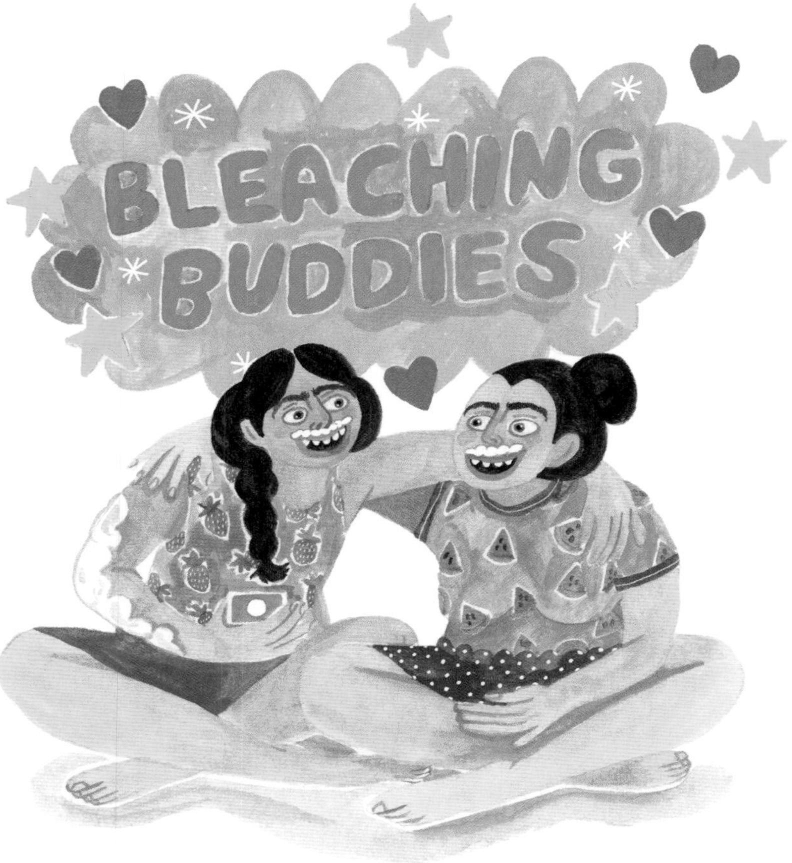
BLEACHING BUDDIES

Maya was the first fellow hairy lady I connected with—she also had upper lip hair! Every few weeks, we'd stand near-naked in the bunk bathroom, chatting casually as we bleached our bodies, inhaling the unmistakable chemical scent as the cream bubbled on our skin.

Maya gave me the confidence and permission to claim that I was hairy. It was just a fact about my body.

After a few years, I grew tired of the whole bleaching routine and slowly became less stressed out about my hair. I finally ditched Jolen after my first year of college, figuring the hour-long bleach session was more trouble than it was worth.

But my arm hair insecurities resurfaced in my early twenties when I moved to New York and started getting into dating apps. I worried that my hair might not make the best first impression.

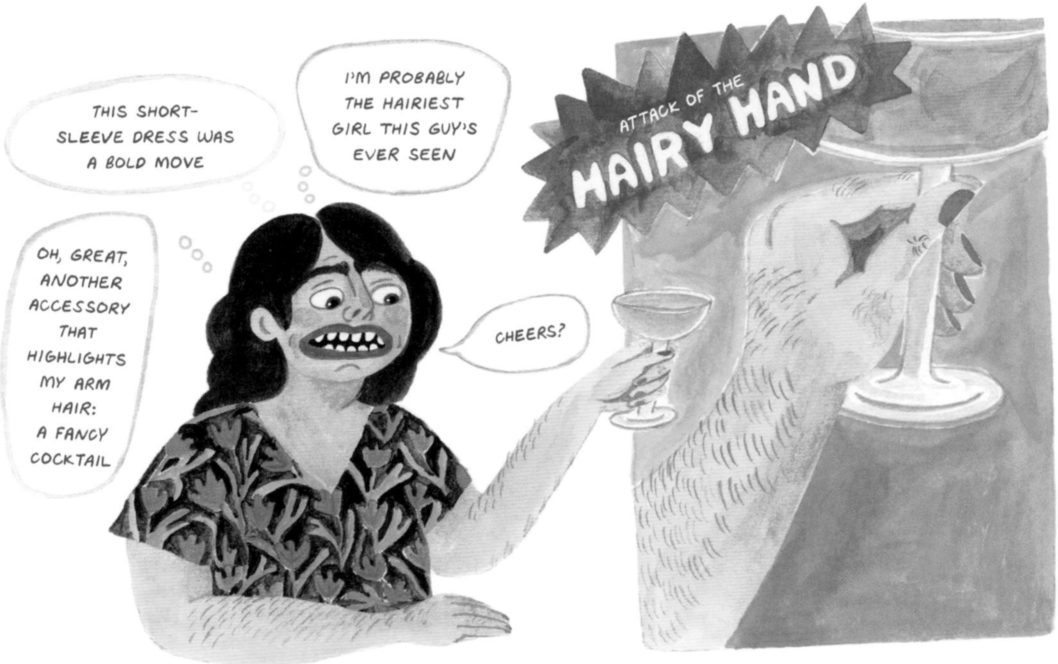

THIS SHORT-SLEEVE DRESS WAS A BOLD MOVE
I'M PROBABLY THE HAIRIEST GIRL THIS GUY'S EVER SEEN
ATTACK OF THE HAIRY HAND
OH, GREAT, ANOTHER ACCESSORY THAT HIGHLIGHTS MY ARM HAIR: A FANCY COCKTAIL
CHEERS?

OK, FIRST OF ALL EVERYONE HAS HAIR. WE'RE MAMMALS!

WE THINK YOUR ARM HAIR IS CUTE!

IF A LITTLE HAIR IS ABLE TO DISTRACT THIS GUY FROM HOW WONDERFUL YOU ARE, RUN!

TO BE REAL, THIS IS THE TIP OF THE BODY HAIR ICEBERG, SO IF THIS GUY HAS ISSUES WITH ARM HAIR THERE'S NO HOPE. AND IT'S HIS LOSS.

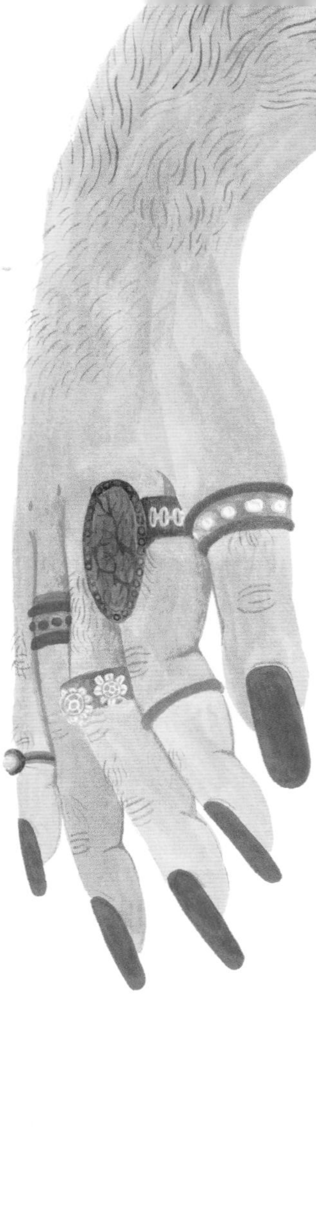

come on VOGUE

LET YOUR ARM HAIRS MOVE TO THE MUSIC

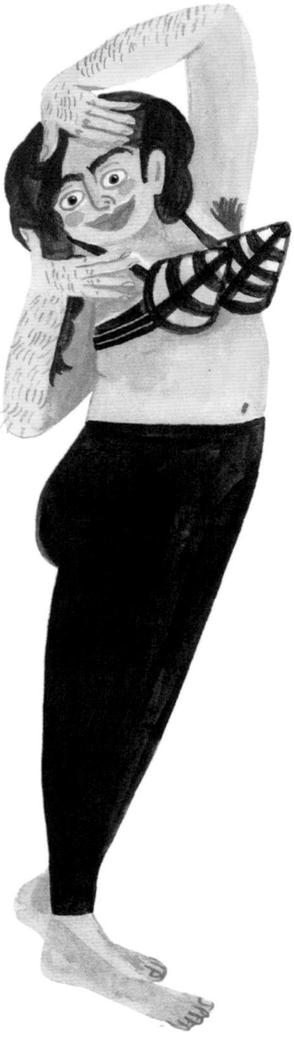

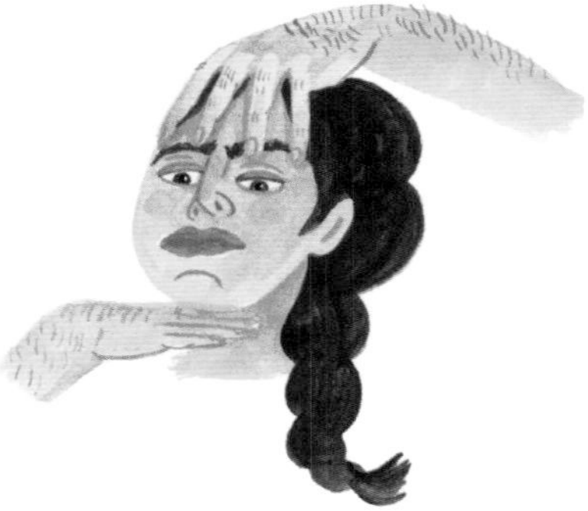

My flowing hairs give my arms character and make me feel like a Semitic goddess.

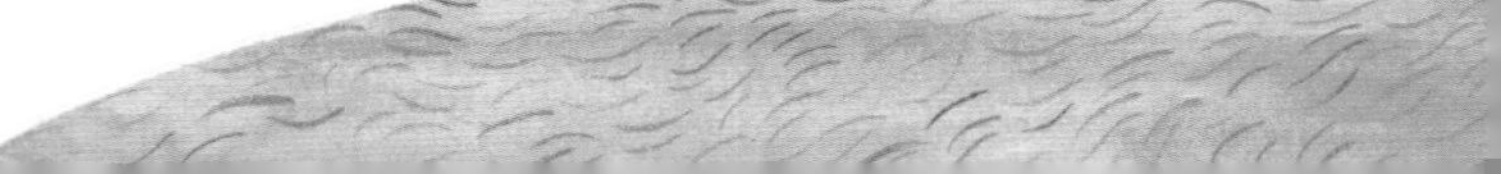

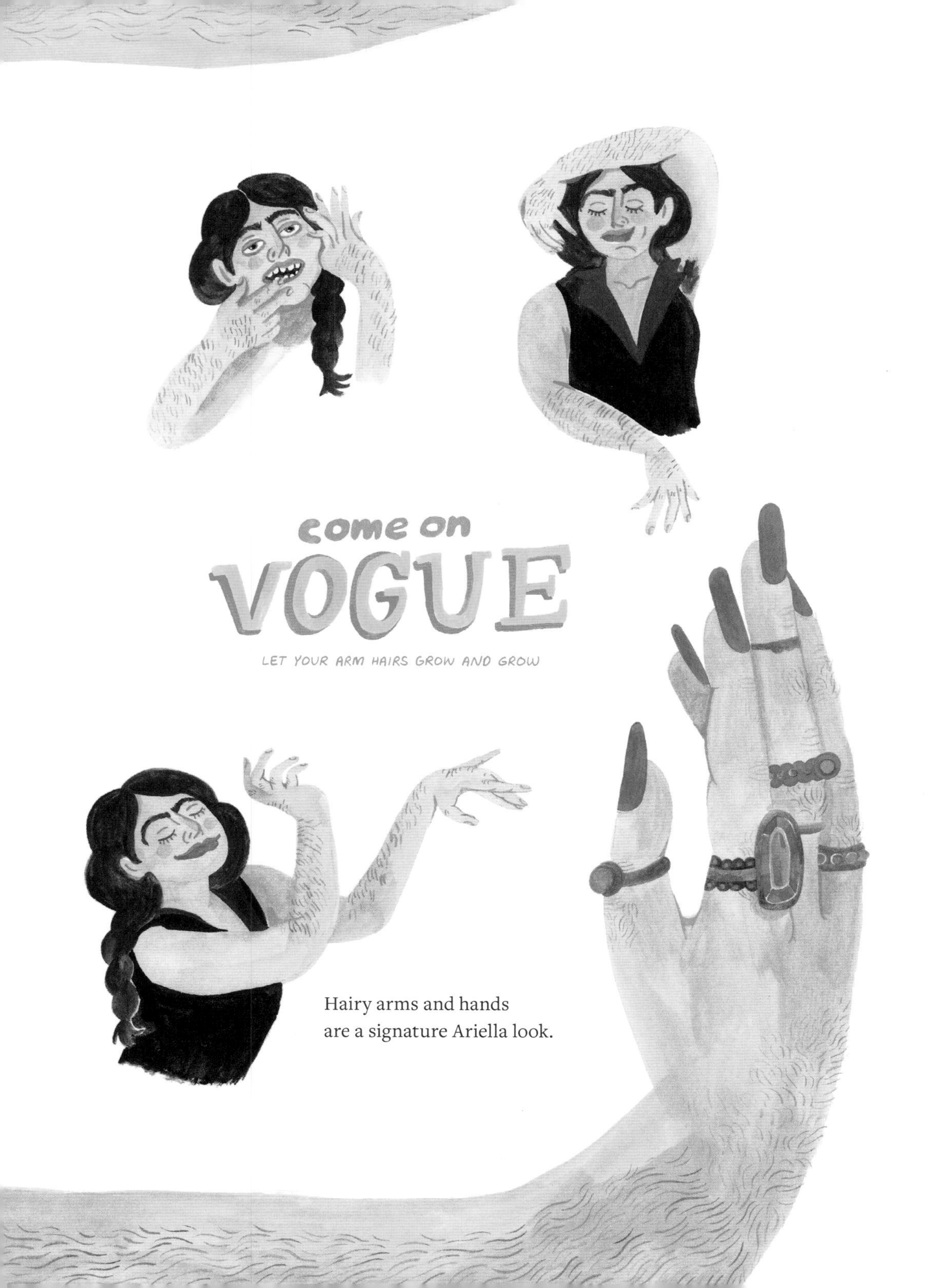
come on
VOGUE
LET YOUR ARM HAIRS GROW AND GROW

Hairy arms and hands
are a signature Ariella look.

TUMMY

A few years ago, I found a home video of myself acting with the most confidence I've ever had. I was six years old, standing in front of a group of people while wearing a bathing suit, demanding a bigger piece of cake. It was Elisha's fourth birthday party and I argued that I should get the biggest piece since I was the oldest guest and therefore had the most room for it in my tummy.

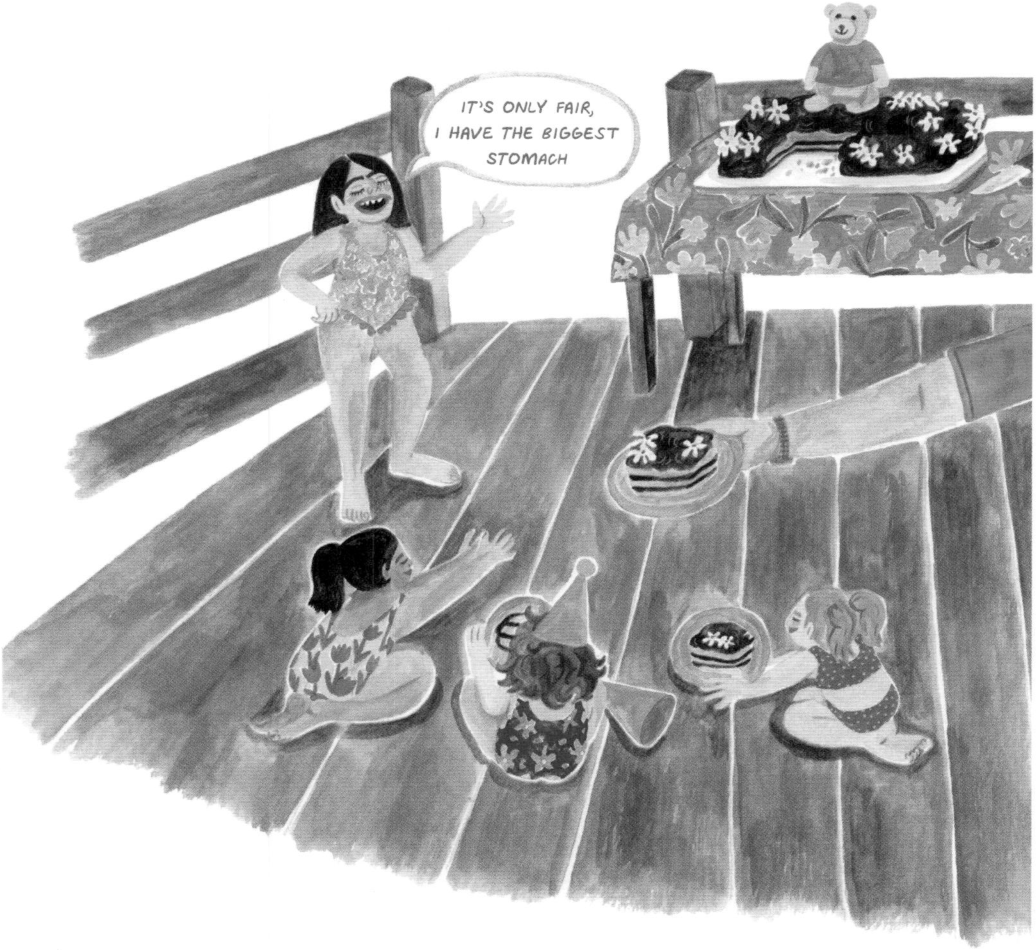
IT'S ONLY FAIR,
I HAVE THE BIGGEST
STOMACH

Watching this in my twenties—a time in which I would never dare call attention to my stomach, never mind boast about its size—I mourned my loss of confidence. This little kickass lady unabashedly enjoyed food, knew what she wanted, and wasn't afraid to ask for it.

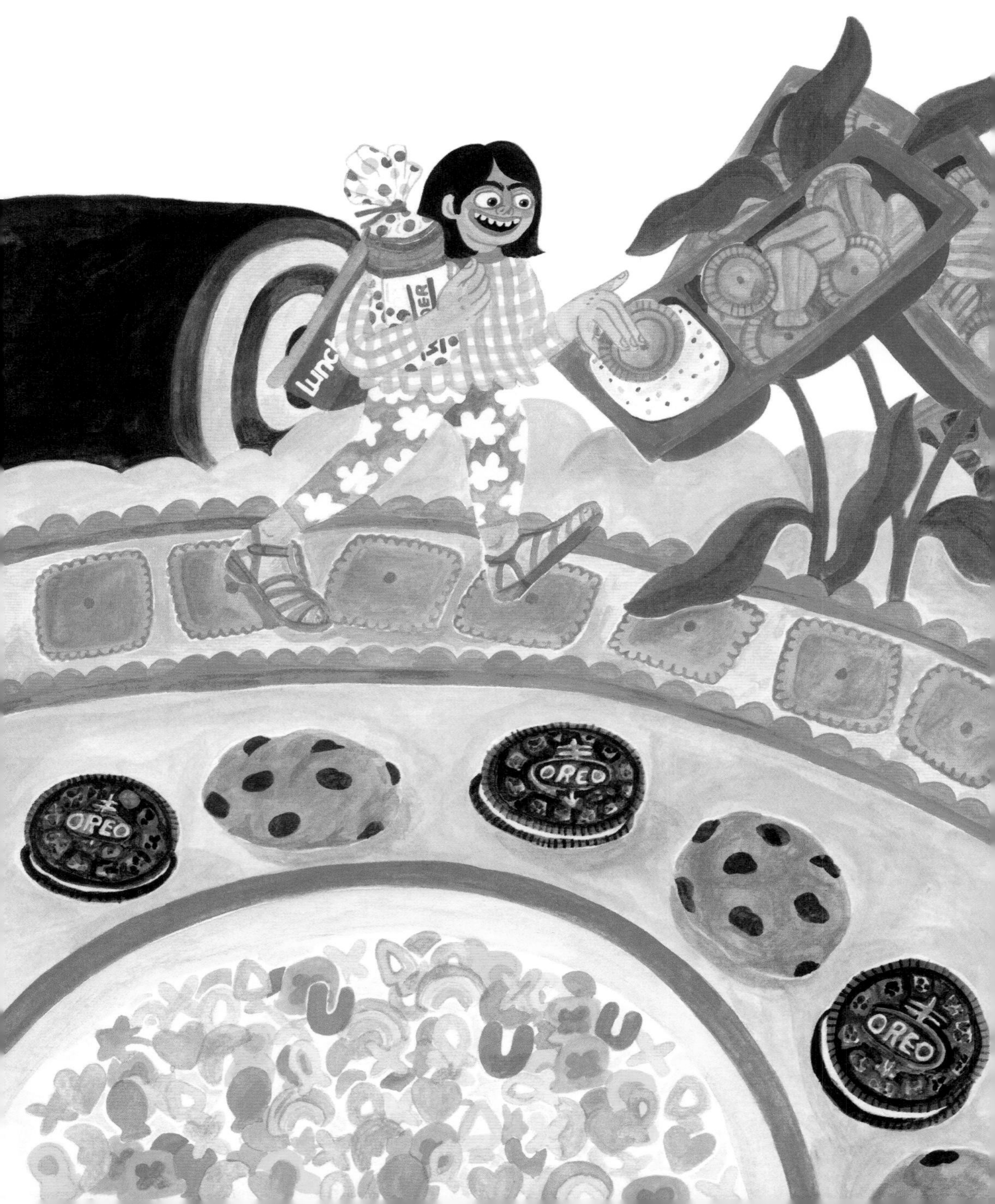
OREO
OREO
OREO
OREO

I had an ongoing fantasy of being trapped in a grocery store overnight, able to taste test every snack in existence!

*THINK NORMCORE WILLY WONKA.

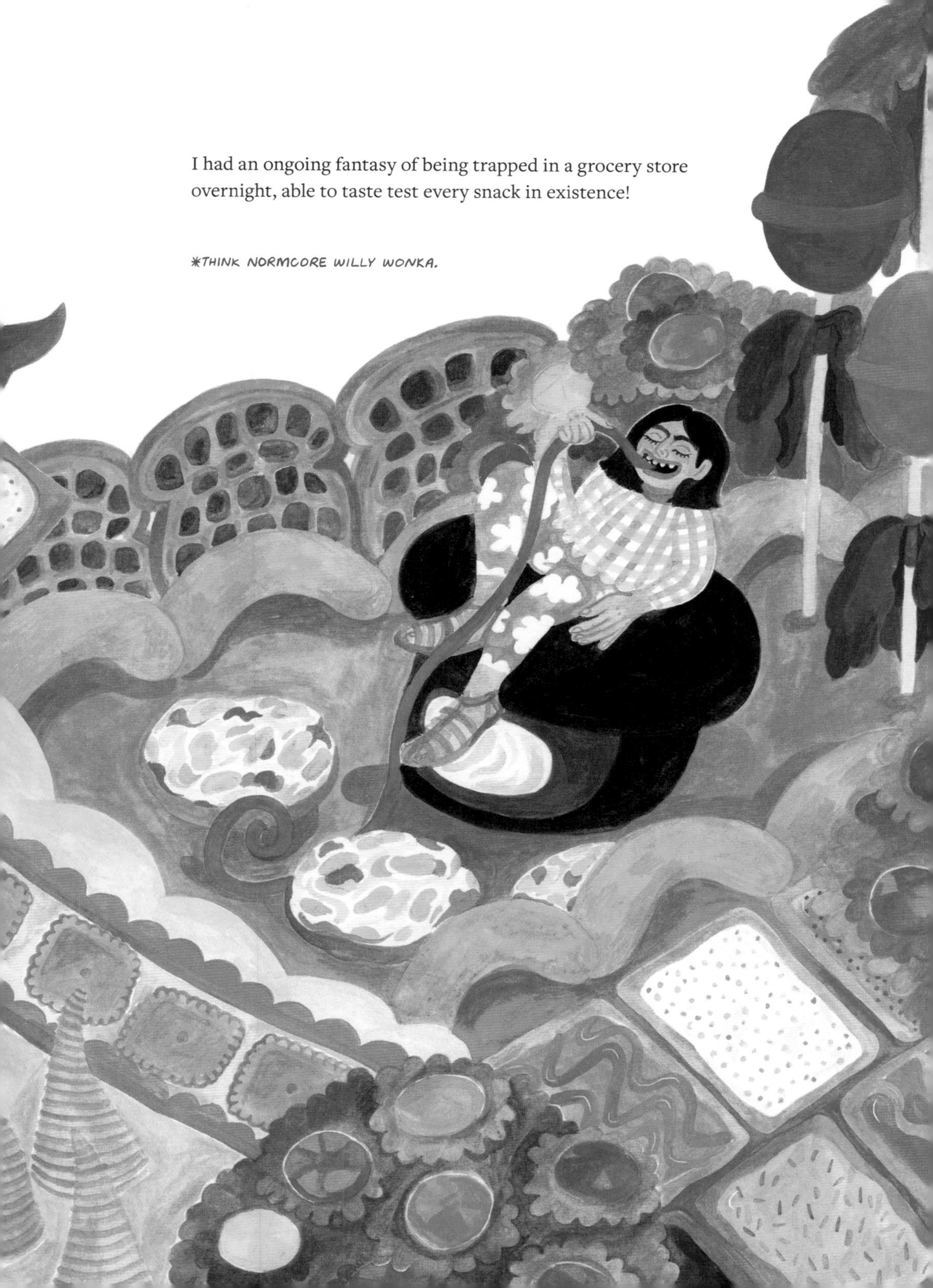

But as early as fourth grade, I internalized that my weight and size would be something I'd be judged by. I began relabeling my pants to read kids' 6S—the same size as the most popular girl in my grade. From then on that number—my pants size—meant a lot.

I joined Weight Watchers in eighth grade and kept with it on and off through college.

Weight Watchers sucked the joy out of food. All the counting made me obsess over my eating habits even more, and any time I wasn't being strategic about my caloric intake, I felt reckless and "bad."

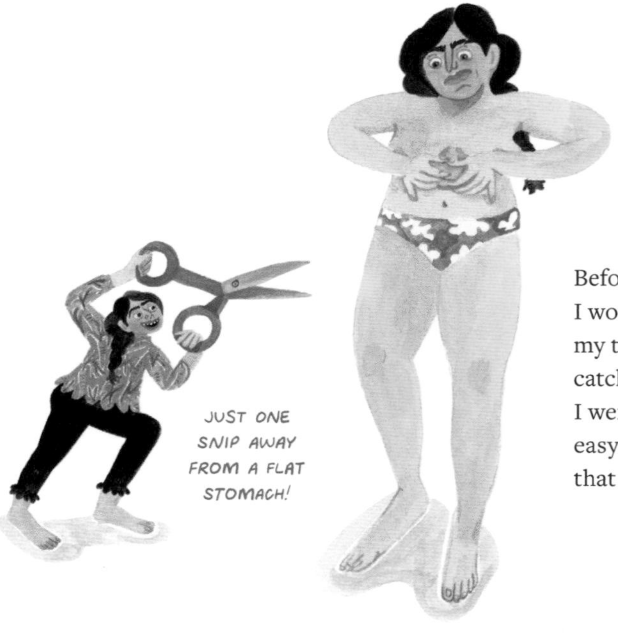

JUST ONE SNIP AWAY FROM A FLAT STOMACH!

Before I got into the shower each night, I would bend over to grab as much of my tummy fat as possible, pull it up, and catch a glimpse of what I'd look like if I were skinny. I fantasized about how easy it would be if I could just cut all that fat off and call it a day.

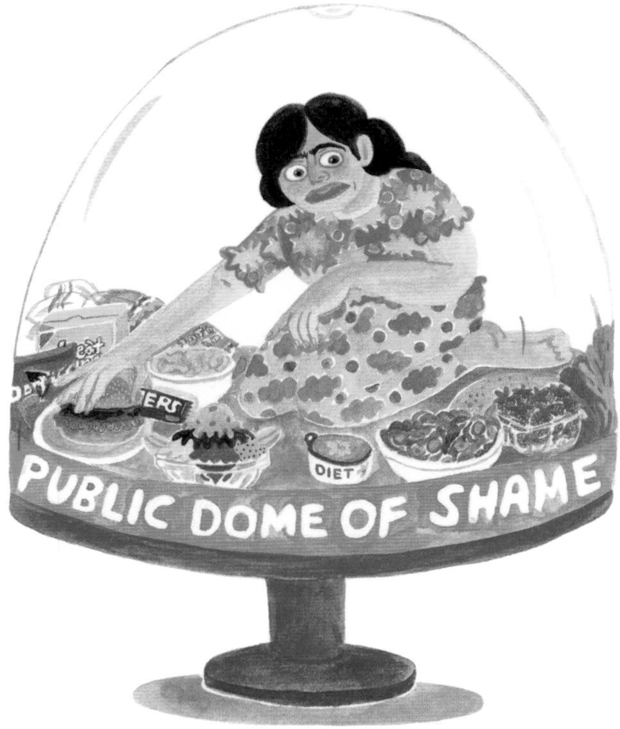
PUBLIC DOME OF SHAME
DIET

The food I ate began to feel like a total reflection of who I was, and I felt like my eating habits were constantly on display.

At camp, all my meals were eaten with others and this was always very stressful for me—especially because boys were around. I didn't like eating in front of them. I kept a roll of rice cakes in my underwear drawer and dug into them once everyone was asleep. Eating my rice cakes under the covers in the dark was true relaxation and bliss.

While some of my friends used the quiet of midnight to sneak out for a secret kissing rendezvous with a crush, I was in bed savoring three-plus rice cakes a night. Instead of swirling my tongue around a boy's mouth, I was sucking on chunks of Quaker Oat greatness.

A GIRL IN MY BUNK ONCE EXPERTLY EXPLAINED (AND DEMONSTRATED) THAT IF YOU SQUISH THE AREAS AROUND YOUR BELLY BUTTON TOGETHER AND IT LOOKS LIKE A BAGEL, YOU'RE EATING TOO MANY CARBS. THAT IMAGE WAS BURNED IN MY BRAIN.

LOX SLIPPERS MIGHT NOT BE THE MOST APPETIZING CONCEPT (AND THEY WOULD RESULT IN A VERY DISTURBING FOOT SMELL), BUT ADD A NICE SLATHER OF CREAM CHEESE SOCKS? LUXURY!

I became my own food and weight watchdog—incredibly judgmental and tough on myself. Each meal became an opportunity to be "good" or "bad," rather than a time to nourish, enjoy, or even indulge myself. Vacations became agonizing because that meant less control over meals and exercise schedules. I began filling journals with diet plans and weight loss goals. I used trips home as milestones, determined to look thinner and thinner each time.

LOOK, I'M SKINNY!

LOW FAT

skinny

ACCEPTABLE GIRL

FOODS RESPONSIBLE, ATTRACTIVE GIRLS EAT:

- SALAD! AND LOTS OF IT!
- VEGGIE STICKS
- BIG MUGS OF GREEN TEA
- GRILLED SALMON
- NONFAT YOGURT

I still sometimes catch myself judging my grocery store haul as I stand in line, assessing what my choices say about me.

I went from publicly declaring my love for cake to stealing precious, sneaky moments with it behind (nearly closed) refrigerator doors.

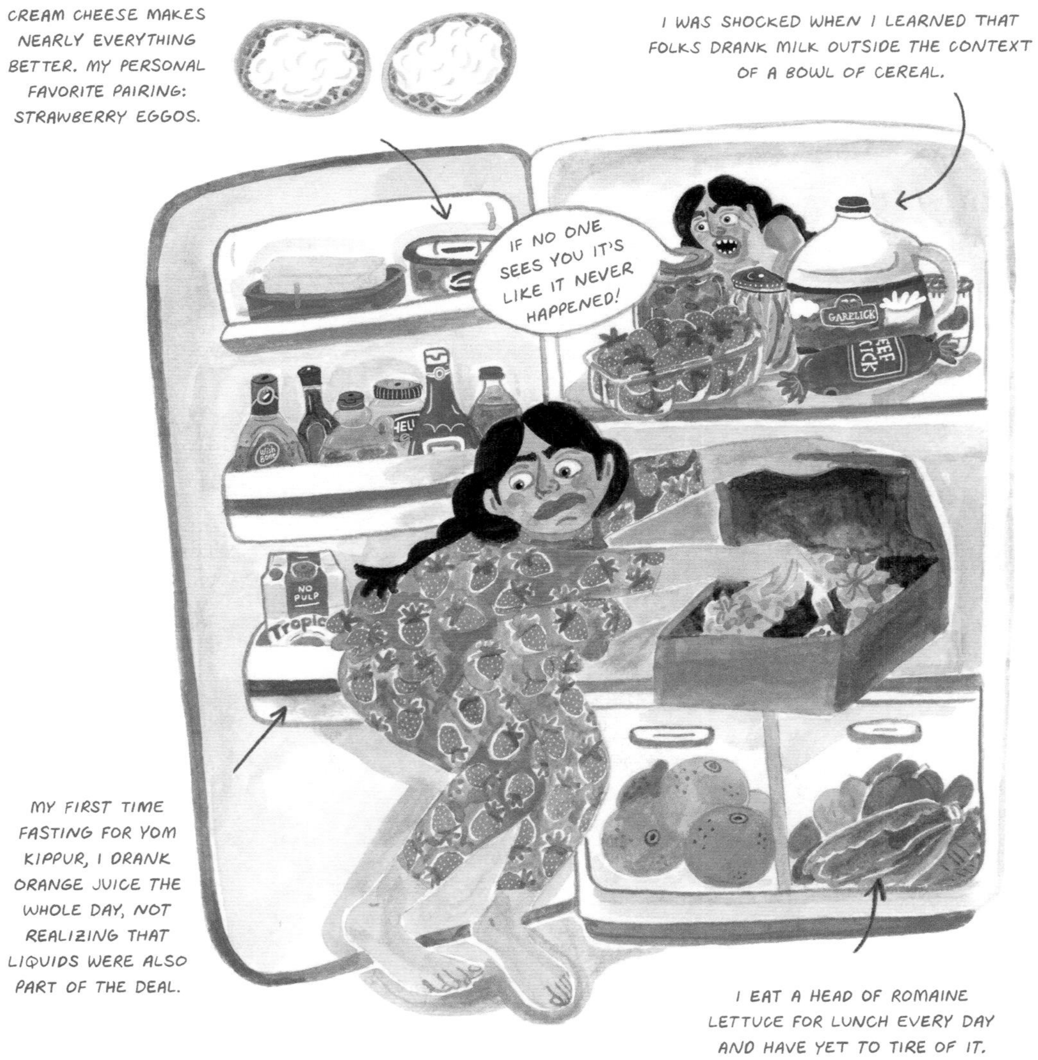
CREAM CHEESE MAKES NEARLY EVERYTHING BETTER. MY PERSONAL FAVORITE PAIRING: STRAWBERRY EGGOS.
I WAS SHOCKED WHEN I LEARNED THAT FOLKS DRANK MILK OUTSIDE THE CONTEXT OF A BOWL OF CEREAL.
IF NO ONE SEES YOU IT'S LIKE IT NEVER HAPPENED!
GARELICK
NO PULP
MY FIRST TIME FASTING FOR YOM KIPPUR, I DRANK ORANGE JUICE THE WHOLE DAY, NOT REALIZING THAT LIQUIDS WERE ALSO PART OF THE DEAL.
I EAT A HEAD OF ROMAINE LETTUCE FOR LUNCH EVERY DAY AND HAVE YET TO TIRE OF IT.

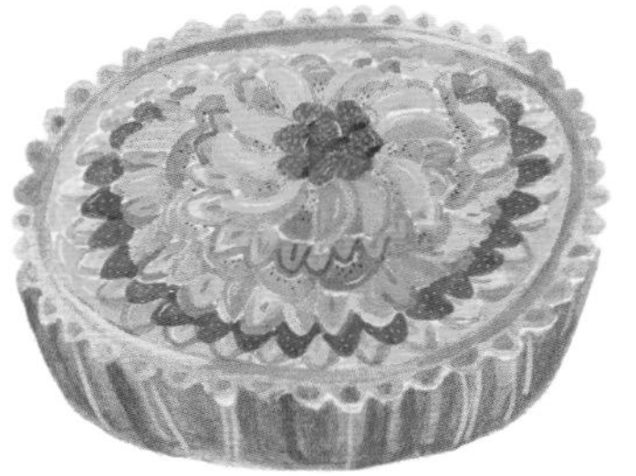

In middle school, I began asking for fruit tarts for my birthday each year instead of the decadent cake I was secretly pining for. In my mind, a traditional birthday cake with thick frosting was far too indulgent for me; I wasn't skinny enough to have real dessert. I didn't actually like the tart that much, so I would just end up eating the fruit coated in sugary gel and never had to worry about eating the leftovers.

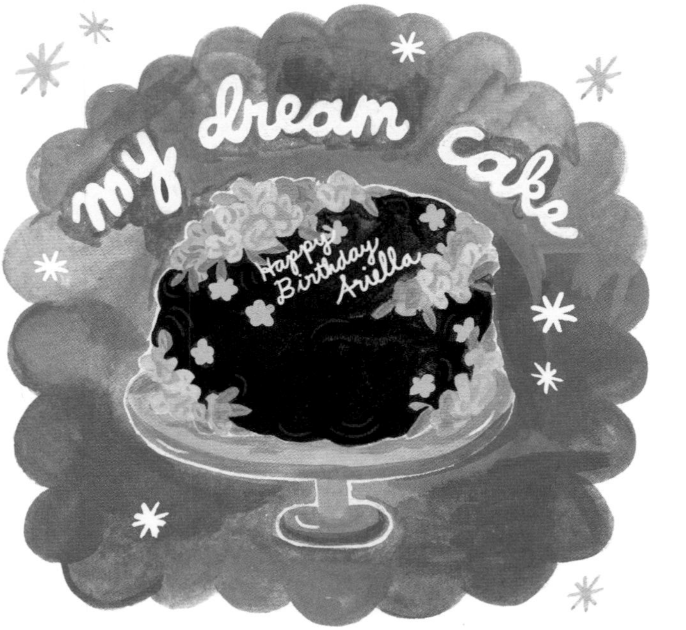
my dream cake
Happy Birthday Ariella

Moist, yellow cake with a fudgy chocolate frosting. Flowers are, of course, a must.

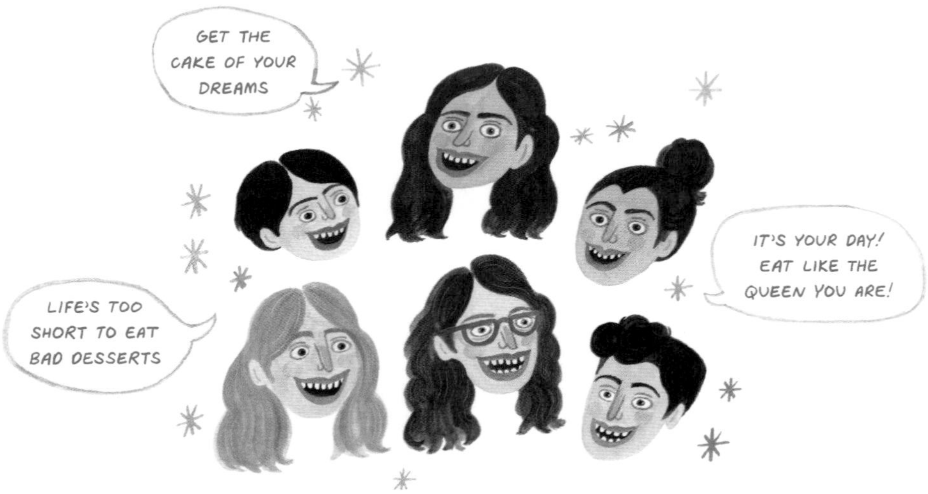
GET THE CAKE OF YOUR DREAMS
IT'S YOUR DAY! EAT LIKE THE QUEEN YOU ARE!
LIFE'S TOO SHORT TO EAT BAD DESSERTS

Finally, on my twenty-third birthday I went for it. I was officially an adult: living in New York City with a job and an apartment. I had arrived. I called in my own cake order from the famous (at least to me—my Grams used to live nearby and I had heard that their cakes were incredible) Two Little Red Hens Bakery on the Upper East Side.

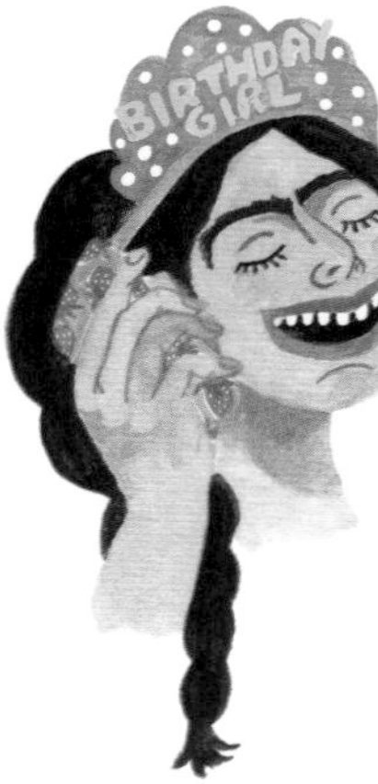
BIRTHDAY GIRL

TLRH: And what would you like written on the cake?

ME: Happy Birthday Ariella

TLRH: Great, and can I get a name for the order?

ME: Ariella

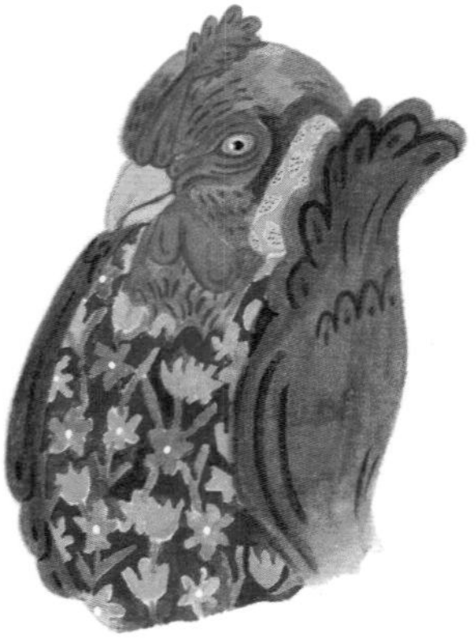

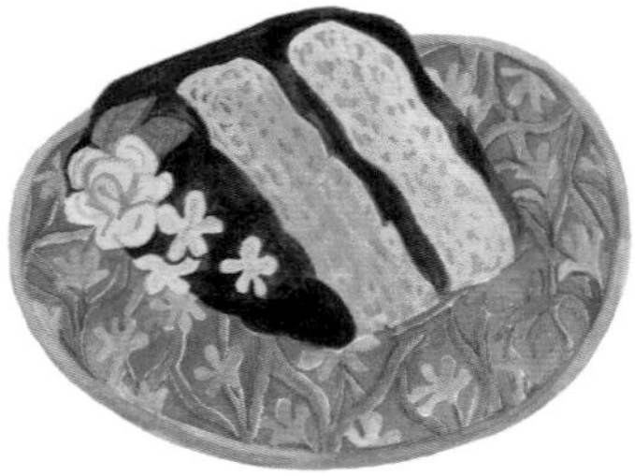

It was dreamy and delicious. I had two and a half slices the day of, and ate the rest over the course of the following week. Sliced, out in the open, and on a beautiful plate.

Reconnecting with The Yentas over meals helped me reconnect with the joy of food. In some twist of fate, we never discuss diets or comment on what anyone decides to order with an "Oh, you're just getting a salad? Wow, you're being so good." These meals heal me, and have slowly relieved the anxiety I have surrounding food.

IF YOU COULD BATHE IN ANY FOOD, *what would it be?*

(A very fun question Jesse asks everyone)

me

Meat sauce: cold leftovers in a plastic container

grams

Her signature mix: Cheerios and almonds, pecans, blueberries, sliced nectarine and pear, Craisins, and skim milk

THIS IS GRAMS'S BELOVED SIDEKICK, MAX. HE'S A GENTLEMANLY SHIH TZU.

118

elisha

Matzoh ball soup (homemade),
and with a book of logic puzzles

mom

Strawberry Jell-O with Cool Whip

*NOT PICTURED: MY
MOM'S THREE
GOLDEN RETRIEVERS
LAPPING IT UP.

alex

Jar of pickles (Vlasic spears)

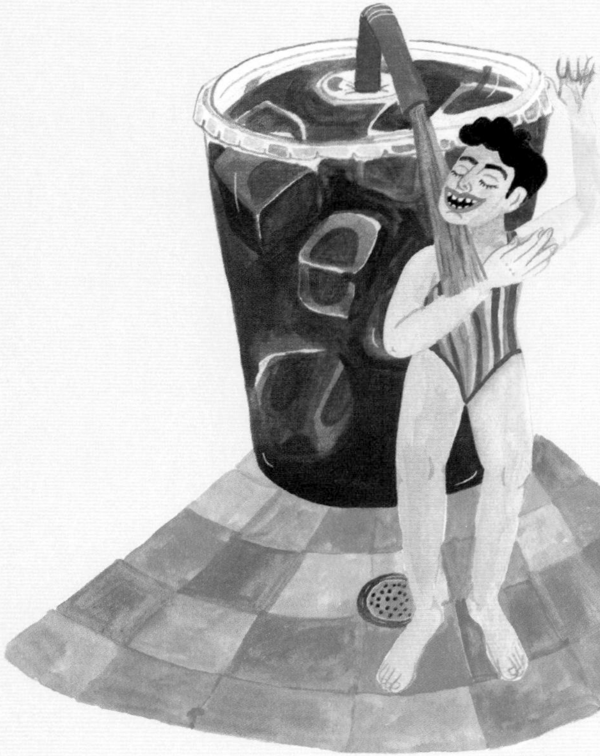

ellie

Cold brew shower. She opted out of the food bath, noting that if she had to pick it would be Greek yogurt—but she would find a less messy way to enjoy it.

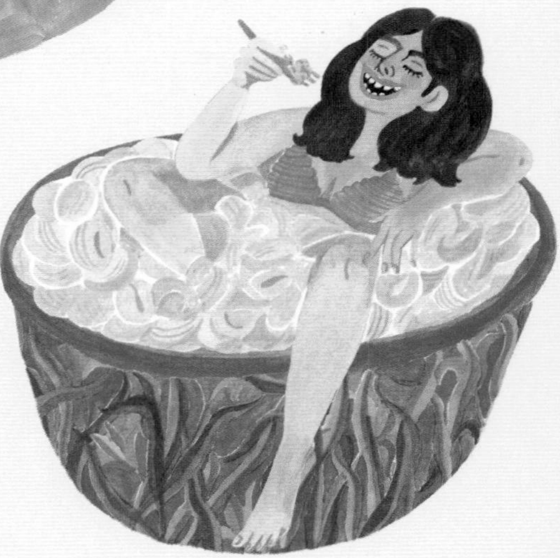

jesse

Annie's Mac & Cheese.
"The juicy cheese taste and the sound when you stir and the noodles suck each other—OMG, heaven."

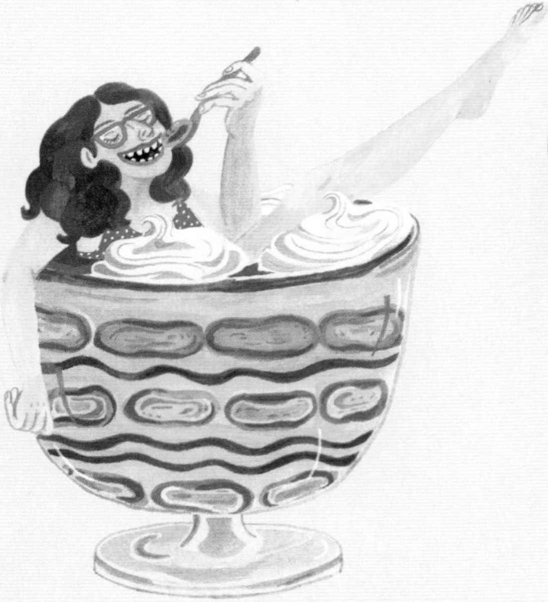

adi

Tiramisu

maya

Sour cream. She is of the mind that a sidecar of sour cream can improve almost every dish. She's not wrong.

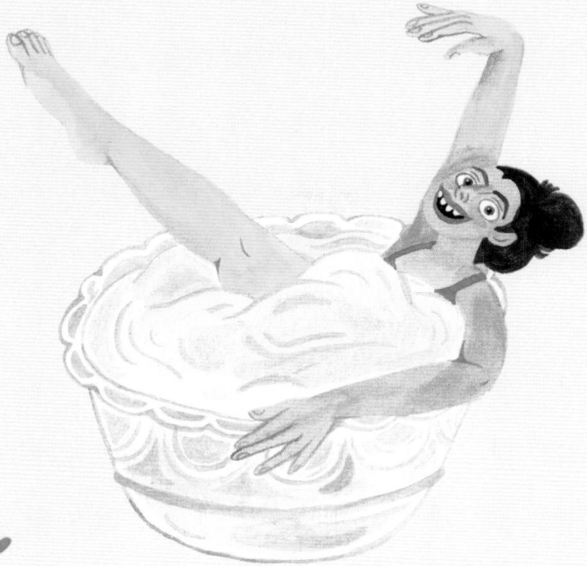

leila

Oatmeal

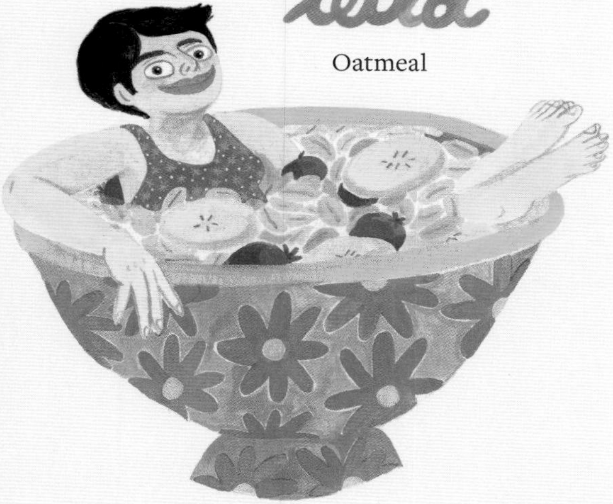

noa

A melting Yasso Bar (mint chip)

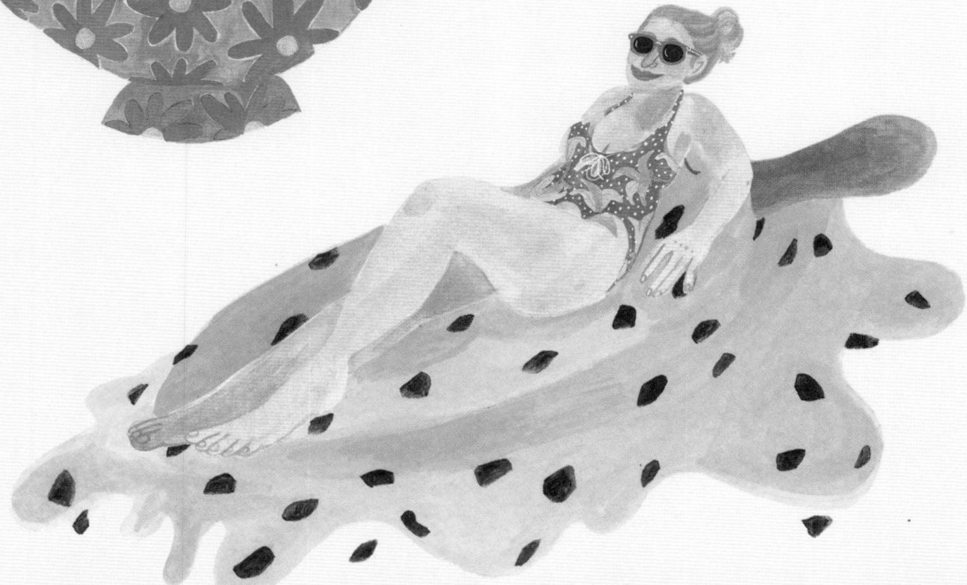

I used to avoid this view at all costs. These days, I like to think my tummy is pretty cute. Soft, friendly, and warm.

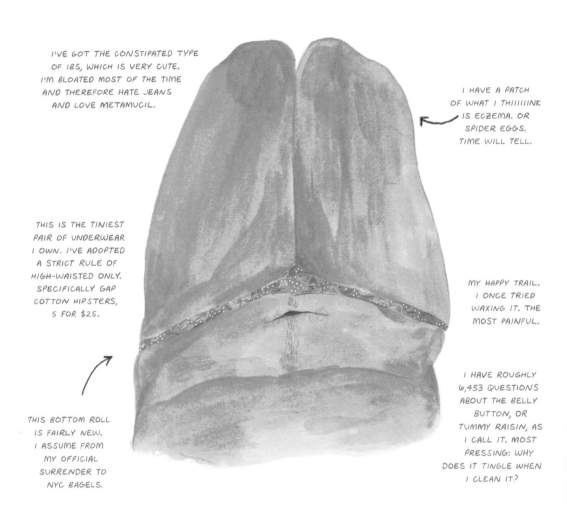

I'VE GOT THE CONSTIPATED TYPE OF IBS, WHICH IS VERY CUTE. I'M BLOATED MOST OF THE TIME AND THEREFORE HATE JEANS AND LOVE METAMUCIL.

I HAVE A PATCH OF WHAT I THIIIIIINK IS ECZEMA. OR SPIDER EGGS. TIME WILL TELL.

THIS IS THE TINIEST PAIR OF UNDERWEAR I OWN. I'VE ADOPTED A STRICT RULE OF HIGH-WAISTED ONLY. SPECIFICALLY GAP COTTON HIPSTERS, 5 FOR $25.

MY HAPPY TRAIL. I ONCE TRIED WAXING IT. THE MOST PAINFUL.

THIS BOTTOM ROLL IS FAIRLY NEW. I ASSUME FROM MY OFFICIAL SURRENDER TO NYC BAGELS.

I HAVE ROUGHLY 6,453 QUESTIONS ABOUT THE BELLY BUTTON, OR TUMMY RAISIN, AS I CALL IT. MOST PRESSING: WHY DOES IT TINGLE WHEN I CLEAN IT?

THE BAND OF HELL: AGGRAVATED MOST BY BRAS AND HOLIDAY WEEKENDS AT HOME, DURING WHICH I EAT NONSTOP FOR AT LEAST THREE CONSECUTIVE DAYS.

(not) GETTING INTO JEANS

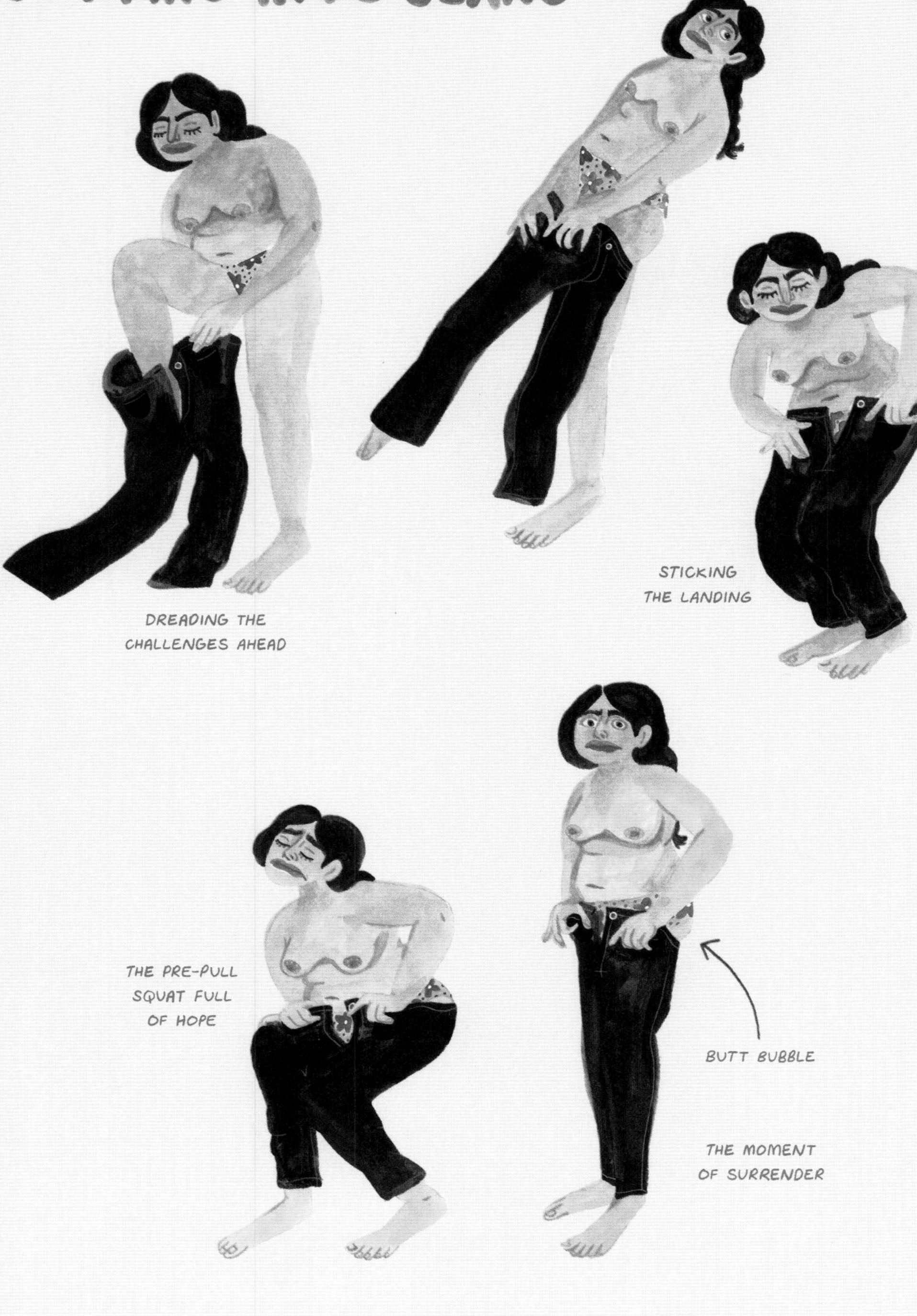
DREADING THE CHALLENGES AHEAD
STICKING THE LANDING
THE PRE-PULL SQUAT FULL OF HOPE
BUTT BUBBLE
THE MOMENT OF SURRENDER

THINGS I'VE EATEN *in one sitting*

Here's a bit of news: it's not unladylike to enjoy food—dare I say mindlessly. Here are the foods I blissfully snack on and for which I often ignore the suggested serving size.

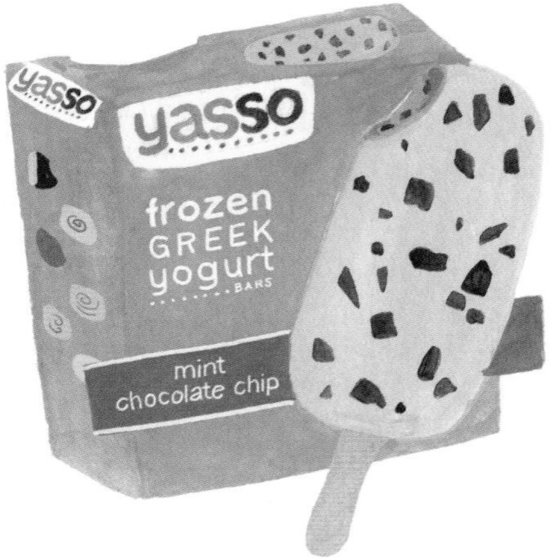

yasso
yasso
frozen
GREEK
yogurt
BARS
mint
chocolate chip

These are delicious and refreshing. With four to a box, it's pretty easy to power through them all. I don't always practice this level of regimentation, but it's a nice treat to ration over four episodes of TV.

Noa's family is famous among The Yentas for always having a freezer filled to the brim with every flavor of Yasso pop. A delicious, heavenly rainbow.

I have to stop myself from purchasing this cereal because when I do, I'm out of commission for the day. Like no other cereal, Peanut Butter Puffins pull me into the most vicious cycle of milk-to-cereal ratios. Before I know it, the plastic bag is out of the box, I'm tipping those sad and tasty crumbs into my bowl, I've gone through a carton of milk, and I'm inconsolably bloated.

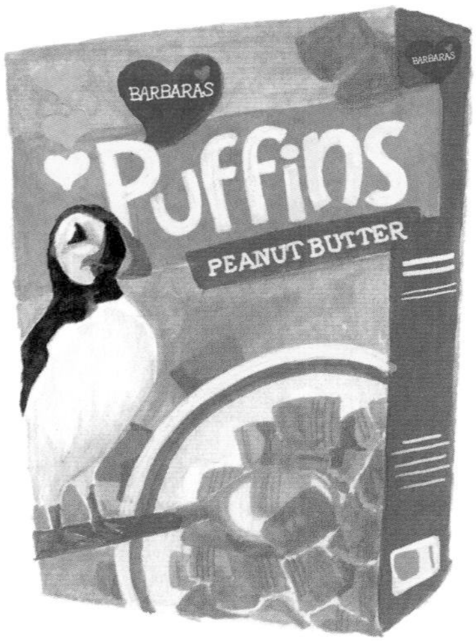

BARBARAS
BARBARAS
Puffins
PEANUT BUTTER

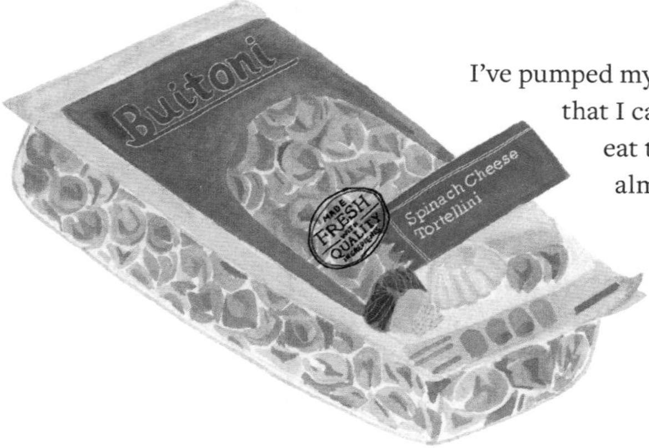
Buitoni
Spinach Cheese
Tortellini

I've pumped myself up for Tinder dates with the promise that I can buy these on my way home. I always eat them with a side of ketchup. The dipping is almost a sensual experience.

Last time I bought these, I started eating them on the way home from the grocery store. Frozen and thawing. I don't trust myself enough to keep an entire tub of cream cheese in my refrigerator, but I'm certain it would be the perfect spread for these waffles.

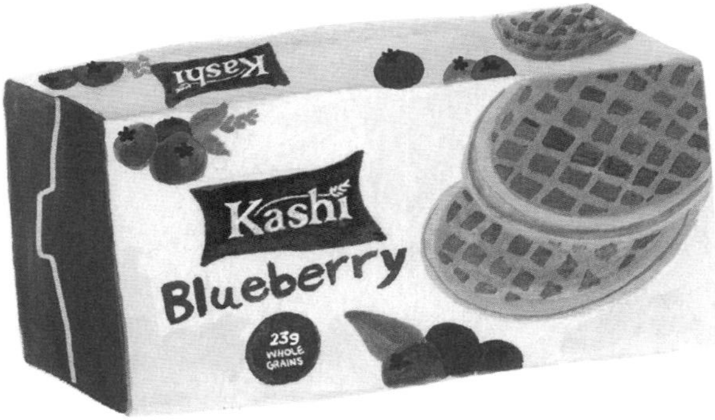
Kashi
Kashi
Blueberry
23g
WHOLE
GRAINS

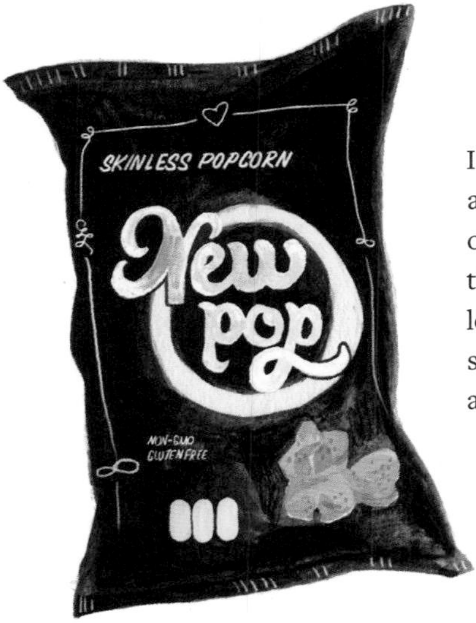
SKINLESS POPCORN
New pop
NON-GMO
GLUTEN FREE

I discovered New Pop in a bodega near my apartment and soon bought out their entire supply. This led to an obsession to find the other select bodegas that carried these vaguely sweet, styrofoam-textured popcorns that look like baby butts (salivating yet?). I'm saddened to share that I haven't seen a bag of New Pop for a while and am unable to find it online. I fear it's been discontinued.

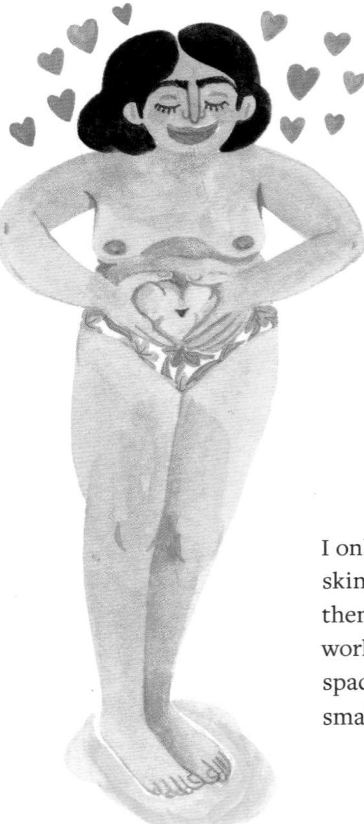

Now in my late twenties, I'm finally letting go of the heavy guilt I used to associate with food, and am learning to love my soft and squishy tummy. It's definitely still a process, but it feels insanely amazing to let go of that harsh inner voice telling me to hate my fat and deny myself delicious food.

I only sometimes try on my pair of skinny shorts (one day I will burn them). When they're too tight, the world doesn't end. I give my body space and permission to get bigger/smaller/softer/jigglier/tighter.

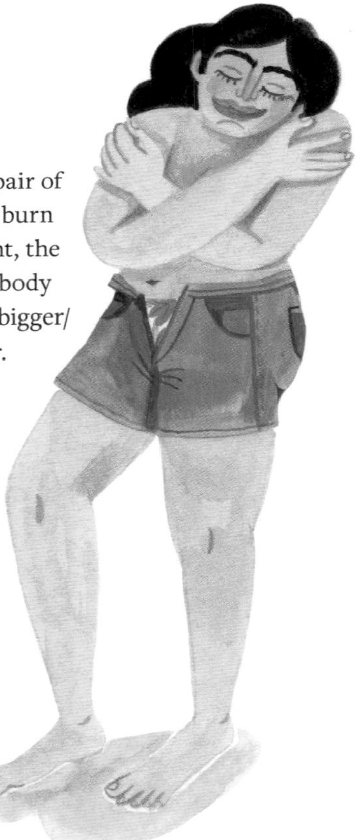

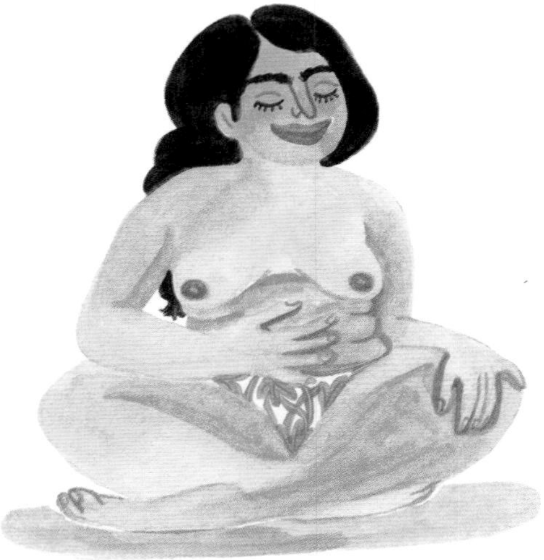

Sometimes I play with my tummy rolls (instead of fearfully avoiding them).

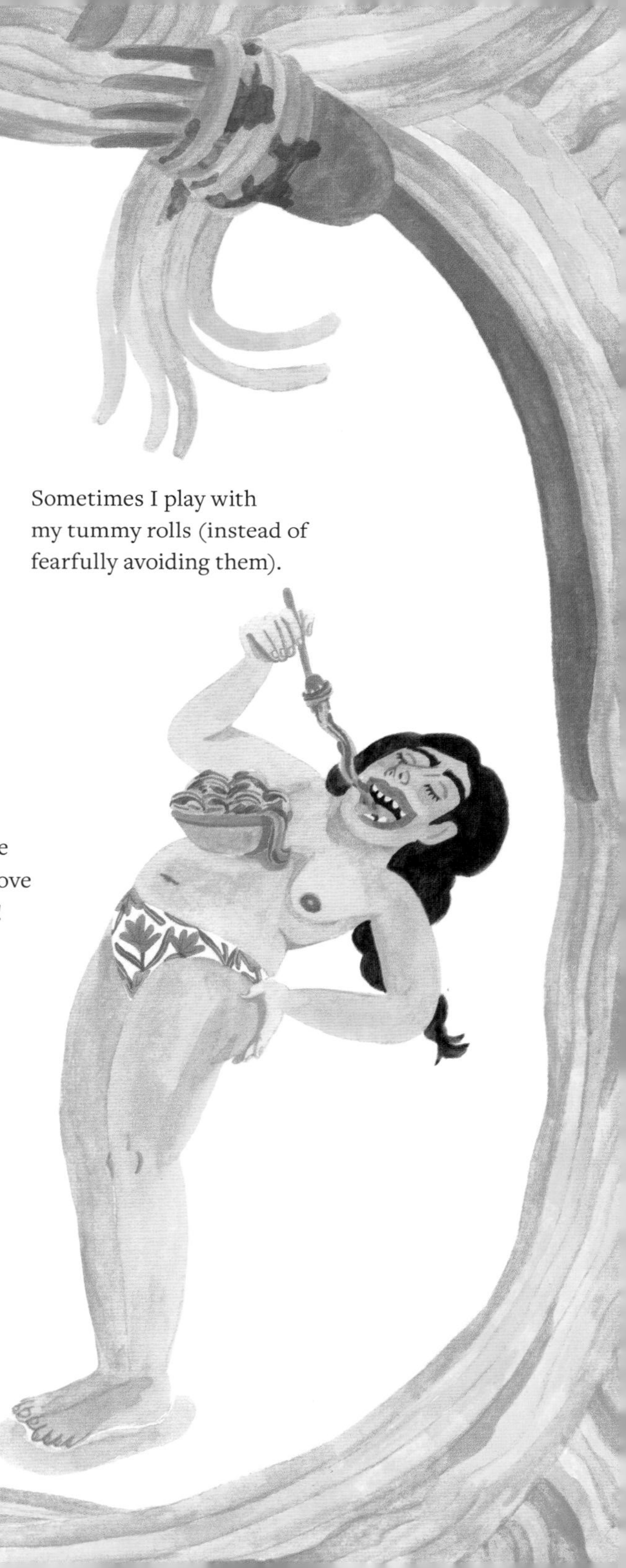

I order pasta when I crave it or want to feel cozy. I love pasta; it's very fun to eat!

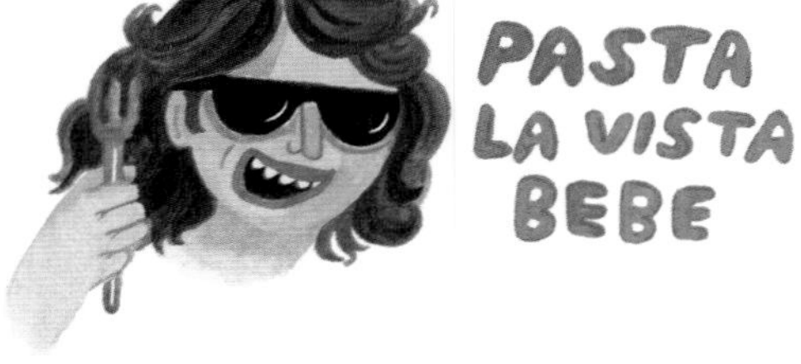
PASTA LA VISTA BEBE

THAT'S HOW ELISHA USED TO ASK US TO PASS THE PASTA AT DINNER

BUTT

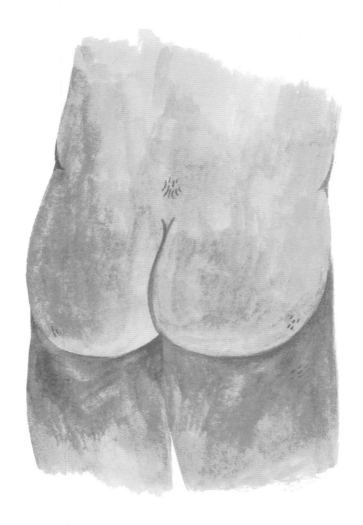

This is my butt. It looks best nude. Jeans simply don't do it justice.

When I was growing up, my parents didn't teach me to use cutesy terms like "bum," "toot," or "number two." In our house, bathroom humor was always a hit.

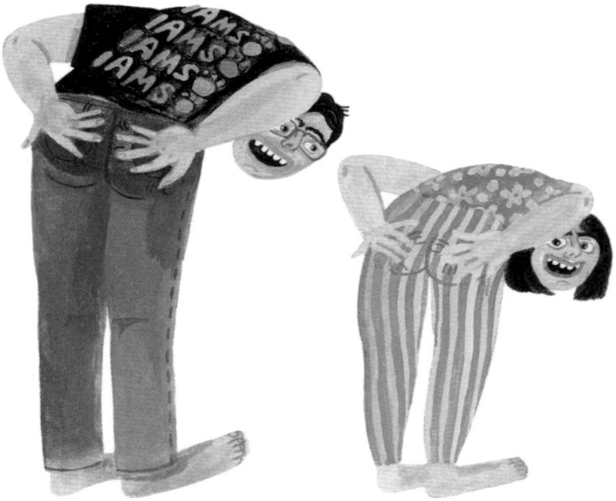
IAMS
IAMS
IAMS
IAMS

AFTER WATCHING ACE VENTURA: PET DETECTIVE TOGETHER, MY DAD AND I LOVED TO RE-ENACT THE SCENE WHERE HE TALKS FROM HIS BUTT.

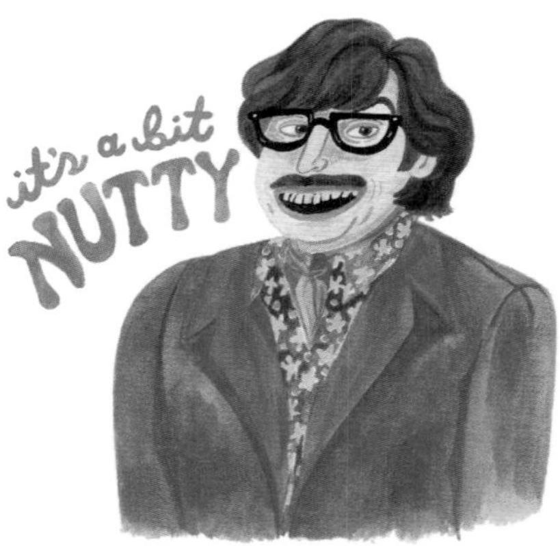
it's a bit
NUTTY

We quoted *Austin Powers* often, specifically the scene where Austin drinks poop, thinking it's coffee.

During long car rides, my sisters and I would craft new lyrics to the diarrhea song.

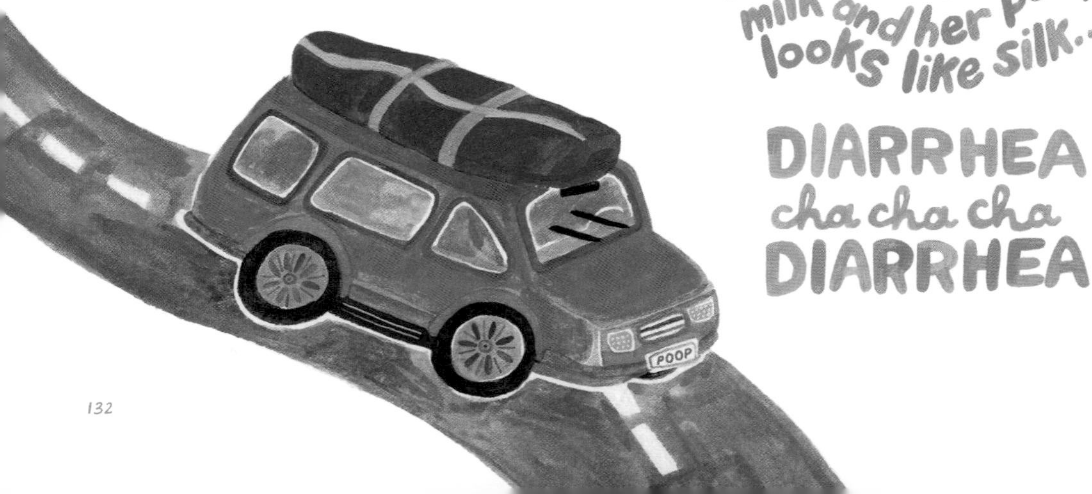
when alex drinks milk and her poop looks like silk...
DIARRHEA
cha cha cha
DIARRHEA
POOP

I was always fascinated by the idea of mooning and I credit my affinity for the act to the scene in *Grease* when Doody, Sonny, and Putzie (those are their names; I looked this up to confirm) pull down their pants at the dance and flash their butts just as the song gets to the lyrics "blue moon." Hilarious.

I was inspired to create this exhibitionist pool game:

THE DOLPHIN DIVE

1) WHILE IN WAIST-DEEP WATER, PULL DOWN YOUR BATHING SUIT BOTTOM SO THE WAISTBAND SITS RIGHT BELOW YOUR BUTT (DOLPHIN DIVE ONLY WORKS WHEN WEARING A TWO-PIECE).

2) BEND YOUR KNEES AS YOU INHALE, AND PREPARE TO PROPEL YOURSELF FORWARD AND INTO THE WATER, HEAD FIRST.

3) TAKE THE PLUNGE. YOUR SPINE ROUNDS, YOUR BODY GLIDES THROUGH THE WATER, AND YOUR BARE BUTT BOBS TO THE SURFACE, WET AND GLISTENING IN THE SUN.

finale!

THE DOLPHIN DIVE WAS GENUINELY RISKY PUBLIC BEHAVIOR, BUT I THOUGHT IT WAS A RIOT.

WHAT HAPPENS IN THE BATHROOM STAYS IN THE BATHROOM

As I got older, I slowly observed that girls were not meant to align themselves with butts, farting, or pooping. Bathroom humor was reserved for boys and simply was not my domain.

When I was six years old, I was put in a time out at my friend's house for using "bathroom words." Butt and poop were not appropriate playroom discussion topics, so I was exiled to the dining room to sit alone, stare at the toile wallpaper, and think about what I'd done.

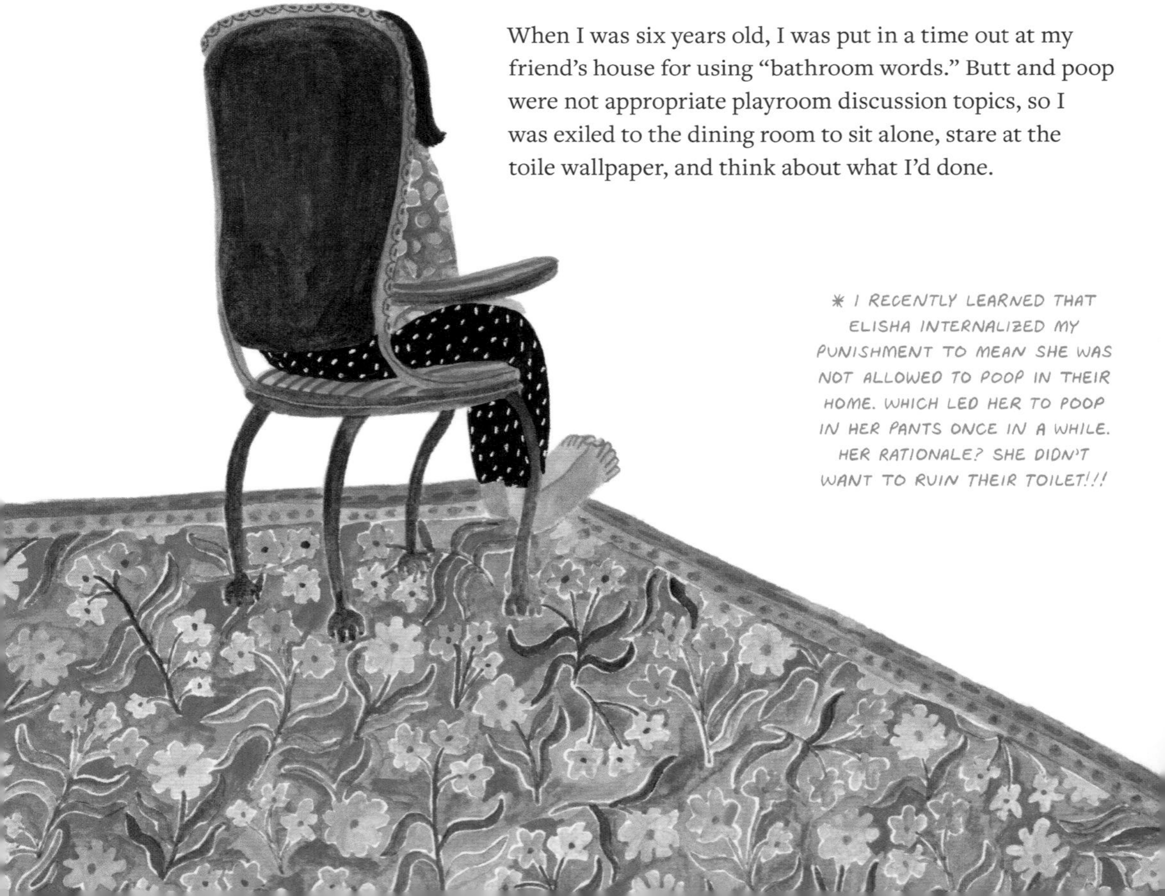

* I RECENTLY LEARNED THAT ELISHA INTERNALIZED MY PUNISHMENT TO MEAN SHE WAS NOT ALLOWED TO POOP IN THEIR HOME. WHICH LED HER TO POOP IN HER PANTS ONCE IN A WHILE. HER RATIONALE? SHE DIDN'T WANT TO RUIN THEIR TOILET!!!

According to teen magazines, pooping was the most shameful thing a girl could do. The embarrassing stories sections were filled with tales in which girls had pooped in a toilet that would not flush and the desperate measures they would take to get rid of the evidence. We read these stories aloud at camp, screaming at the horror of it all.

One memorable case was a girl who had pooped at her boyfriend's parent's house when she was meeting them for the first time. When her poop didn't flush, she scooped it out of the toilet and threw it out the window. This window was—unbeknownst to her—located above the kitchen skylight downstairs, and she had essentially thrown her poop into her boyfriend's and his parents' faces. The lesson? Don't ever poop! It will always end badly! Be afraid of poop forever!

LOOK OUT BELOW!

As a teenager, I abandoned my love for mooning (probably for the best) and felt that be to seen on the toilet was to be tossed into an unending hole of humiliation. One night when my youngest sister, Alex, was having a sleepover party, one of her friends walked in on me going to the bathroom. I was totally mortified and upset. I spent the night in my bedroom, sure that her friends were making fun of me the whole night. I logically knew I wasn't the only human to have ever used a toilet before, but in the moment I felt like a total aberration. The freak in the corner with her pants down.

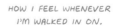

HOW I FEEL WHENEVER I'M WALKED IN ON.

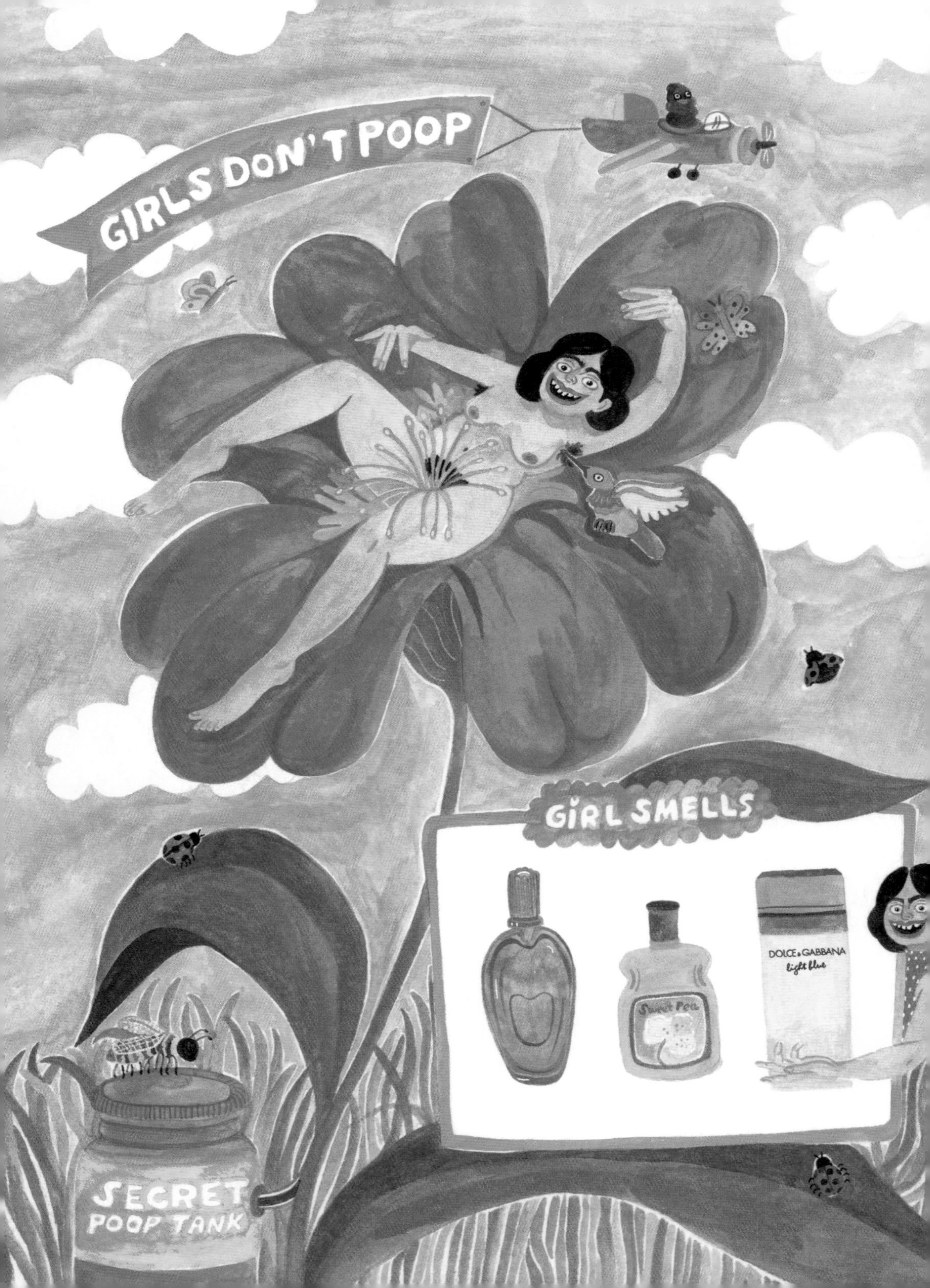
GIRLS DON'T POOP
GIRL SMELLS
Sweet Pea
DOLCE & GABBANA
light blue
SECRET
POOP TANK

Our butts don't actually serve any functional purpose at all. They're merely ornamental (just like every other part of our body!) pouches of fat that come in varying shapes, sizes, and degrees of roundness that determine what type of jeans we ought to buy.

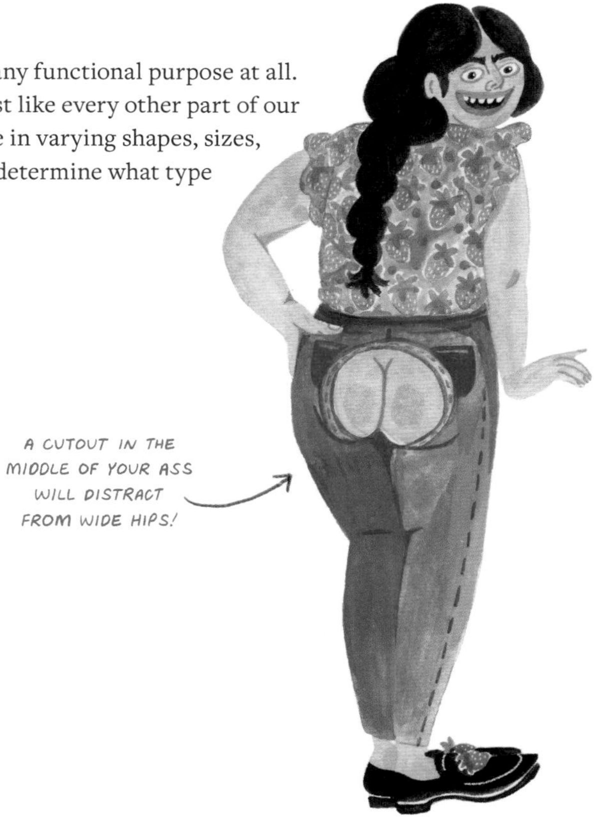
A CUTOUT IN THE MIDDLE OF YOUR ASS WILL DISTRACT FROM WIDE HIPS!

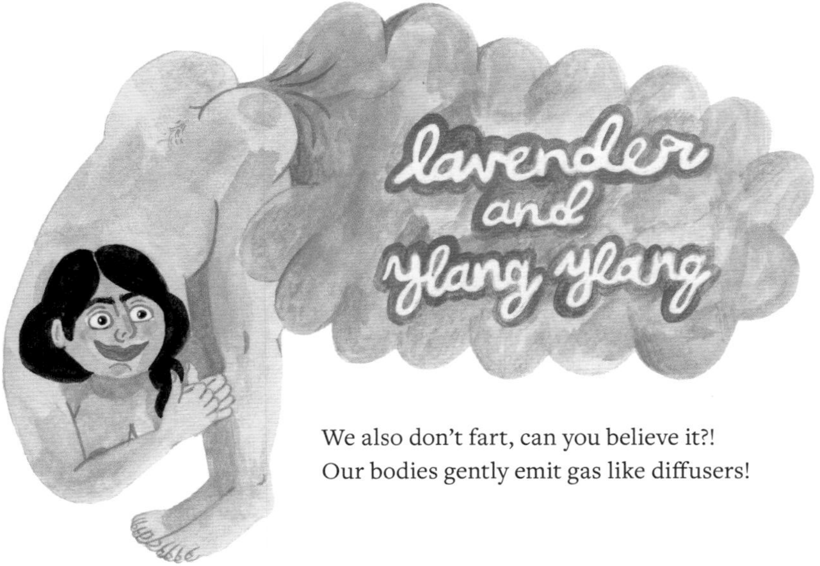
lavender and ylang ylang

We also don't fart, can you believe it?! Our bodies gently emit gas like diffusers!

POOP STANDOFF

We try to hide these human traits from each other. Women's bathrooms house one of the most intense competitions of all time: the poop standoff. Two women in neighboring stalls, fighting to be the last one standing (sitting, or squatting), free to let out their poop and all sounds that come with it in total privacy. Like all other parts of our life we work hard to disguise with illusions of non-human perfection, silencing farts and easing out poops take a lot of work. I've broken a sweat engaging in such a charade.

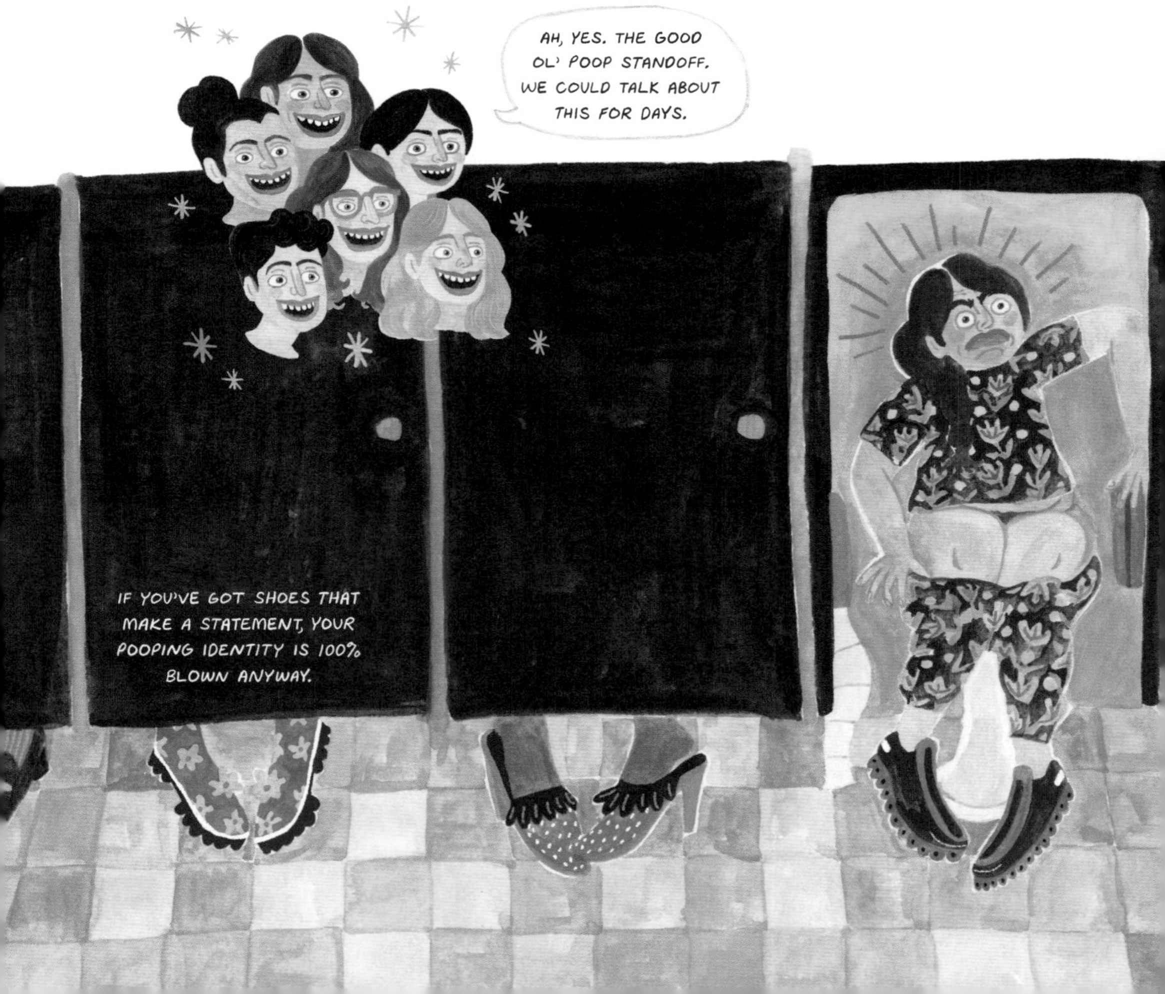
AH, YES. THE GOOD OL' POOP STANDOFF. WE COULD TALK ABOUT THIS FOR DAYS.
IF YOU'VE GOT SHOES THAT MAKE A STATEMENT, YOUR POOPING IDENTITY IS 100% BLOWN ANYWAY.

LIVE
THE OFFICE BATHROOM

Good evening, reader, it's me reporting live from the office bathroom where The Yentas are sharing their experiences in one of the most grueling competitions of our time.

BREAKING THE SILENCE

hello from the other siiide...
Hello
Adele
0:05
-4:50

I once accidentally starting playing Adele's "Hello" out loud on my phone while waiting it out. Note to self: never try to pull down pants while holding your phone.

CROSSING TERRITORY LINES

One day at the office in the middle of a standoff, Jesse dropped her phone across the borderline, into the (occupied) stall next to her.

The battle came to a truce when her neighbor slid the phone back over to Jesse's stall.

INTIMIDATION AT THE BORDER

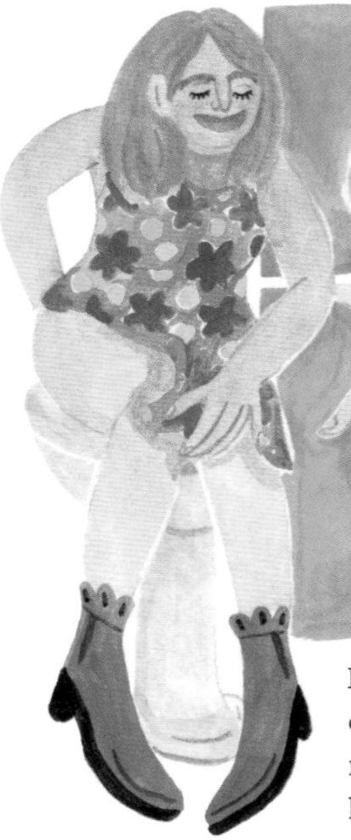

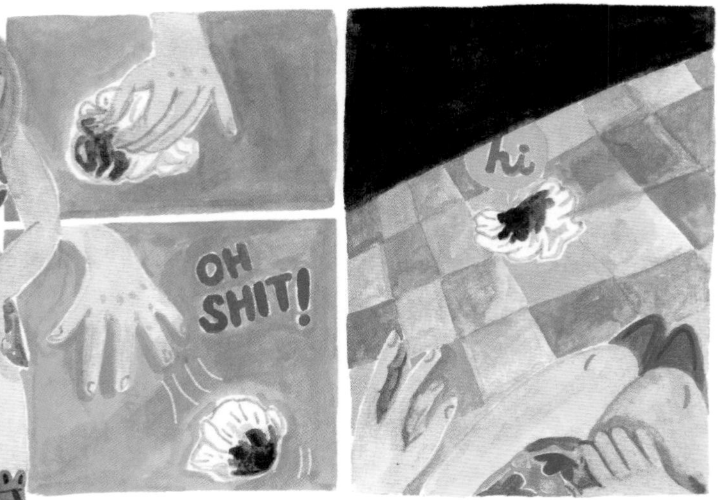
OH SHIT!
hi

Noa once dropped her toilet paper, poop side facing up, on the floor right underneath the barrier. Someone was in the next stall. She spent the entire day trying to figure out who had witnessed her crime.

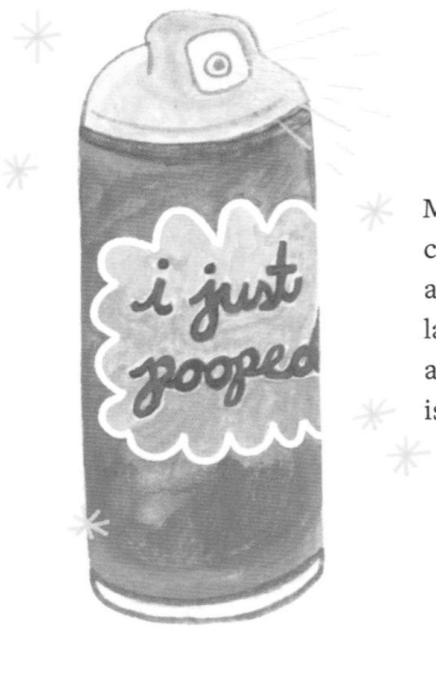
i just pooped

HOT TAKE

Maya's thoughts on air freshener: it does nothing but cover you in its thick "deodorizing" scent, and therefore alerts everyone to the fact that you have just taken a very large, very smelly shit. Her advice: stink up the bathroom and get out. No hard feelings; that's what the bathroom is for anyway. It's got a door. Leave it all behind.

MANIFESTO

Women poop. We propose that instead of being ashamed, we should join together in celebration and acknowledgment of that fact (Pooping is a gift, really. One that should not be taken for granted). Let's embrace those sneaky, aggressive farts that escape us, ricocheting off the surprisingly acoustic toilet bowl, and pass the baton of toilet paper to our neighbors, cheering them on as they cross the finish line. Just think how beautiful it would be to proudly emerge from your stall and offer your running mate a (sudsy, freshly washed) high five, instead of waiting until the coast is clear to show your face. Women of the working world: embrace your work poop!

✳ TO BE CLEAR, WE'RE NOT ADVISING YOU
TO BLOW DIARRHEA PROUDLY EVERYWHERE YOU
GO, OR PUBLICLY BRAG ABOUT EACH HEALTHY
BOWEL MOVEMENT YOU HAVE. IT'S JUST
THAT TALKING ABOUT POOP, FARTS, AND BUTTS
HAS FELT OFF-LIMITS TO US GALS A
ND THERE'S A LOT OF MATERIAL TO MINE
HERE! WE'RE GROSS TOO!

POOP *is for* MULTITASKING

In a busy, rushed world, a good poop is a reliable and effective way to take a minute. It's a unique moment where you are truly forced to do nothing but sit where you are and simply be. Take your time! My favorite ways to take advantage of a good, long poop:

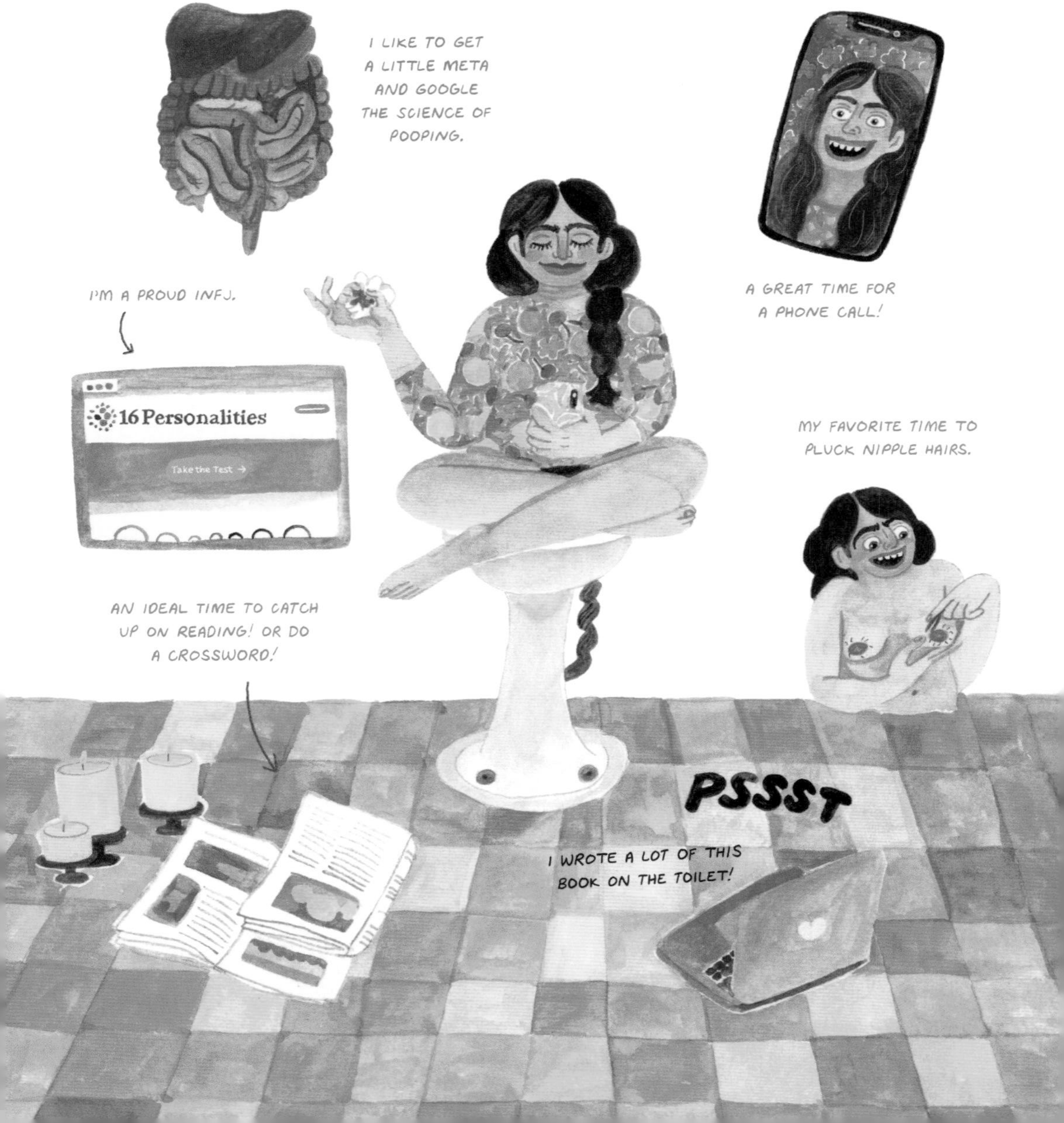

I LIKE TO GET A LITTLE META AND GOOGLE THE SCIENCE OF POOPING.
A GREAT TIME FOR A PHONE CALL!
I'M A PROUD INFJ.
16 Personalities
Take the Test →
MY FAVORITE TIME TO PLUCK NIPPLE HAIRS.
AN IDEAL TIME TO CATCH UP ON READING! OR DO A CROSSWORD!
PSSST
I WROTE A LOT OF THIS BOOK ON THE TOILET!

A TOUGH POOP TRANSFORMS ME INTO
A TAP DANCER, FURIOUSLY STOMPING
THROUGH THE PAIN AS I WAIT FOR RELIEF.

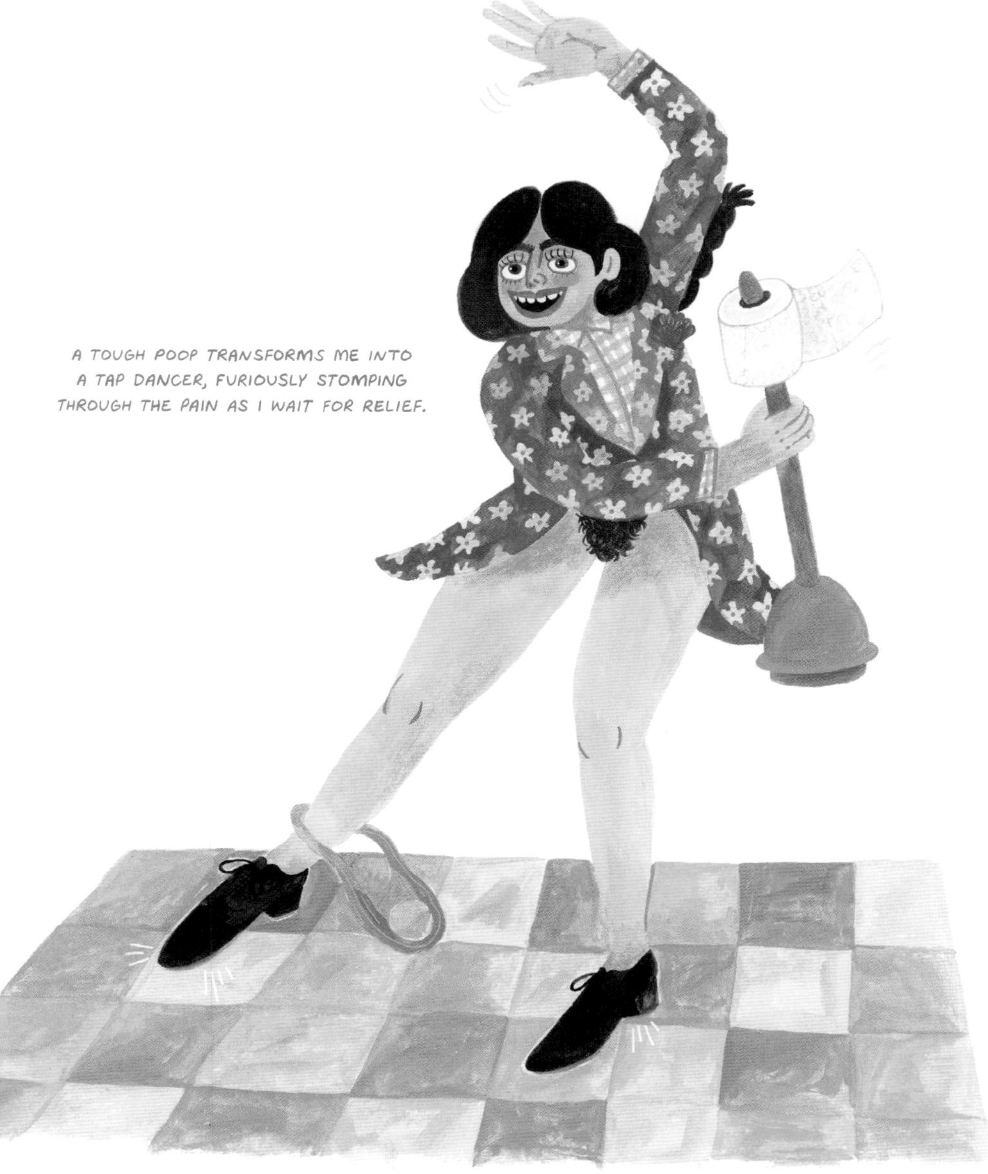

YENTA TIPS FOR STAYING REGULAR

① THE SQUATTY POTTY

Though not the most attractive accent to a bathroom, this object genuinely changed our lives. Apparently, our toilets don't set us up for the best possible pooping posture. The Squatty Potty fixes that.

DIY:

TOILET PAPER FOOTREST
* BONUS: A GREAT REMINDER WHEN YOU NEED TO RESTOCK!

IF YOU HAVE A VERY SMALL BATHROOM LIKE MINE (OR LONG LEGGY LEGS LIKE ALTERNATE UNIVERSE ME), YOU CAN USE THE WALL OPPOSITE YOU FOR LEVERAGE.

REALLY HEEL-Y HEELS OR WEDGE-Y WEDGES.

2 A FIBER POWER/SUPPLEMENT

A few of us (including yours truly) suffer from chronic constipation and take a daily dose of psyllium husk fiber to keep things moving.

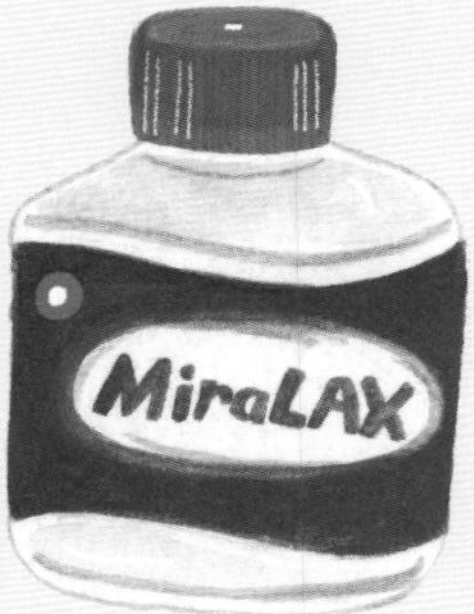
MiraLAX

MAYA AND LEILA BOTH SWEAR BY MIRALAX.

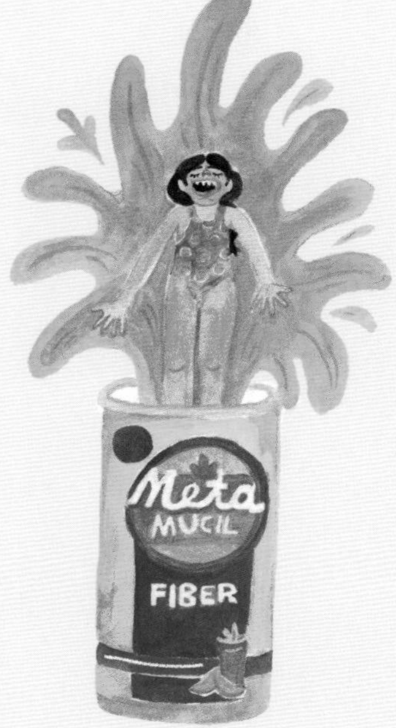
Meta
MUCIL
FIBER

I'M A METAMUCIL GAL— IT'S JEWISH TANG!

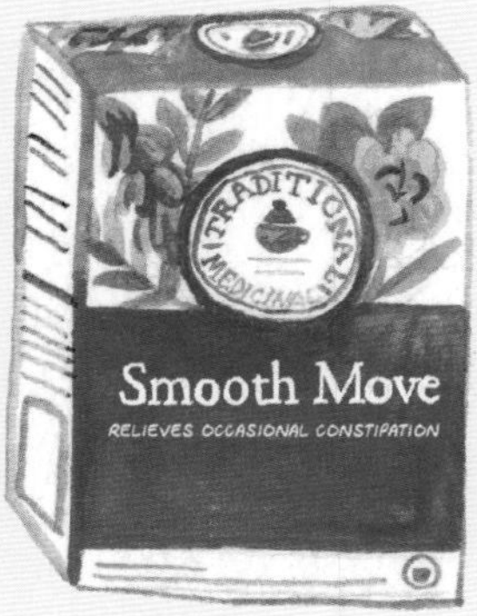
TRADITIONAL MEDICINALS
Smooth Move
RELIEVES OCCASIONAL CONSTIPATION

3 LAXATIVE TEA

When I find myself in a really intolerable situation, I drink this tea before I go to bed. I can absolutely count on a full emptying the next morning.

TRAVEL POOPS? good luck

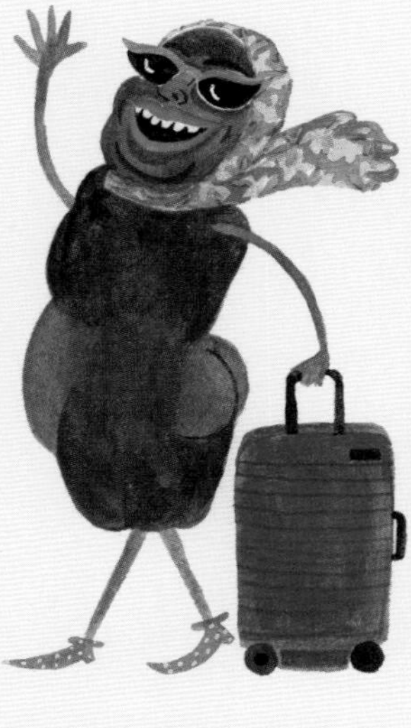

SHE'S GOT AWAY BRAND LUGGAGE, OF COURSE.

TRAVEL POOPS ARE AN ART. A SKILL. I KNOW NO ONE WHO HAS MASTERED THIS.

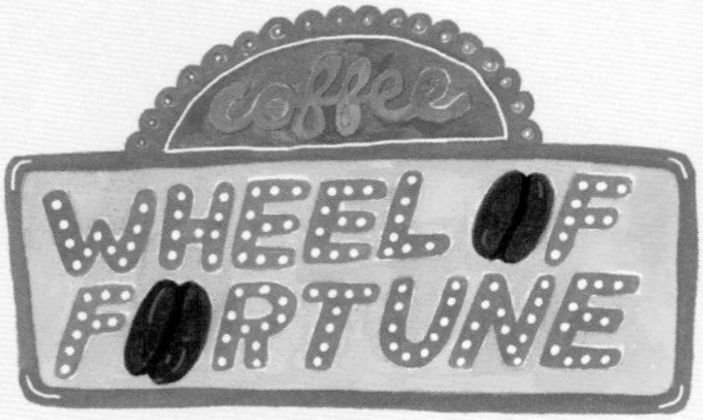
coffee
WHEEL OF FORTUNE

What type of bowel adventure will this morning mug inspire?

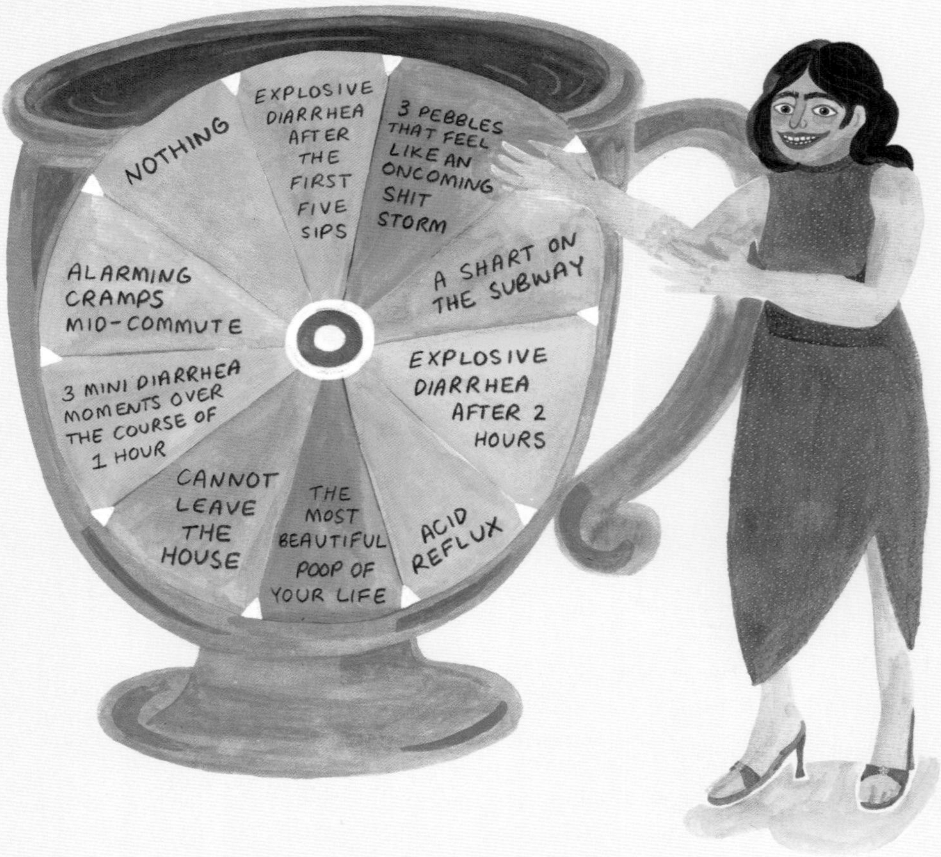
NOTHING
EXPLOSIVE DIARRHEA AFTER THE FIRST FIVE SIPS
3 PEBBLES THAT FEEL LIKE AN ONCOMING SHIT STORM
A SHART ON THE SUBWAY
EXPLOSIVE DIARRHEA AFTER 2 HOURS
ACID REFLUX
THE MOST BEAUTIFUL POOP OF YOUR LIFE
CANNOT LEAVE THE HOUSE
3 MINI DIARRHEA MOMENTS OVER THE COURSE OF 1 HOUR
ALARMING CRAMPS MID-COMMUTE

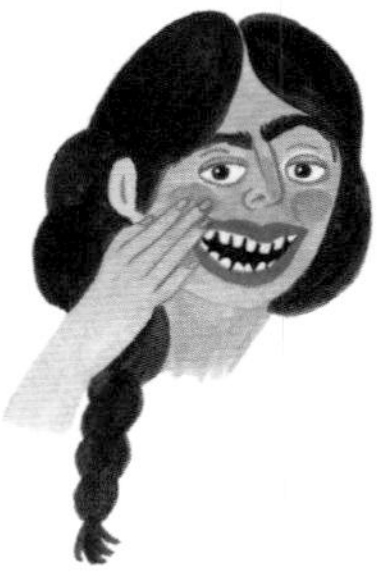

and i hate to tell you: GIRLS FART

The most adorable ways to let 'em rip

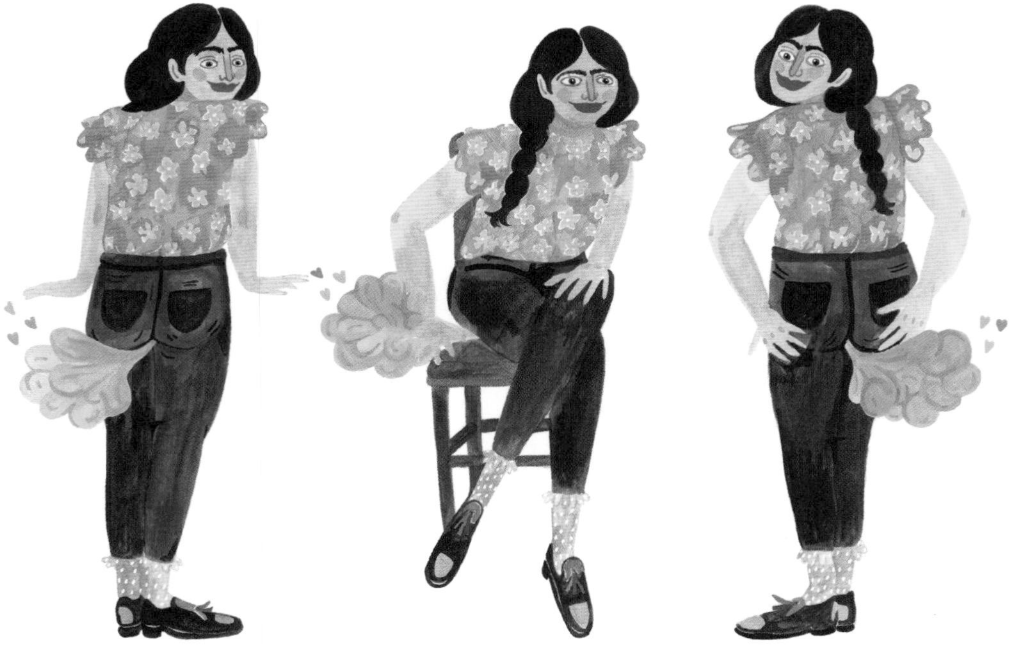

1. The squeeze & toot
2. The subtle lift & lean
3. The charming butt cheek pull

TYPES OF FARTS:

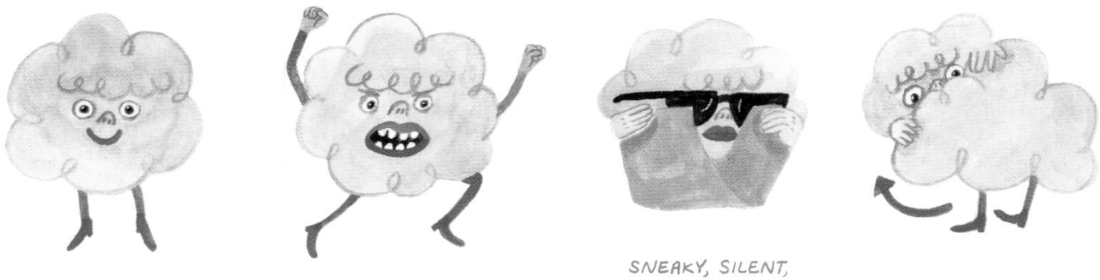

CUTE 'N' AIRY

LOUD AND RAGING

SNEAKY, SILENT, AND SINISTER

GOES INWARD SOMEHOW?

farting IN PUBLIC

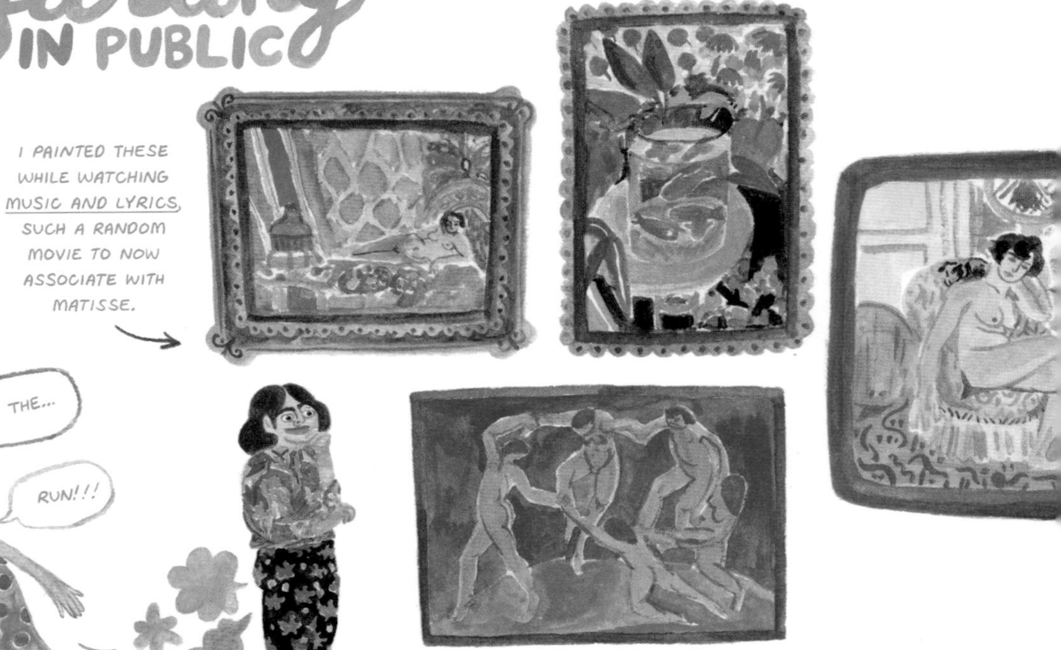
I PAINTED THESE WHILE WATCHING MUSIC AND LYRICS, SUCH A RANDOM MOVIE TO NOW ASSOCIATE WITH MATISSE.

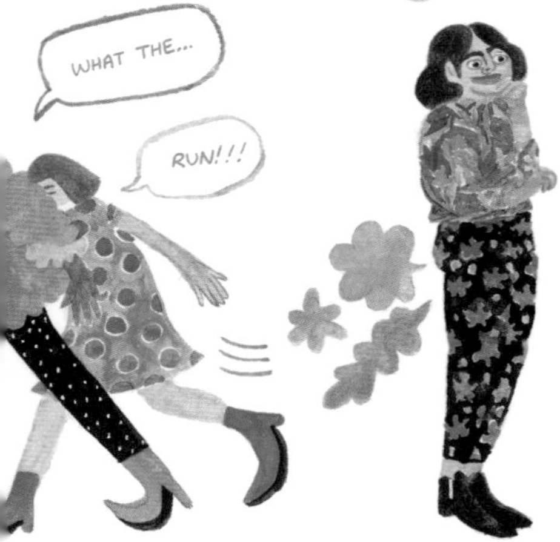
WHAT THE...
RUN!!!

I once farted in the middle of a very crowded area of the Met. Everyone around me scattered. I was pretty embarrassed about the impact I'd had, but what a tactic! There was no denying the fart, but no one knew it was me, and there I was with a once-packed room all to myself!

YOGA CLASS

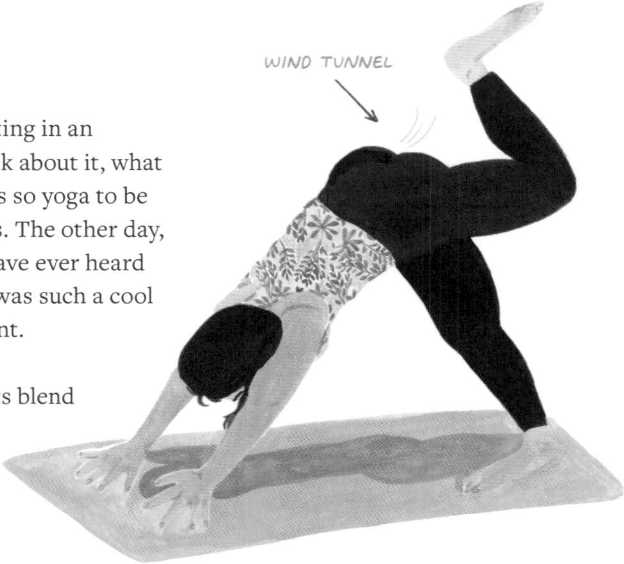
WIND TUNNEL

I used to avoid this activity for fear of farting in an otherwise silent room. But when you think about it, what better space to accidentally let one go? It's so yoga to be accepting of the humanness of our bodies. The other day, some guy let out truly the biggest fart I have ever heard in public, and not one person laughed. It was such a cool "we're all adults and humans here" moment.

Equally accepting is a sound bath. All farts blend seamlessly with the vibrating bowls.

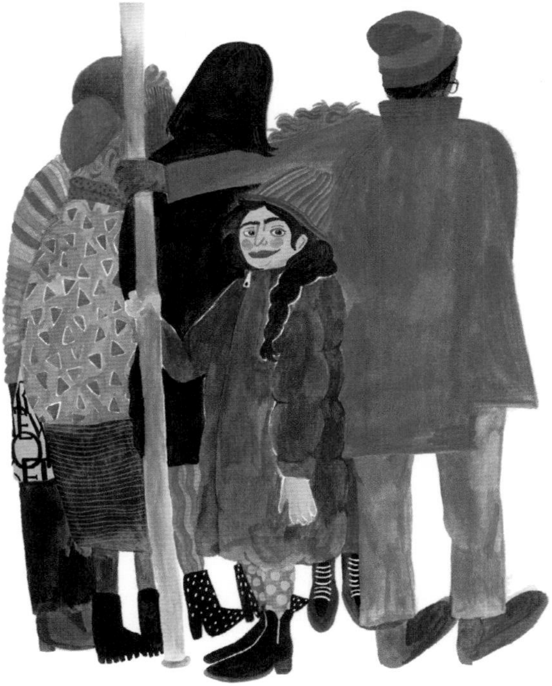

MID-COMMUTE

Farting on the subway is definitely not ideal, but I figure I'm so short that maybe my farts are below detection level. Or do they, like heat, rise?

*ALONG WITH DOWN, MY WINTER PARKA IS LINED WITH MY FARTS— POCKETS OF SWEET SWEET GAS IN EVERY PUFFY QUADRANT.

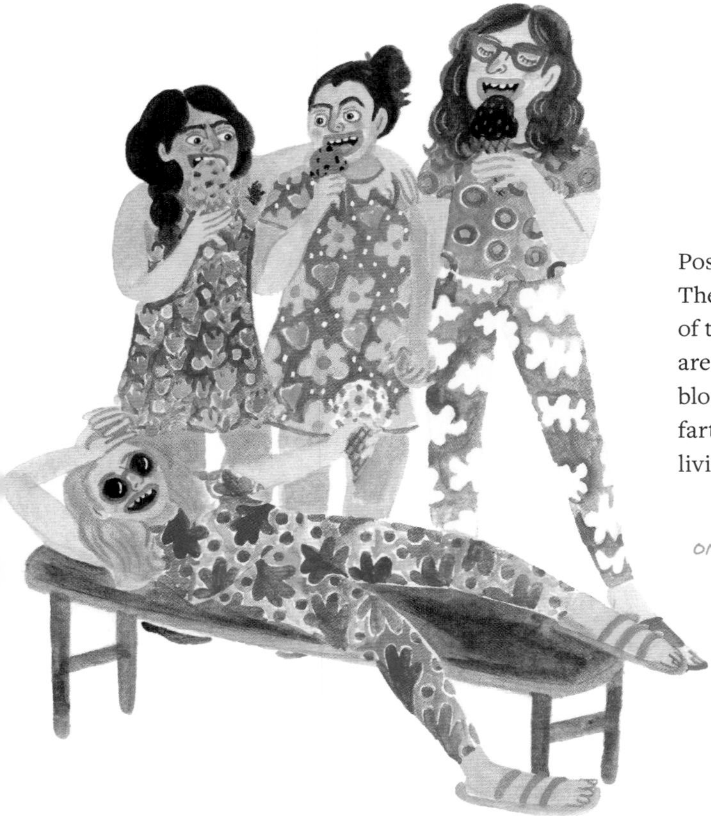

OUT ON THE TOWN

Post-meal ice cream cones with The Yentas are inevitable, regardless of the fact that six out of seven of us are lactose intolerant. We walk off the bloat farting in unison. Anonymous farty walks are my favorite aspect of living in a city as dense as New York.

NOA ONCE HAD TO LAY DOWN ON A BENCH MID-FART-FILLED WALK DUE TO GAS PAIN AND BUYER'S REMORSE.

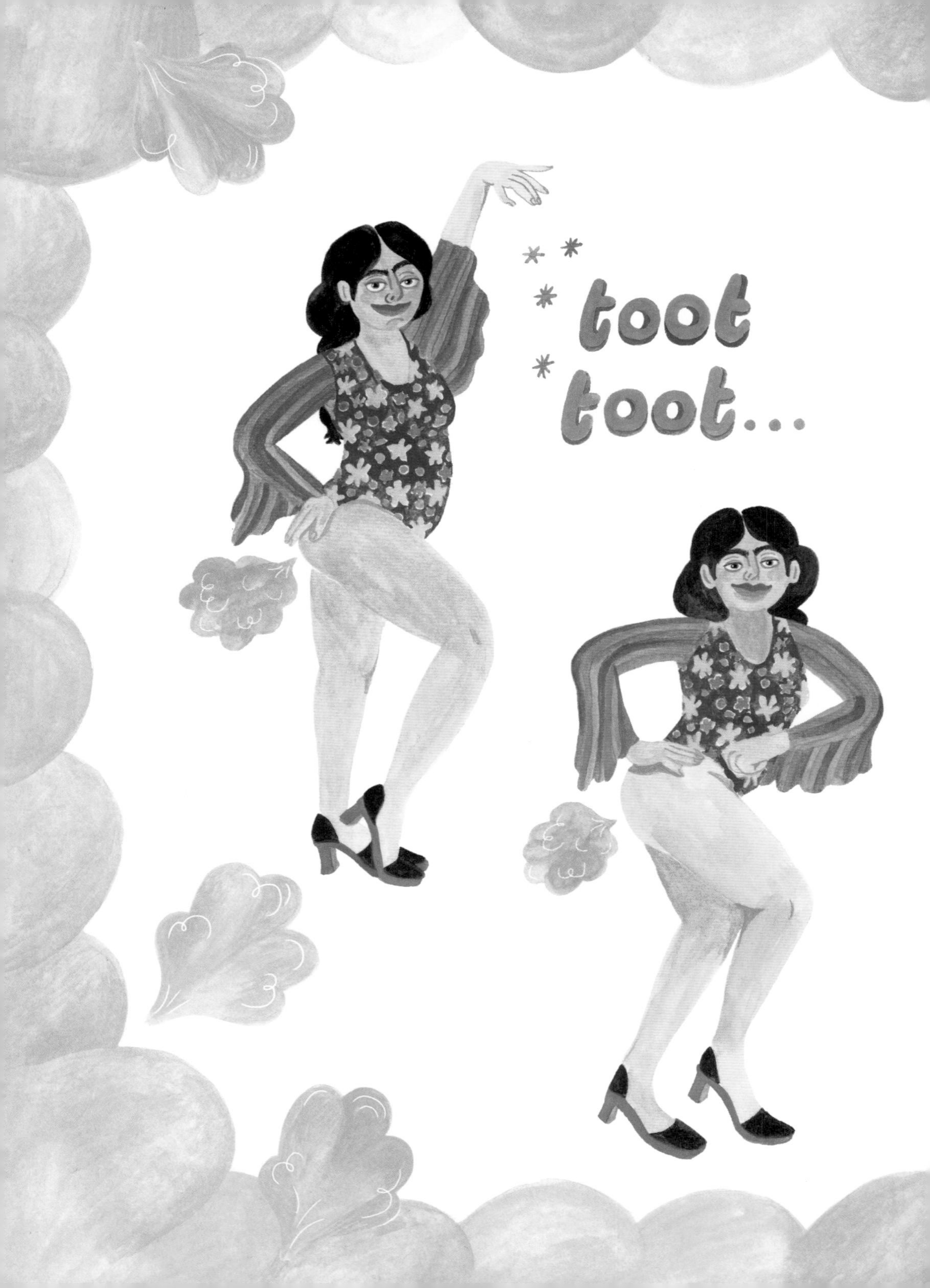
toot
toot...

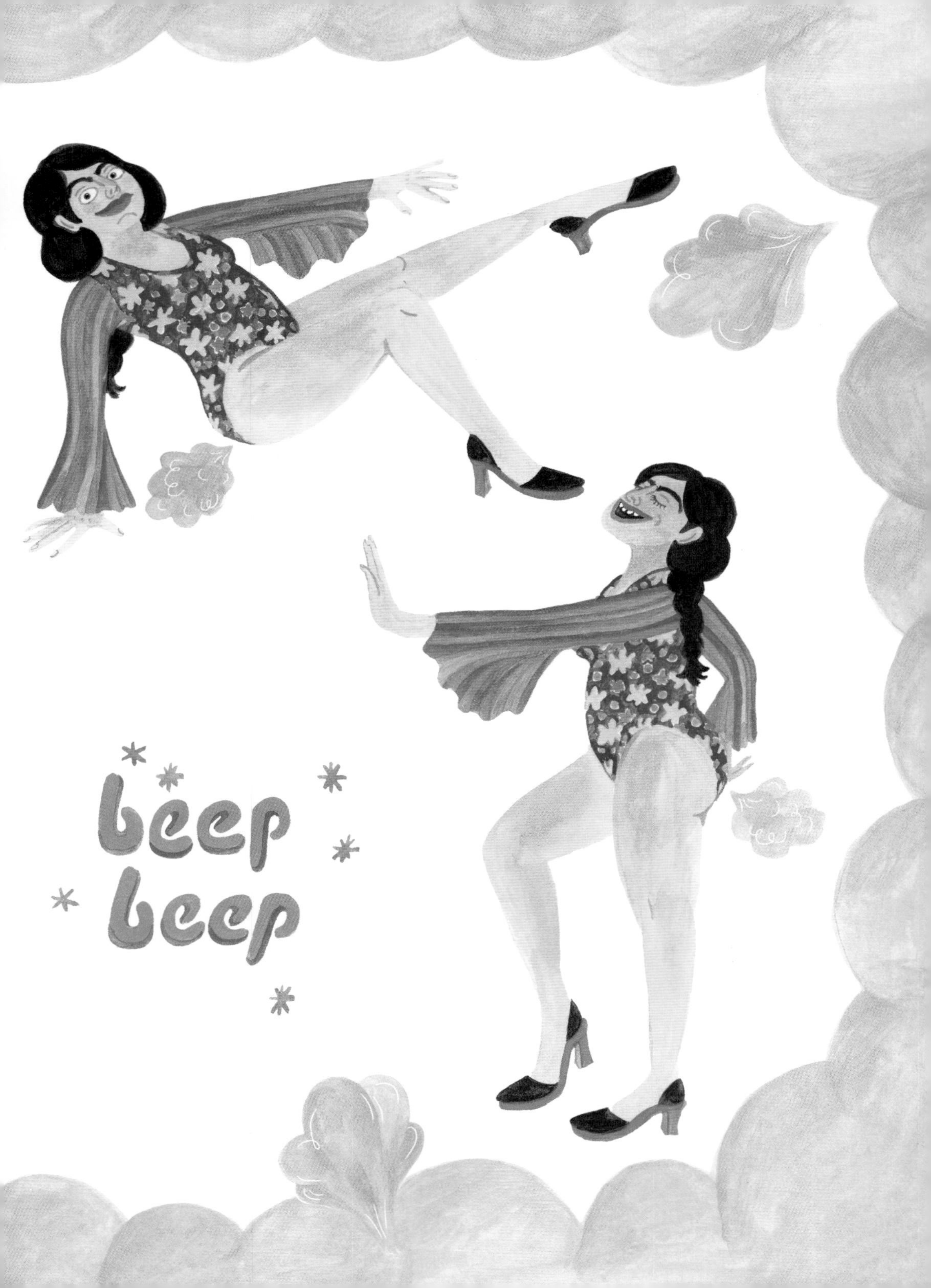
beep
beep

VAGINA

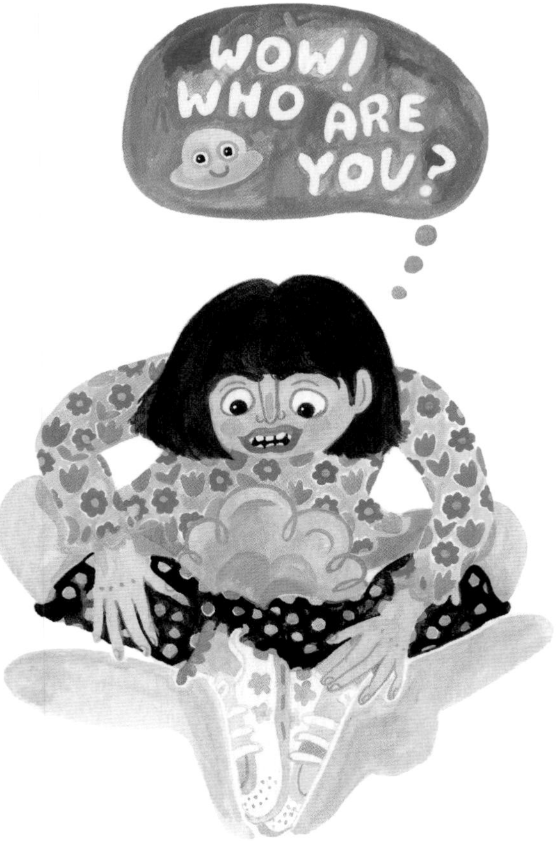
WOW! WHO ARE YOU?

WELL, LABIA, TO BE ANATOMICALLY EXACT

I found my first chicken pox on my vagina. I made this enchanting discovery one afternoon in preschool when I set up shop in a low-traffic corner of my JCC classroom to investigate a small itch. I'll never forget the moment I slid my pants below my knees, hunched over, and came face to face with a bubble-wrap-looking alien that had made itself at home on my once smooth private parts.

"Confident" might not be the word I'd use to describe an adult who inspects her vulva in public, but I love how matter-of-factly I approached it. My vagina was just like any other part of my body, mine to explore.

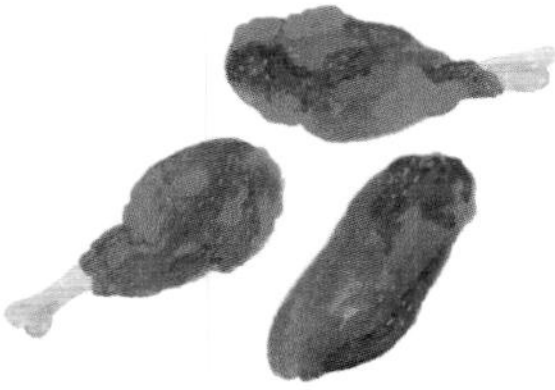

CHICKEN POX WERE THE TALK OF THE TOWN IN PRESCHOOL, BUT I DIDN'T UNDERSTAND EXACTLY WHAT THEY WERE AND, BEFORE HAVING CHICKEN POX MYSELF, I IMAGINED IT WAS A CONDITION WHERE YOUR SKIN TOOK ON THE TEXTURE OF FRIED CHICKEN SKIN.

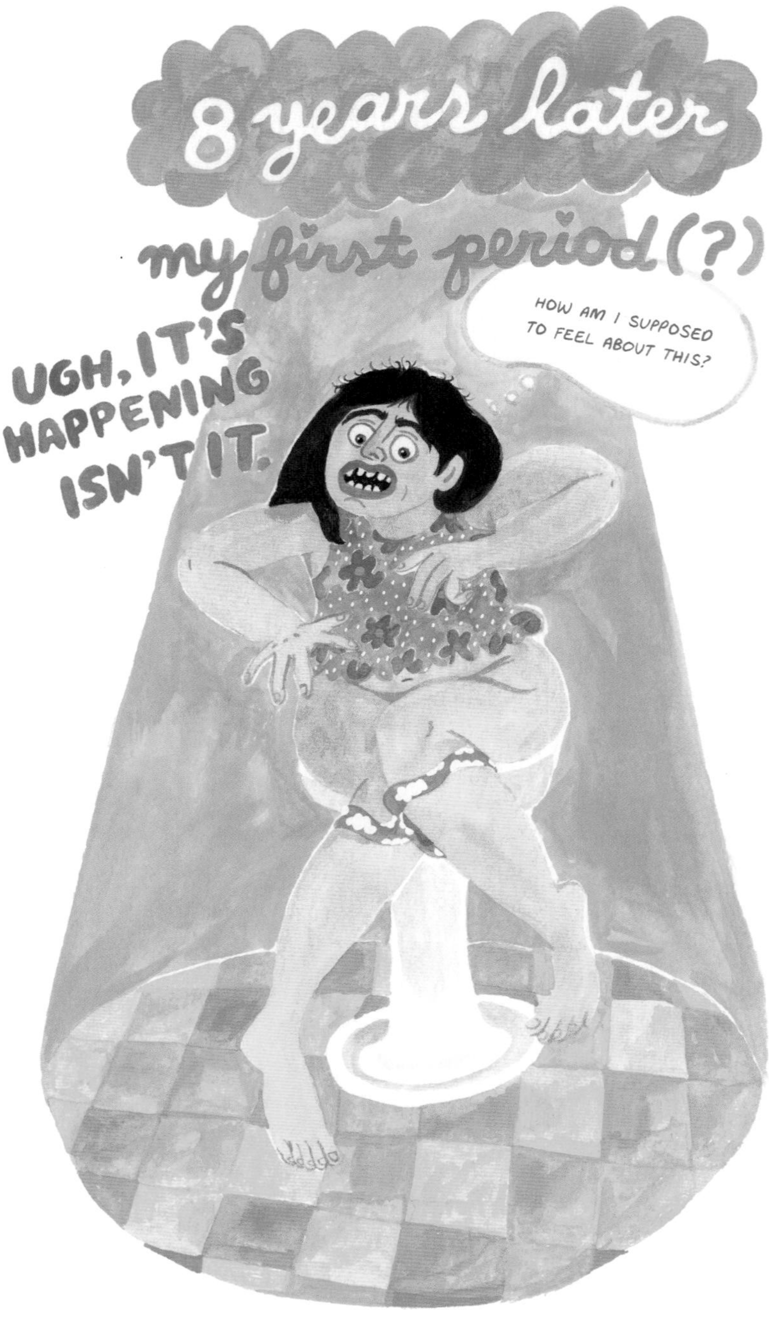
8 years later
my first period (?)
UGH, IT'S HAPPENING ISN'T IT.
HOW AM I SUPPOSED TO FEEL ABOUT THIS?

Flash-forward to fifth grade, when I officially lost all interest in knowing what was going on in or aroud my vagina.

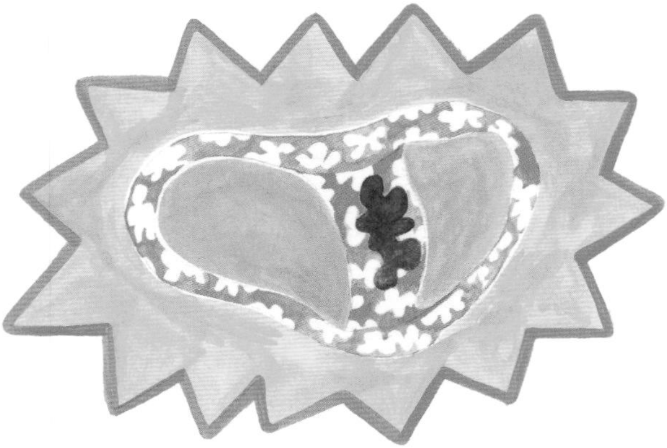

One night after school, I went to the bathroom to pee and when I pulled down my underwear I was forced to finally accept the truth that my life with periods had begun. According to the various "you're becoming a woman" books I had, I knew it was only a matter of time—the boobs were in and the pubes had emerged—but I was in full denial.

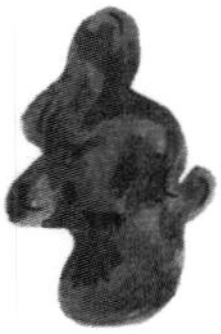

*NO ONE TOLD ME THAT MY FIRST PERIOD WOULD ACTUALLY BE BROWN

I didn't realize how much I was dreading my period until I got it. I was totally freaked out. None of my friends had gotten theirs yet (at least not to my knowledge) and I felt completely at my period's mercy. I decided I could either a) talk about my body with my mom and gain access to the materials I needed to keep this situation under control or b) avoid dreaded talk with Mom and kick off my period with a bang, bleeding freely everywhere.

My mom never said anything to make me feel ashamed of my body and, if anything, always encouraged open dialogue, yet I had somehow internalized the secrecy of menstruation and couldn't imagine telling my mom this news face to face. I think part of that, too, was not wanting to see her reaction in person. At twelve, a mom reaction had the power to quickly pull me over the edge into deep humiliation. So, with full body shaking, I took out my box of camp stationery and wrote my mom a letter. I folded it up neatly and placed it on her pillow.

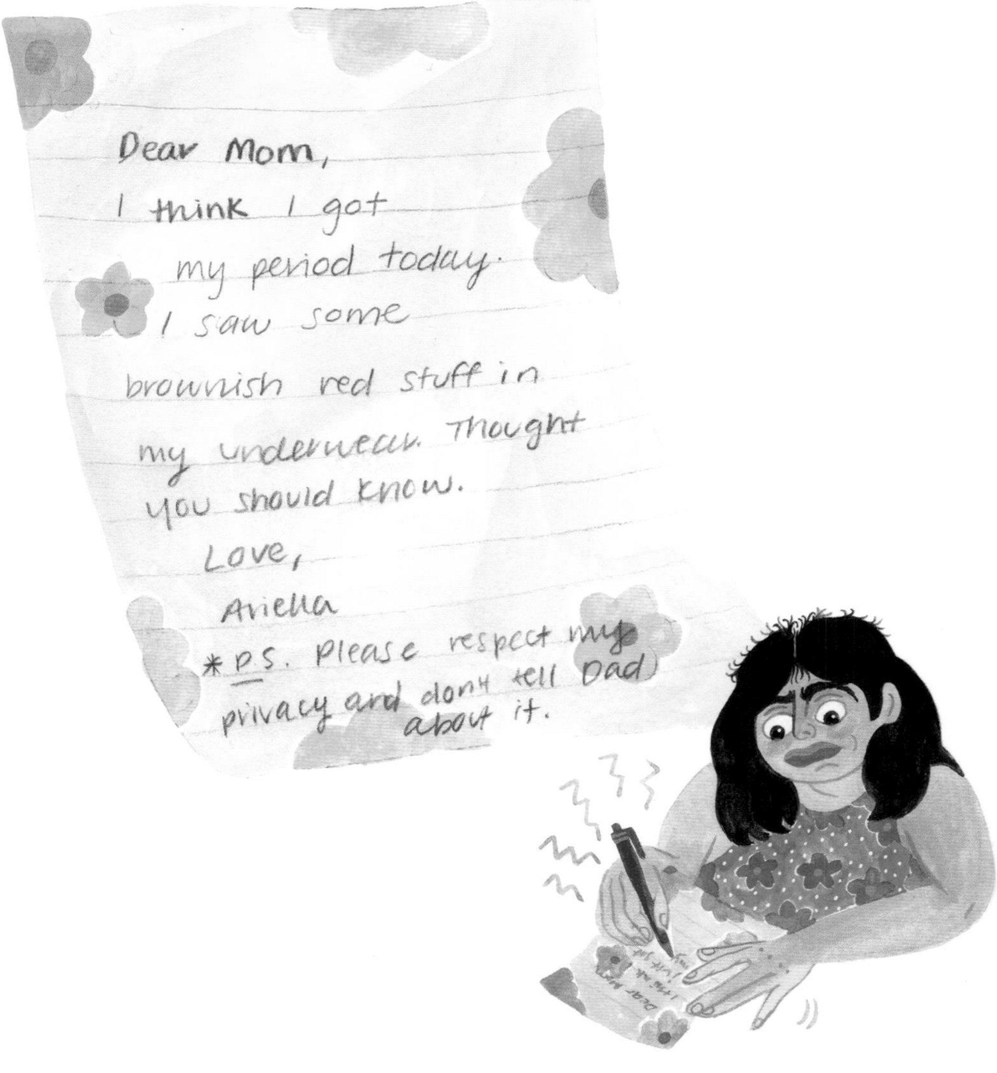
Dear Mom,
I think I got
my period today.
I saw some
brownish red stuff in
my underwear. Thought
you should know.
Love,
Ariella
*P.S. Please respect my
privacy and don't tell Dad
about it.

menstruating & MORTIFIED

I spent that first year with my period in constant embarrassment, sitting through early rounds of sex-ed classes thinking I was the only person aside from the teacher who had actually gotten her period.

Our sex-ed teacher used a classroom chair to demonstrate how propping a leg up on a toilet can be a great way to make sure the tampon goes in correctly. The theatrics of it all made me feel totally insane and alone—as if everyone somehow knew the demo was just for me.

※ I TAKE A LESS ATHLETIC APPROACH TO TAMPON INSERTION BUT APPRECIATE HER ENTHUSIASM FOR PERIOD EDUCATION.

THIS TEACHER ALWAYS ATE TUNA FOR LUNCH. THE SMELL ADDED AN ON-POINT LAYER TO THE WHOLE EXPERIENCE.

Despite having ample coaching on how to use a tampon, I stuck to pads. I wanted as little contact with my bleeding vagina as possible. In fact, I tried to completely ignore that I had my period altogether and made no effort to predict or prepare for its arrival each month. I preferred this stressful and frantic recurring scenario: the dull onset of cramps followed by that familiar, terror-inducing warm rush of goop that signaled it was time to make a run for it. In the middle of class I'd have to abruptly excuse myself and waddle to the bathroom, praying my blood hadn't already seeped through and created a menstrual tie-dye on the back of my pants. Once in the safety of a stall, I'd construct my signature DIY pad using almost an entire roll of impossibly thin toilet paper.

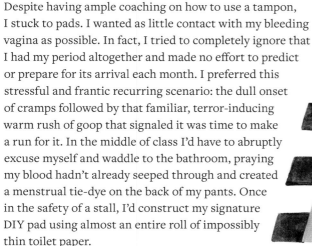

PERIOD FAIRY

PSA: If only we had one to grant us our period wish list.
I mean, how fun would this be!

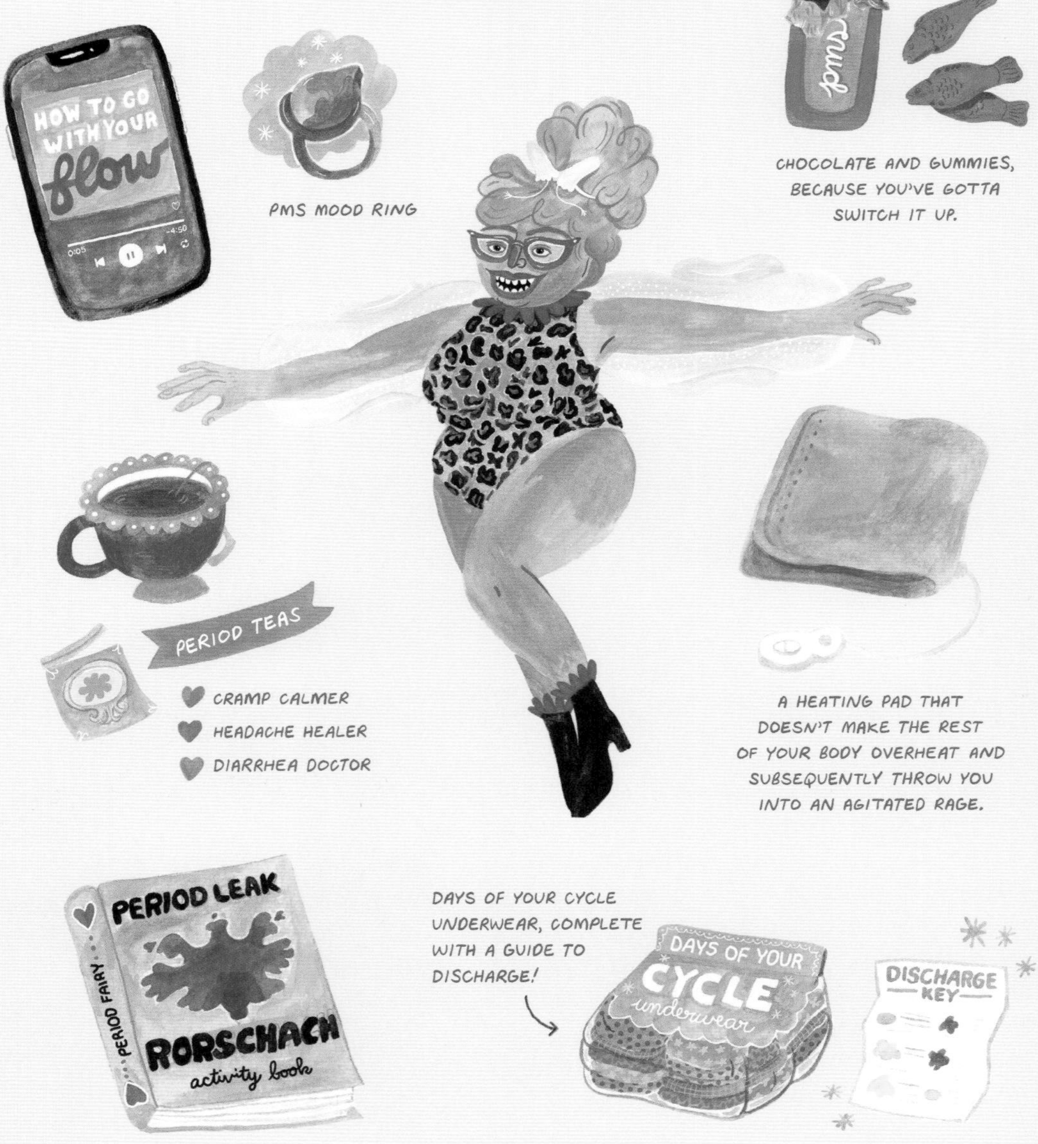
HOW TO GO WITH YOUR flow
PMS MOOD RING
CHOCOLATE AND GUMMIES, BECAUSE YOU'VE GOTTA SWITCH IT UP.
PERIOD TEAS
CRAMP CALMER
HEADACHE HEALER
DIARRHEA DOCTOR
A HEATING PAD THAT DOESN'T MAKE THE REST OF YOUR BODY OVERHEAT AND SUBSEQUENTLY THROW YOU INTO AN AGITATED RAGE.
PERIOD LEAK RORSCHACH activity book
PERIOD FAIRY
DAYS OF YOUR CYCLE UNDERWEAR, COMPLETE WITH A GUIDE TO DISCHARGE!
DAYS OF YOUR CYCLE underwear
DISCHARGE KEY

my leak log

Literally not one person ever warned me that periods
(especially in the beginning) go fucking rogue. My victims:

OK, WOULD BE A GREAT SPIN ON
MY BEST FRIEND'S WEDDING.
GET HOLLYWOOD ON THE PHONE.

A linen-ish coral skirt I wore to my best friend's Bat Mitzvah
(where I sat on a white seat for the service—thankfully
it was wipeable!). I went home to change and came back for
the brunch—in a black skirt this time.

On a Friday after school, I was standing
in my friend's kitchen eating challah when
she gently alerted me to the fact that I had
leaked onto the front—*the front*—of my
khaki pants. A nice and bizarre period leak
to pile onto the already sad experience
of wearing khakis.

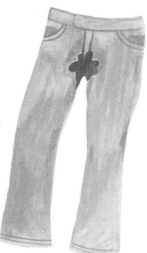

ON FRIDAYS, WE HAD TO WEAR
DRESS PANTS, DRESSES, OR SKIRTS.
THESE ONES FROM OLD NAVY WERE
BIZARRELY FLATTERING.

In college, I bled onto the corner of someone's World Market
throw pillow at a party. Once I noticed the stain I quietly
got up, grabbed my coat, and went back to my dorm room.

Silver lining: I discovered that the silent exit is totally doable.
It's now my trademark move.

the backseat
RED TENT

When I was growing up, my family spent most winter vacations skiing in Maine on a mountain that was a five-hour drive from home. These car rides were typically hellish, with my two sisters and I fighting about the strange breathing sounds someone was making, or screaming/nail pinching/hitting when any of us accidentally violated our strict rule to keep arms and legs within the bounds set by the seams of our respective seats. One year though, we had a new family car that had two rows of back seats. We rotated who got to sit alone, and I had the space to myself for the drive up.

There I was enjoying the rich world of my daydreams when I was interrupted by that familiar gooey and warm rush. With no warning at all, my period had hit at full force. I was not prepared and was too embarrassed to ask my mom to stop at a drugstore and buy me pads.

Luckily, I was sharing the back row with a fresh roll of plush toilet paper. We always had some spares floating in the car in case of emergency—my mom was dealing with what we now know was undiagnosed celiac disease, so roadside poops were far from rare.

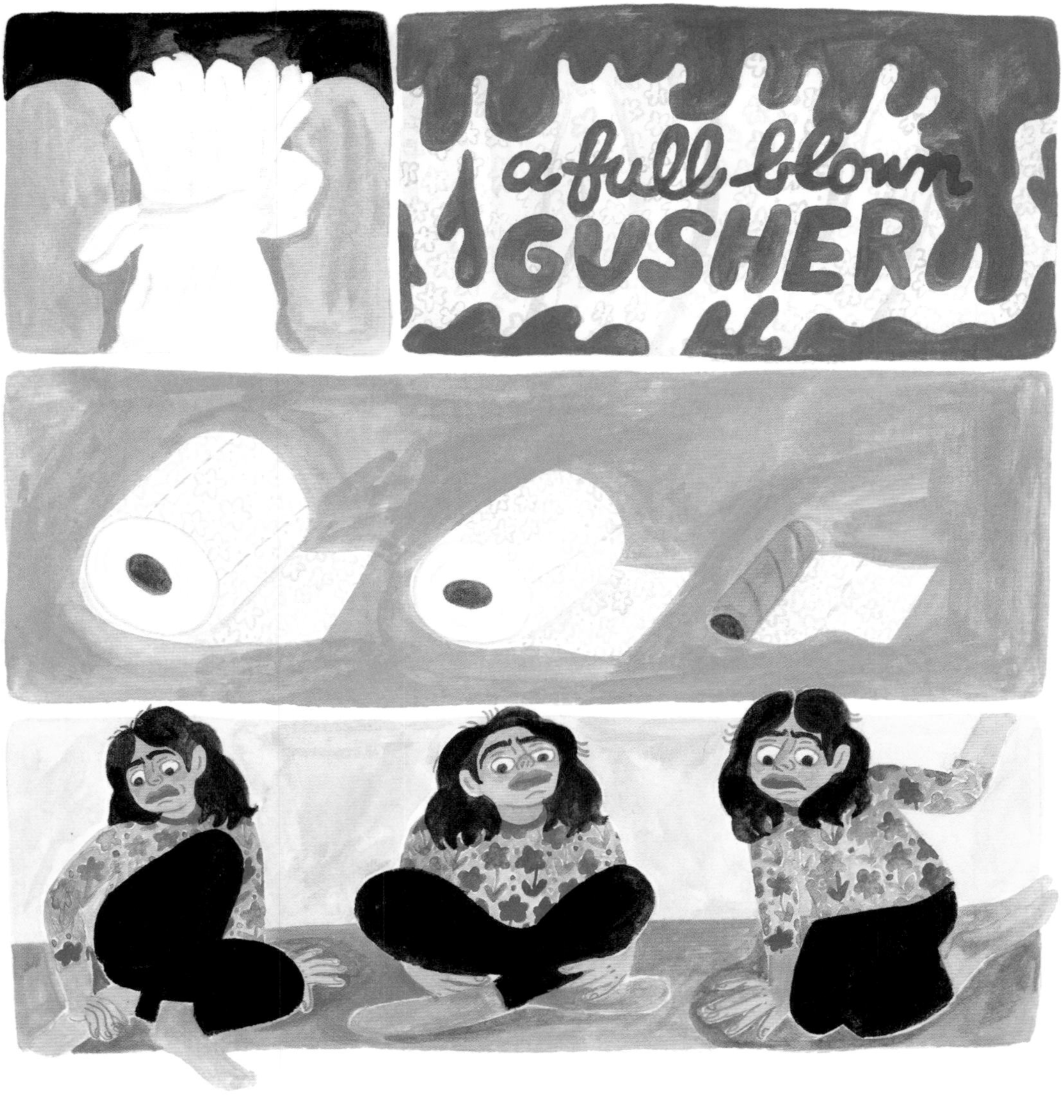
a full blown
GUSHER

I rationed out the roll to make sure I didn't go through it too quickly, used gas stops to restock (though gas station toilet paper may as well be air—literally the least effective toilet paper of all time), and I experimented with different sitting positions that kept my butt from ever making weighted contact with the seats.

My family was totally unaware of the drama that was unfolding just inches behind them. My underwear and leggings were absolutely ruined, bloody shreds of toilet paper were multiplying, and I must have smelled revolting. As much as I wanted to deny it, this episode definitely left its subtle blush-toned mark on the car. Even the thickest of long underwear can only soak up so much blood.

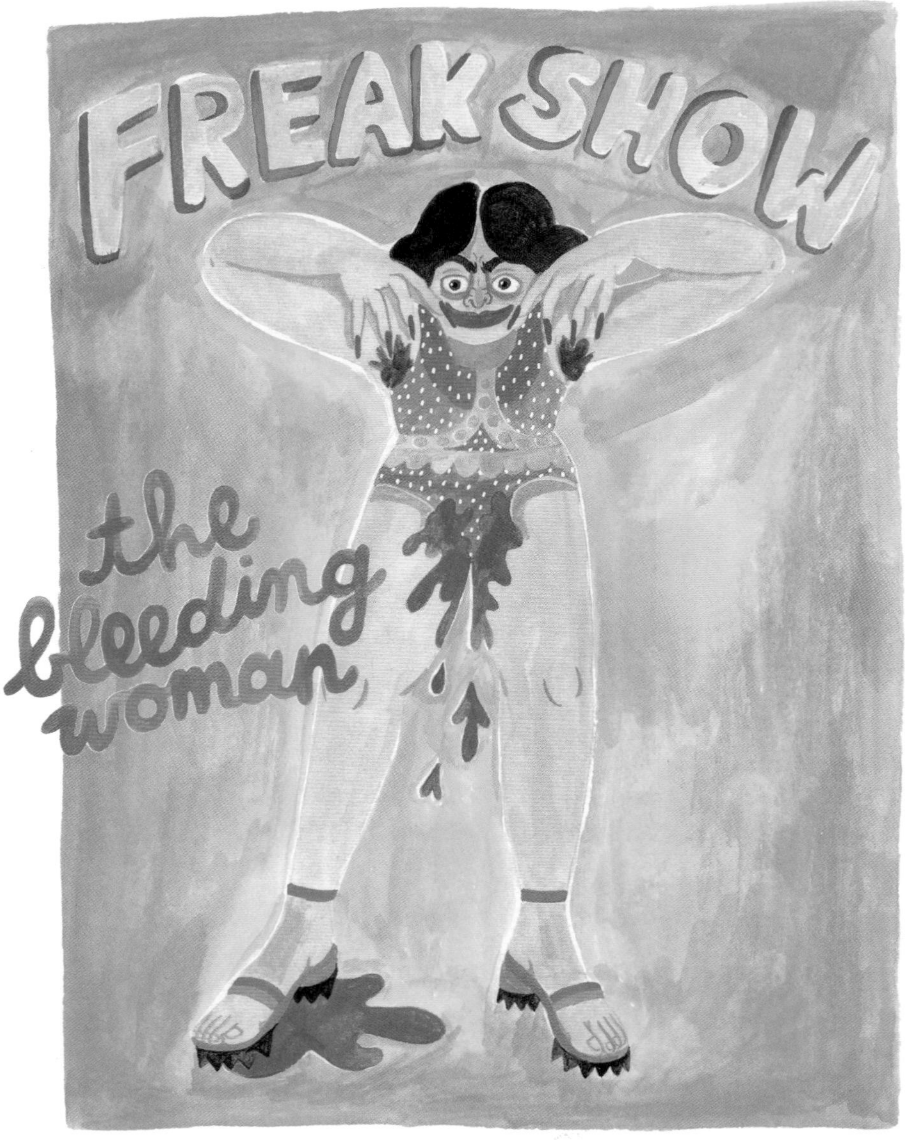
FREAK SHOW
the bleeding woman

My period clearly wasn't traveling well, and my first summer at camp was nearing. I had no idea what I was going to do when it came time to take this blood-drenched show on the road again.

I still had no idea if any of my friends had gotten their periods yet, and in my mind I was going to be all alone in my mess with no washing machine or unused cabinets I could toss ruined underwear into.

SOME WORST-CASE SCENARIOS

I will bleed through all my underwear for the month.

Squirrels will find said underwear and drag them out into the open for all to see.

DO ALL ANIMALS LIKE PERIOD BLOOD, OR JUST DOGS?

I will bleed into my bathing suit in front of everyone (boys included!) because I can't wear pads in the lake.

THE TAMPON

In my mind, tampons were the scary, real deal leak-blockers. They were adult and the only low-profile way to keep my period in check. It was time.

I NOW KNOW THAT MY PERIOD IS A FREAKING SNAKE AND OFTEN CHOOSES TO SOMEHOW FLOW AROUND A TAMPON.

TAMPON FIASCO!

My first experience with tampons was everything I feared it would be: sweaty, scary, and complicated. I was initially fooled into thinking it would be smooth sailing after I—with a little bit of clumsy navigation—slid the tampon up and into my vagina with ease. The mayhem came four hours later when the dangling string went red and it was time to take the tampon out. It was stuck. Yes, totally and completely stuck inside me, gripping onto some part of my vagina for dear life.

I called my mom at her office in a panic.

Per my mom's suggestion, I soaked myself in a hot bath. Our thought was that my muscles were probably clenched and I needed to relax to retrieve the tampon.

Fifteen minutes later, I'd become a soggy bath raisin and still no luck. I was forced to move into a phase I had tried at all costs to avoid: self-inspection. Looking into my vagina was truly the last thing I wanted to do.

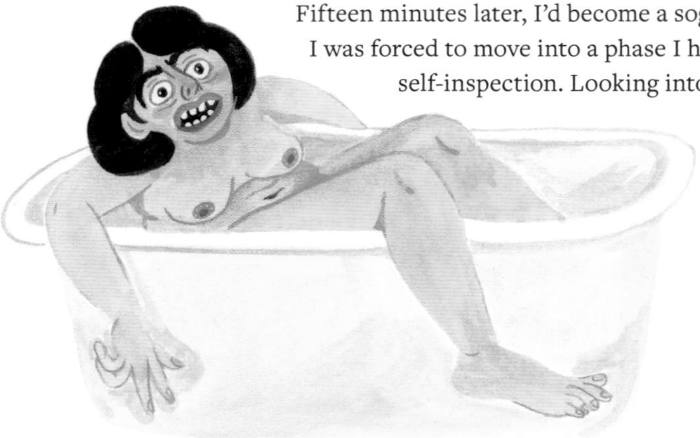

*CUE IMAGES OF THE SCARY SAND LION FROM ALADDIN.

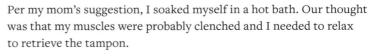

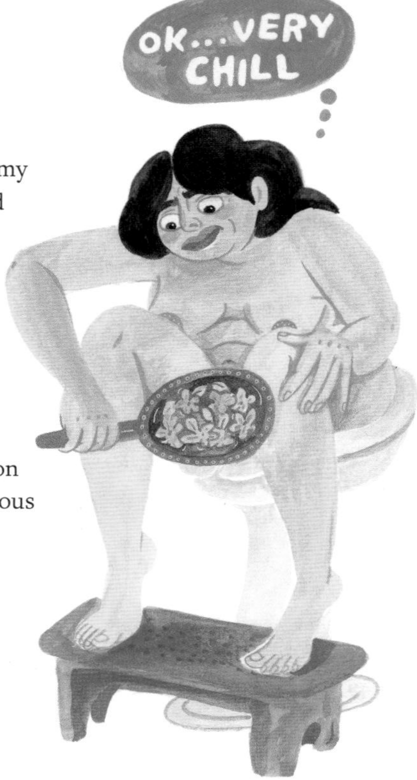
OK... VERY CHILL

Through my investigation, I was horrified to find that my tampon was securely straddled on either side of a band of tissue. To get it out, I had to push one side of the tampon up deeper into my vagina and nudge it over the mystery band.

It was official: I was an alien with a psycho vagina.

After doing some research, I found out that the band was actually a part of my hymen and the whole situation had a name: I had a "septate hymen," and it was notorious for making tampon use a bit of a nightmare. Knowing this brought me a lot of comfort, but not quite enough comfort to try and try again until I got it right.

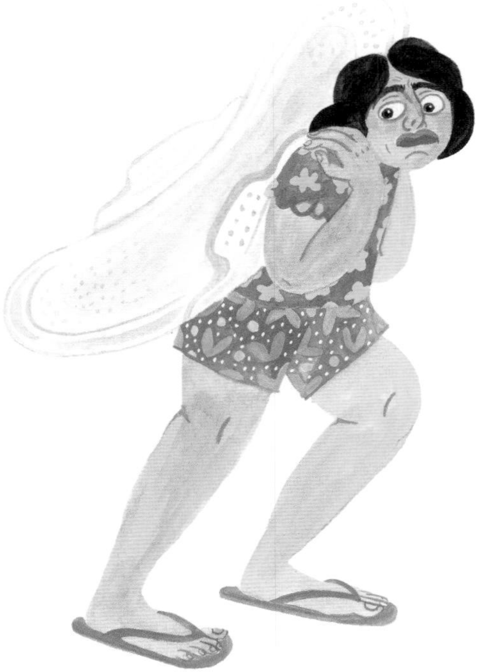

OK, SO... PADS IT IS

Off I went to camp with my pack of super long, heavy flow, overnight pads in tow, feeling doomed to a sticky and bloody summer of embarassment and isolation.

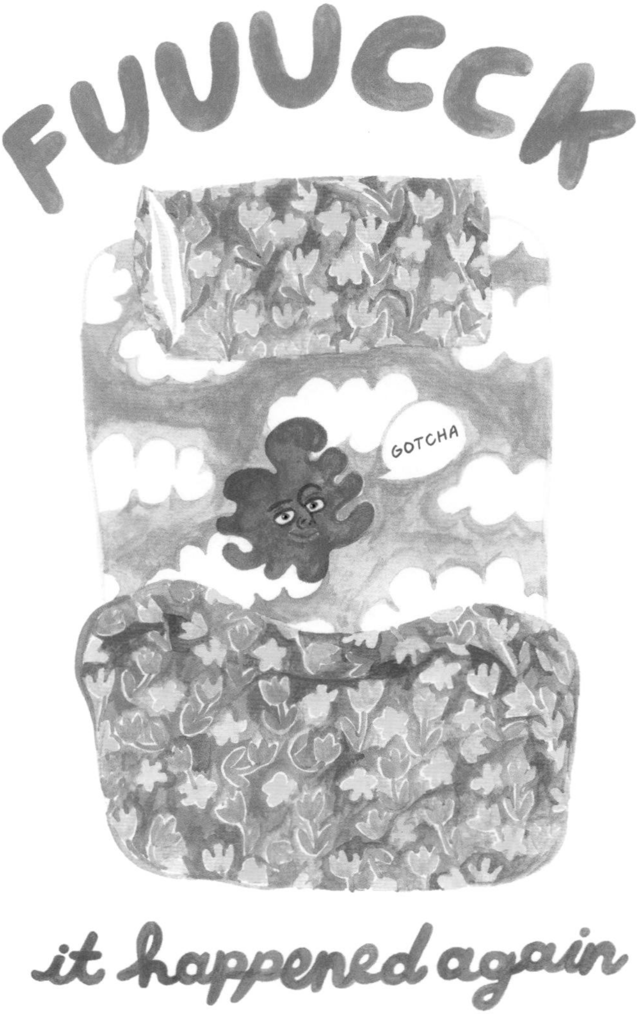
FUUUCCK
GOTCHA
it happened again

But then something magical happened: one morning during the first week of camp, I woke up to a frustrated outburst from the girl sleeping next to me. Her period had leaked all over her bed and she was pissed. If I had leaked my bed that early in the summer, I would have panicked silently, frantically stripped my sheets and thrown them in the trash, and written a letter home to my mom telling her she must come pick me up at her earliest convenience.

Luckily, this girl's coping mechanism was to make as much of a scene as possible, and this scene exposed the fact that at least half that bunk was very familiar with period-soaked sheets.
The massive leak opened the floodgates for conversation. Whispers about our periods grew into full-blown, bunk-wide discussions. And just like that, I found community where I had initially thought I was all alone.

My bunkmates soon became my closest friends and period guardian angels:

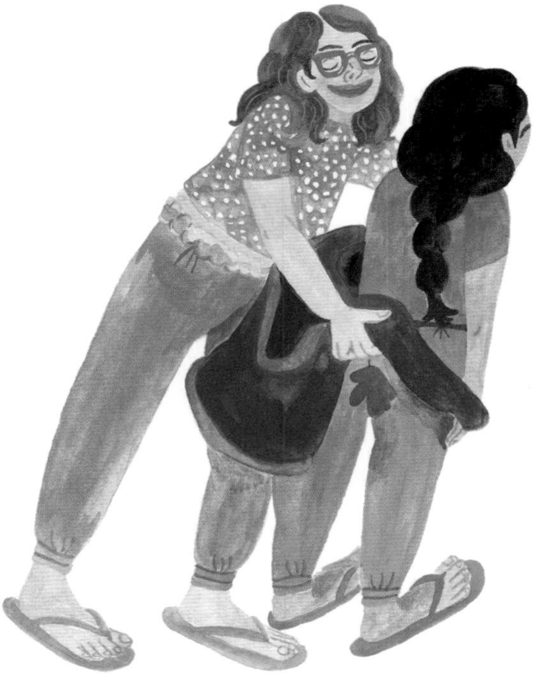

One afternoon on a camping trip, the back of my sweatpants were, unbeknownst to me, beginning to resemble a crime scene. Adi swiftly and subtly brought me my sweatshirt and tied it around my waist to cover it up.

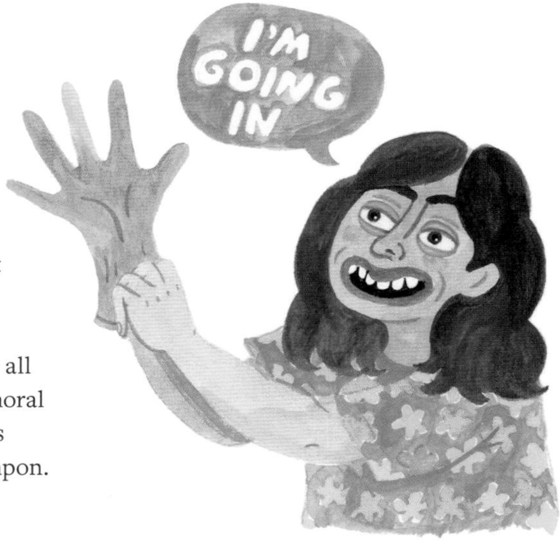
I'M GOING IN

The most legendary Yenta moment was when Jesse crawled into the bathroom stall with a girl who had lost sight of her tampon string. We all crowded in the bathroom to lend moral support as Jesse reached inside this girl's vagina to extract the lost tampon.

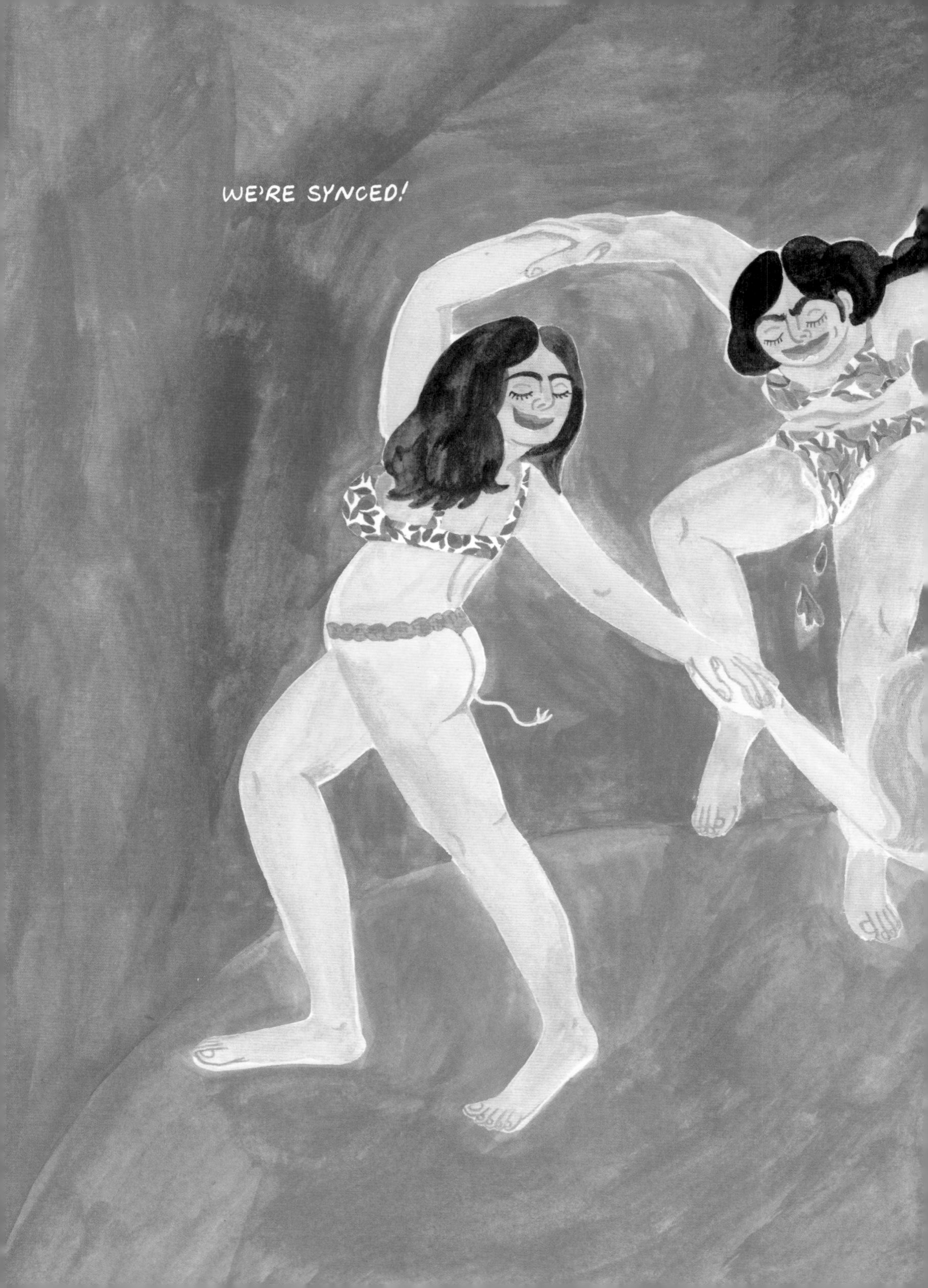
WE'RE SYNCED!

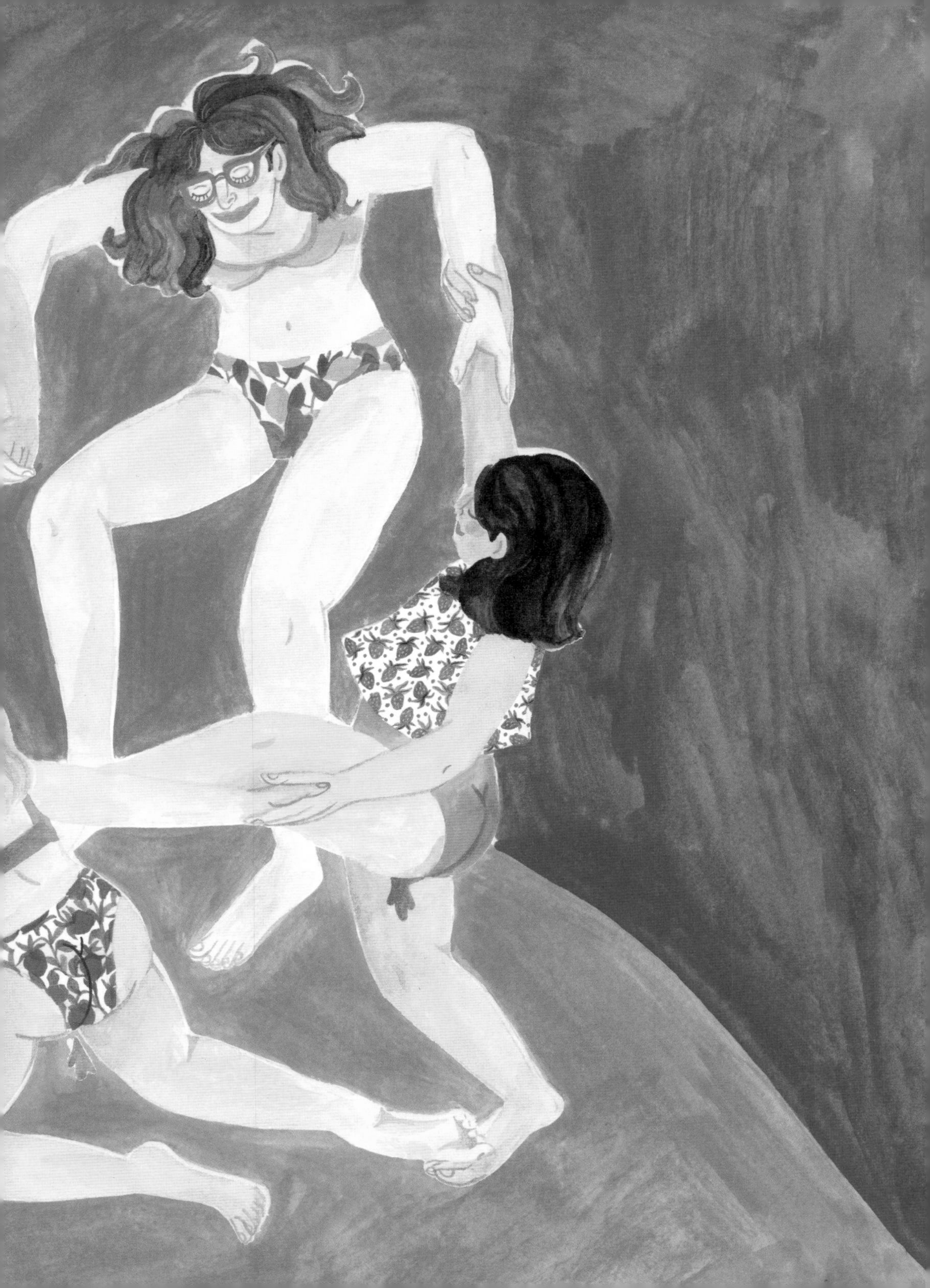

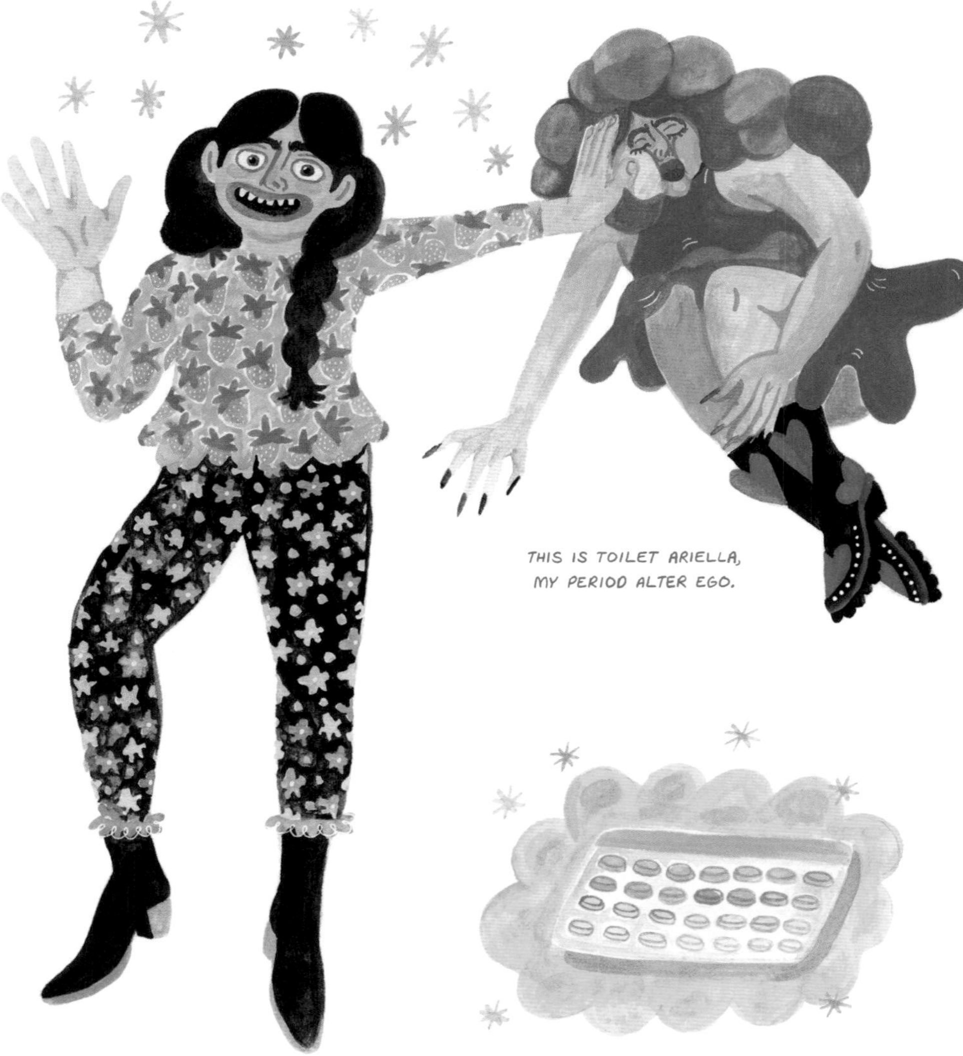
THIS IS TOILET ARIELLA,
MY PERIOD ALTER EGO.

The period positivity I'd soaked up over the course of six summers at camp flew out the window when I had my first boyfriend at twenty-three. Suddenly, my period was once again something I'd pretend did not exist. I had made strides in accepting my period on a personal level, but bringing someone else into the mix was out of the question. To avoid the whole period sex conversation, I used my birth control pills to skip my period altogether. That way, I'd never burden my boyfriend with my gross bloody body. How sweet of me!

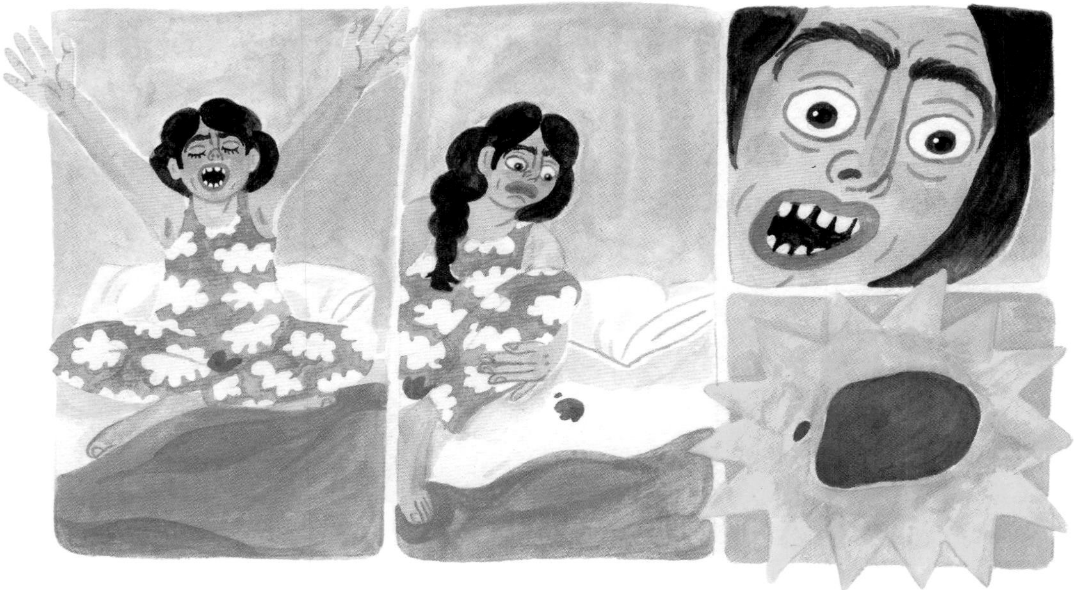

We'd been together for an entire year—yes, one full year—before my period ever became part of the picture. One week I had miscalculated my pills, and I woke up in his bed to find an adorable little leak on his white sheets.

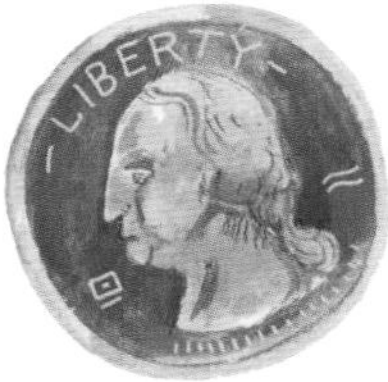
LIBERTY

The blood spot was the size of a quarter, but in the moment it felt enormous. I was mortified and apologized profusely, offering to buy him a new set of sheets.

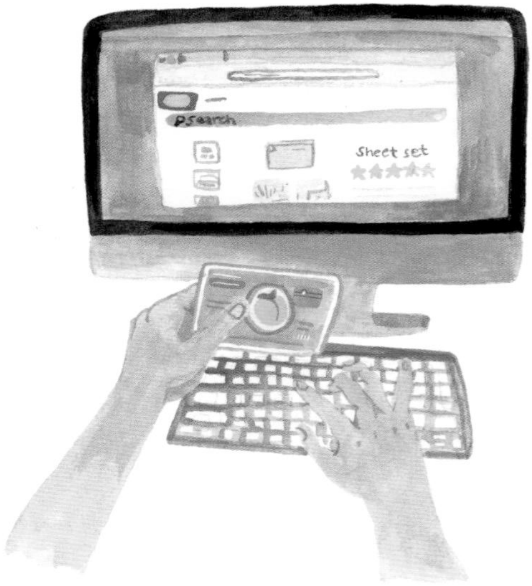
Search
Sheet set

HE LET ME BUY HIM A NEW SET OF SHEETS

This boyfriend was an incredibly kind person and I genuinely wish him only the best, but this twenty-eight-year-old butthead took me up on my offer and Gchatted me a link to the IKEA sheets I could order him later that morning.

In the moment, I thought nothing of it. I was so embarassed by my body that it felt like the right thing to do. I had ruined his sheets, and this was my way to make it up to him.

Only when I recounted the event to The Yentas did I start to recognize how the whole situation made me feel unsupported. I know there was not malintent there, but my boyfriend essentially validated my shame.

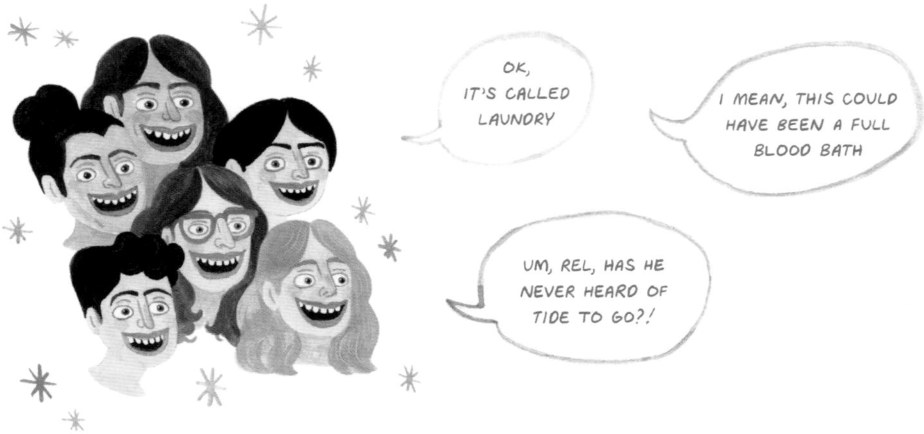
OK, IT'S CALLED LAUNDRY
I MEAN, THIS COULD HAVE BEEN A FULL BLOOD BATH
UM, REL, HAS HE NEVER HEARD OF TIDE TO GO?!

LOOK, HE'S LUCKY.

My period could have engulfed him.
He truly could have woken up

DRENCHED IN MY BLOOD.

I started to feel my perspective shift. The Yentas made me realize just how uncomfortable I clearly still was with my period, and how thrilling it could be to fully embrace every little drop of it.

From that point forward, I challenged myself to become more comfortable talking about my period. After that relationship eventually ended, I jumped back into dating with the goal of being much more candid about my body. I never wanted to feel stuck in isolation and shame with someone ever again. At first, I took a very "fake it till you make it" approach, cheekily inserting my period into conversation whenever I could (this was easier to do with strangers, when the stakes were a lot lower).

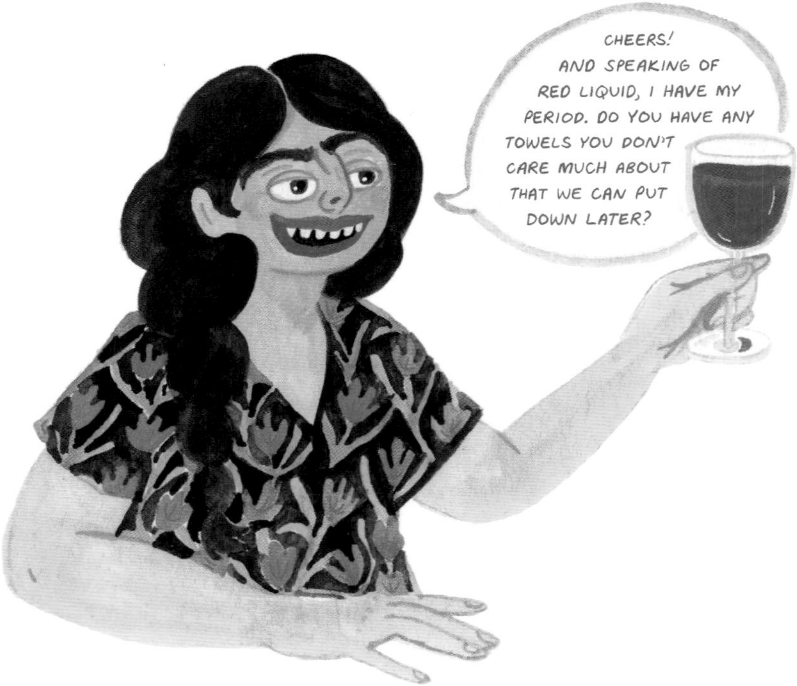
CHEERS! AND SPEAKING OF RED LIQUID, I HAVE MY PERIOD. DO YOU HAVE ANY TOWELS YOU DON'T CARE MUCH ABOUT THAT WE CAN PUT DOWN LATER?

Soon, the way I spoke with The Yentas about my period became how I genuinely felt about my period.

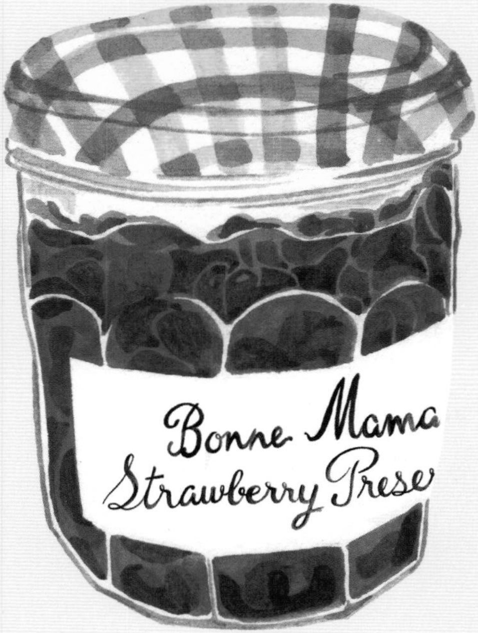
Bonne Mama
Strawberry Prese

MY PERIOD GLOBS ARE *gorgeous* MUCH LIKE SPOONFULLS OF *luxurious* *jam*

toilet ariella
SUPER POWERS

💜 An intense flood of tears just from watching a person hug their dog on the subway, or thinking about how much I love my mom, or marveling at how wild it is to be alive on this planet.

💜 Diarrhea storm that instantly unblocks a week's worth of consitipation. No matter how constipated I am, I can always rely on my period for a thorough emptying. The catch? Period poops eject my tampon every time.

💜 Willpower to trek through any type of treacherous weather at midnight to buy emergency cookies from the nearest bodega.

＊ CAN CRUSH THE BOX OF COOKIES IN UNDER AN HOUR.

BACK TO NATURE FUDGE
MINT COOKIES ARE
A GIFT TO HUMANITY.

I think my period turns me into Garfield? I always need lasagna. Chocolate cake for the sweet cycle. Then repeat.

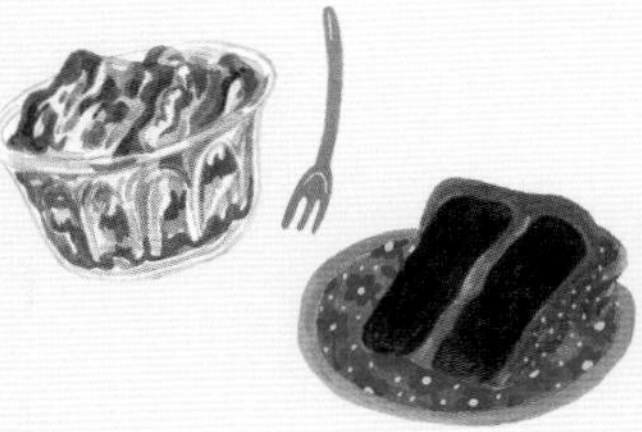

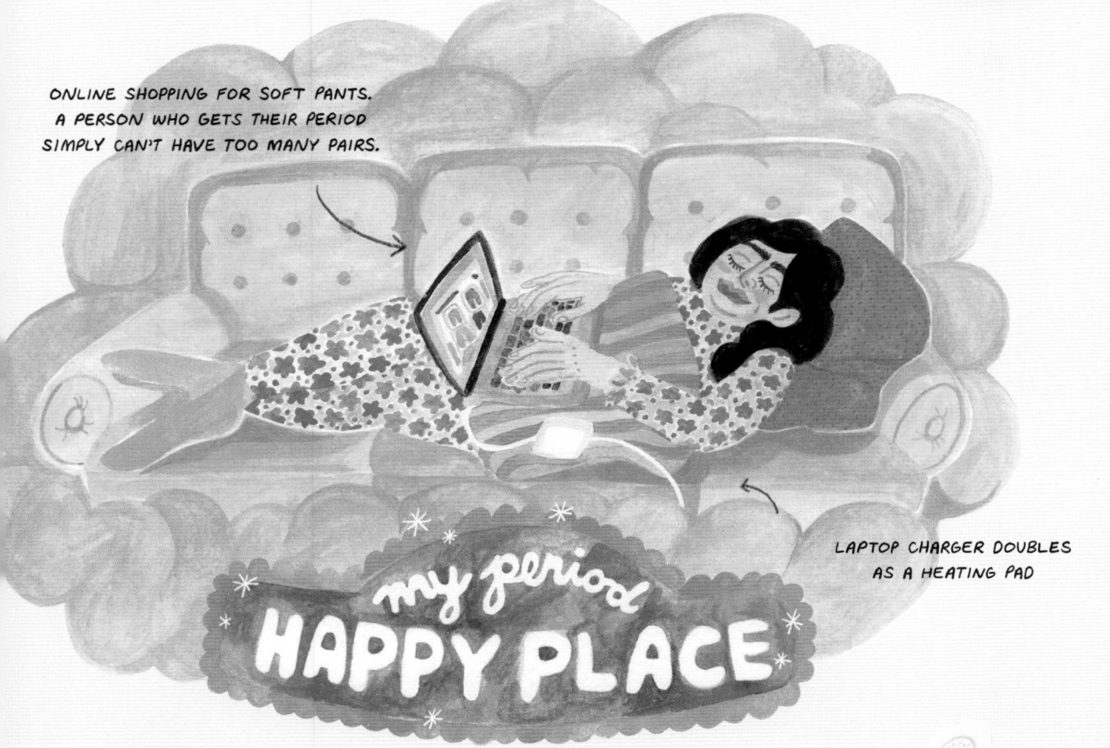
ONLINE SHOPPING FOR SOFT PANTS. A PERSON WHO GETS THEIR PERIOD SIMPLY CAN'T HAVE TOO MANY PAIRS.
LAPTOP CHARGER DOUBLES AS A HEATING PAD
my period
HAPPY PLACE
*

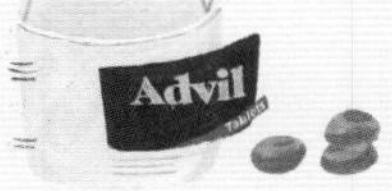
Advil

When I was a teenager, I'd walk laps around the kitchen screaming about my cramps.

Performance art, really.

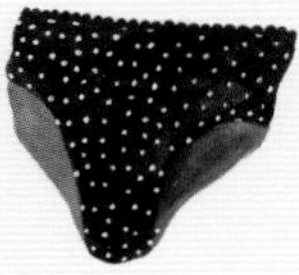

High-rise black cotton underwear

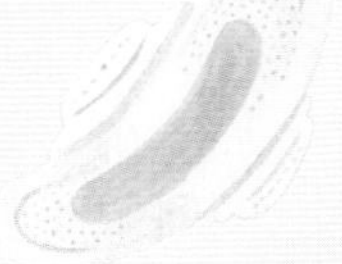

I know they aren't stellar for the environment, but I will always love pads. Yes, they feel like diapers, but there's nothing quite as comfortable as knowing you're prepared for any menstrual drip (or in my case, a full cannonball).

* LARGE CHUNKS OF ALONE TIME ARE VITAL. THOUGH WHEN THE SENTIMENTAL PHASE OF MY PERIOD KICKS IN, SNUGGLES WITH GREAT FRIENDS ARE INCREDIBLY SOOTHING.

let's talk DISCHARGE

It's not celebrated enough, and The Yentas and I are particularly fascinated by the myriad textures and forms it can take:

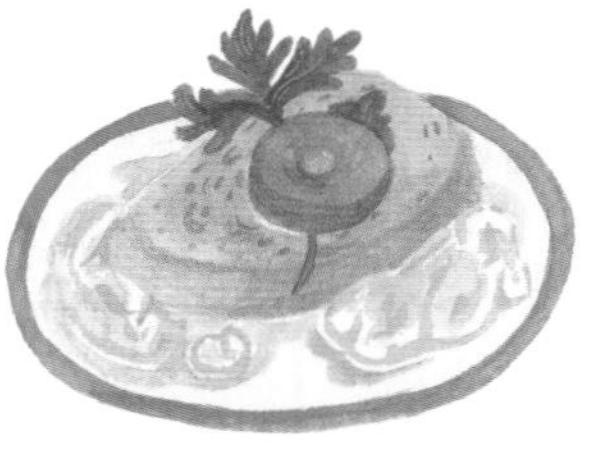

Gefilte Fish Jelly:
For those unfamiliar, it's much like the gelled juices of leftover chicken. Yum.

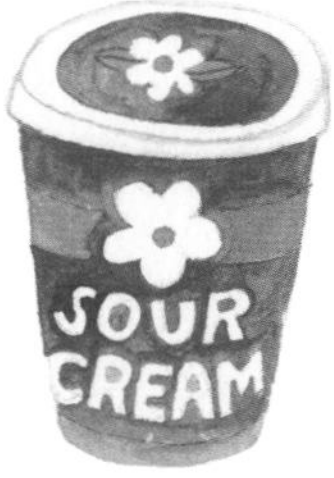
SOUR CREAM

Sour Cream:
A classic.

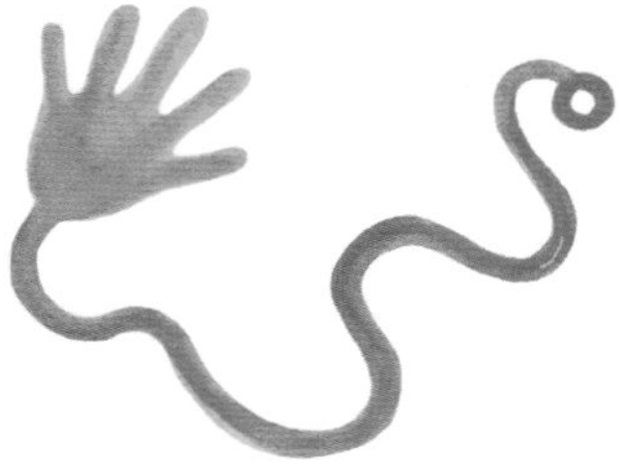

Hand Slime:
A nice touch of nostalgia (and my personal favorite).

Most Yenta gatherings are over meals, so naturally discharge comes up at the dinner table. One night, our server came to clear away our dishes just as our discharge conversation reached its peak. Mid-conversation, Maya licked the last remaining trace of sour cream from her ramekin before surrendering it to the cleanup and we all lost it.

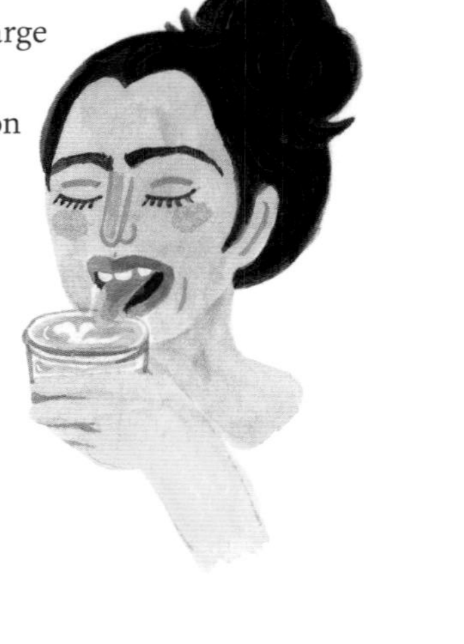

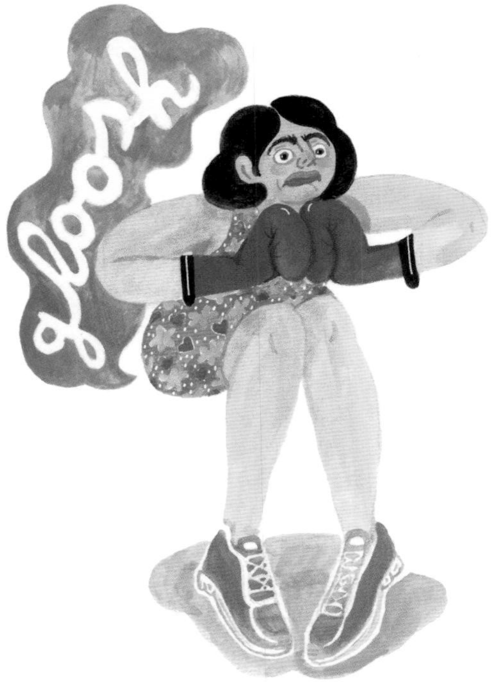
gloosh

Three years ago, I decided to go off of birth control pills and recalibrate. My teenage-level cramps came back in full swing, my skin did some funky things, and I was introduced to a level of discharge I had never experienced before.

On my birthday that year, I treated myself to a kickboxing class. Mid-class, I felt a huge rush of something. Not pee, and not blood, but something definitely released.

When I got to the locker room after class, I began to undress for my shower. I'm not super sheepish, so I just pulled down my pants, out in the open. That's when I was met with the most extreme hand slime discharge I'd ever seen.

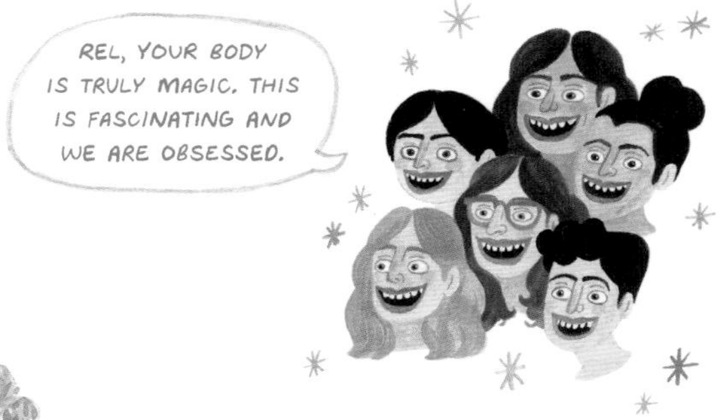
REL, YOUR BODY IS TRULY MAGIC. THIS IS FASCINATING AND WE ARE OBSESSED.

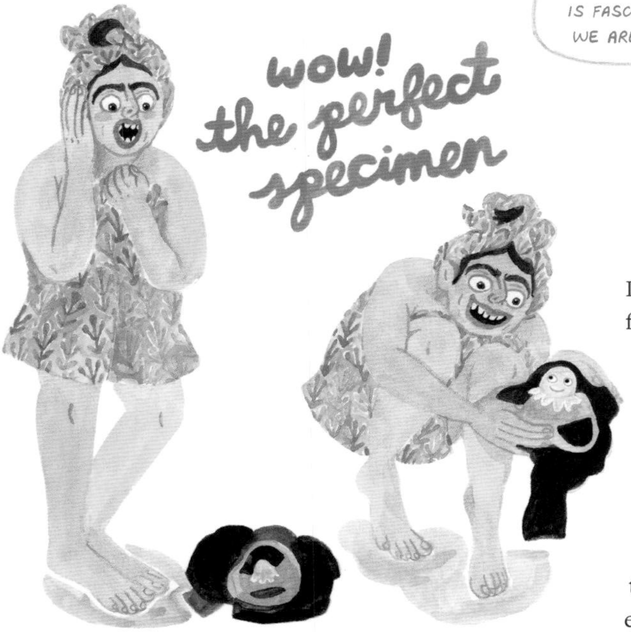
wow!
the perfect specimen

I had produced a fully formed, clear flubber. There it sat in my underwear, staring up at me. I quickly snatched her up and ran into a bathroom stall, attempting to conceal, inspect, and then dispose of the creature before anyone caught sight of it.

The Yentas were very disappointed to learn that I had not collected photo evidence of the event.

Open conversations with The Yentas about my vagina made me less fearful of all her twists and turns and more inclined to explore.

THE WAY I PAINTED MY VAGINA HERE
REMINDS ME OF SNUFFLEUPAGUS
AND I LOVE THAT FOR HER.

Full disclosure: my vagina is still not a part of my body I particularly enjoy looking at, but the more I pay attention to her the more I learn and the more curious I become.

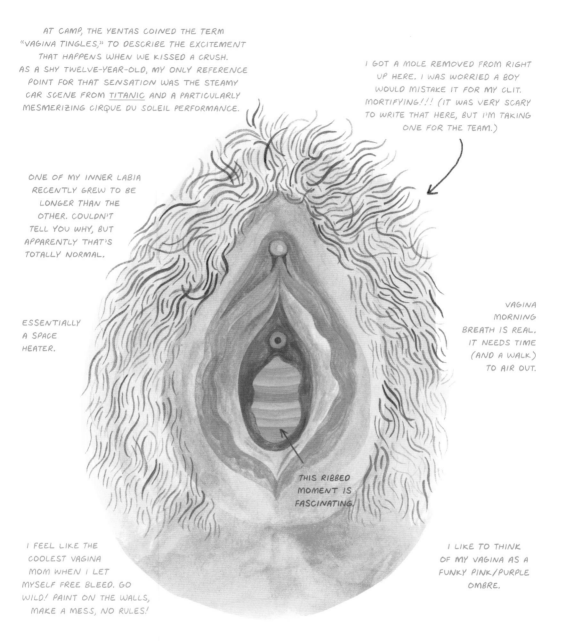

AT CAMP, THE YENTAS COINED THE TERM "VAGINA TINGLES," TO DESCRIBE THE EXCITEMENT THAT HAPPENS WHEN WE KISSED A CRUSH. AS A SHY TWELVE-YEAR-OLD, MY ONLY REFERENCE POINT FOR THAT SENSATION WAS THE STEAMY CAR SCENE FROM <u>TITANIC</u> AND A PARTICULARLY MESMERIZING CIRQUE DU SOLEIL PERFORMANCE.

I GOT A MOLE REMOVED FROM RIGHT UP HERE. I WAS WORRIED A BOY WOULD MISTAKE IT FOR MY CLIT. MORTIFYING!!! (IT WAS VERY SCARY TO WRITE THAT HERE, BUT I'M TAKING ONE FOR THE TEAM.)

ONE OF MY INNER LABIA RECENTLY GREW TO BE LONGER THAN THE OTHER. COULDN'T TELL YOU WHY, BUT APPARENTLY THAT'S TOTALLY NORMAL.

ESSENTIALLY A SPACE HEATER.

VAGINA MORNING BREATH IS REAL. IT NEEDS TIME (AND A WALK) TO AIR OUT.

THIS RIBBED MOMENT IS FASCINATING.

I FEEL LIKE THE COOLEST VAGINA MOM WHEN I LET MYSELF FREE BLEED. GO WILD! PAINT ON THE WALLS, MAKE A MESS, NO RULES!

I LIKE TO THINK OF MY VAGINA AS A FUNKY PINK/PURPLE OMBRE.

My very own cyclops opera singer.

A UTI IS THE AVANT-GARDE PERFORMANCE OF A LIFETIME. FULL-BODIED, SHRILL, AND ABSOLUTELY CHAOTIC.

pubic hair

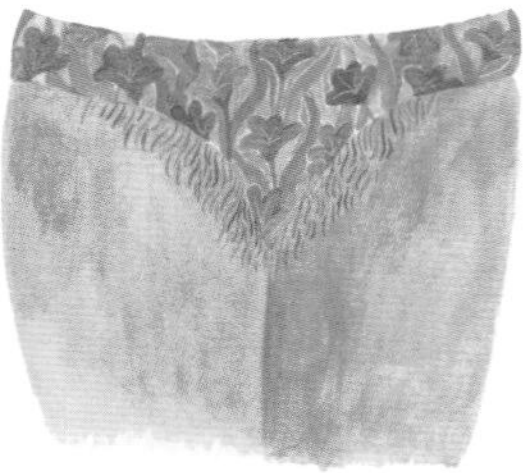

Though my time at camp made me more comfortable with my period, it introduced a new and different (and itchy) layer of vagina shame: the bikini line. Cursed be the day you wear a bathing suit and see a few wiry hairs make a run for it, outside the bounds of your swimsuit bottoms and into the light of day.

SHAVING

At camp, a bikini line shave was all the rage and I jumped on the bandwagon.

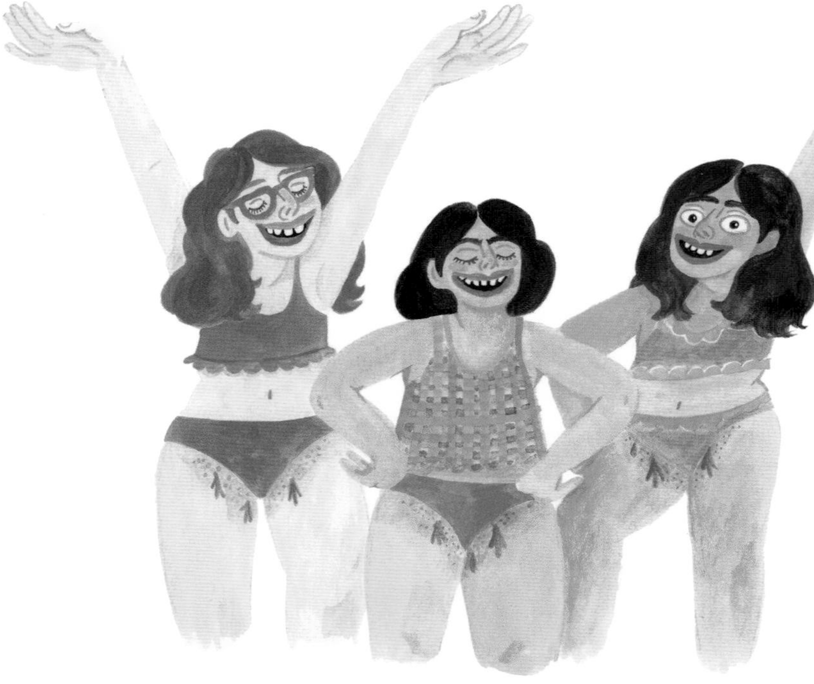
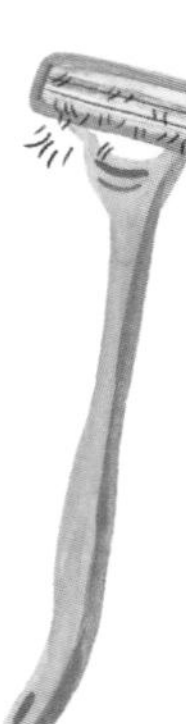

There we were, bunk G6, beach ready with bleeding bikini lines.

WAXING

Not loving the razor burn that resulted from summers of shaving, my more mature college self decided it was time to graduate to a bikini wax. Mind you, I wasn't ever wearing bathing suits at school and I was not having sex. This bikini (and sometimes full Brazilian) wax was just for me. As if men around me could sense how long my pubes were through my jeans. Not at all to say one can't enjoy a smooth situation alone, just for themselves. I had taken on the belief that in order to exude a sense of beauty or desirability, I simply had to be hairless. A dress-for-the-job-you-want kind of situation.

I voluntarily and repeatedly laid on a sheet of paper under a very bright light, legs splayed on either side of me, vulva fully exposed to a complete stranger, staring at the ceiling and digging my fingernails into my hands as hot wax ripped off chunks of my hair. I paid money for this service. It made me feel like more of a woman, and I thought of it almost as a form of self-care.

what a treat!

cute lil' UNDERWEAR

There was a span of time when, much like getting a bikini wax, I felt a thong was just innately more womanly than any other type of underwear. This is how I really feel about all the cute panty options out there:

I HATE THIS WORD

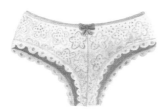

Very many questions about the "cheeky" cut. In my experience, they create immediate and severe wedgies.

I thought these cute "shortie" underwear would make me look and feel like Cameron Diaz in *Charlie's Angels*. Unfortunately not the case. These also come with that stiff, thick, (supposedly) elastic waistband that I hate.

No thong of mine has survived a full month of wear. They never make it out of the laundry (or my butt crack—and inevitably vagina) alive. Anytime I wear one, I end up pulling the center string out of my butt to rest on the side of my butt cheek.

I CURRENTLY BUY MY UNDERWEAR A SIZE TOO BIG SO I CAN PULL THEM UP TO MY BOOBS.

I bought a pair of dainty high-waisted underwear on a whim, thinking I would hate them. Turns out, they're kind of fun! Surprisingly comfortable. But they ended up crumpled in the corner of my room for a few months because they weren't machine-washable.

✳ THE WHOLE HAND WASHING THING FEELS REALLY CUMBERSOME TO ME. PLUS MY BATHROOM SINK IS USUALLY COATED WITH A FILM OF METAMUCIL AND/OR TOOTHPASTE, NOT EXACTLY THE MOST HOSPITABLE ENVIRONMENT FOR DELICATES.

the joy of being SINGLE

WOO HOOO!

it's just me, i can let it all go! burn the fancy underwear and let those pubes grow!

Once I started having sex at twenty-two, waxing and lace felt like much deeper necessities. I had someone to look "pretty" for, and how awful would it be to burden someone with my pubic hair! It eventually became clear to me that these grooming rituals were for someone else's benefit, not my own. I scrambled to fit impromptu waxes into my schedule when spontanous date plans popped up, and I began to resent the secret extra time and effort I felt I had to invest in these relationships. Singledom was freedom—a vacation from all of that pressure.

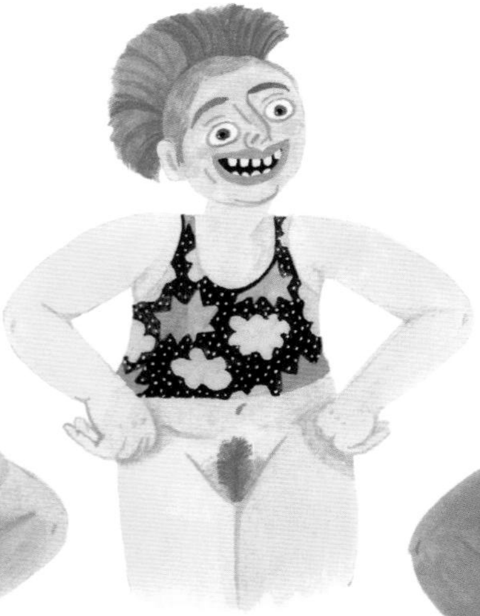
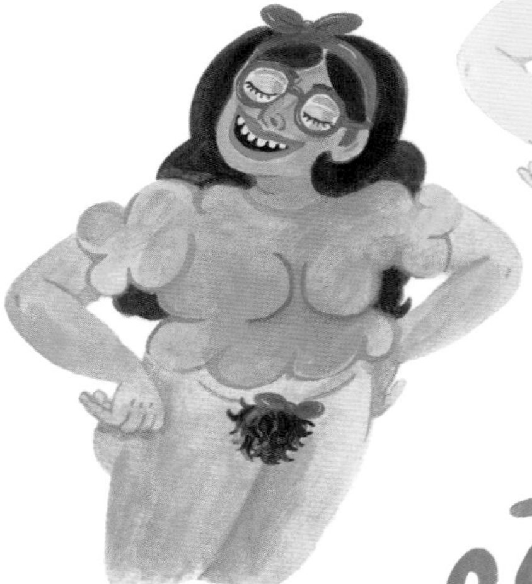
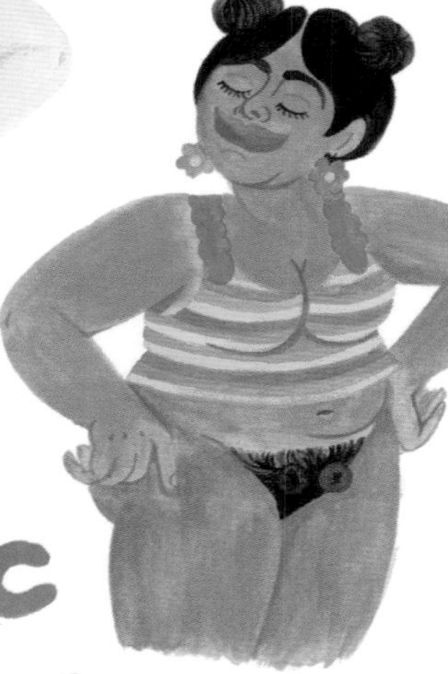

pubic hairdos

Double the hair, double the fun!

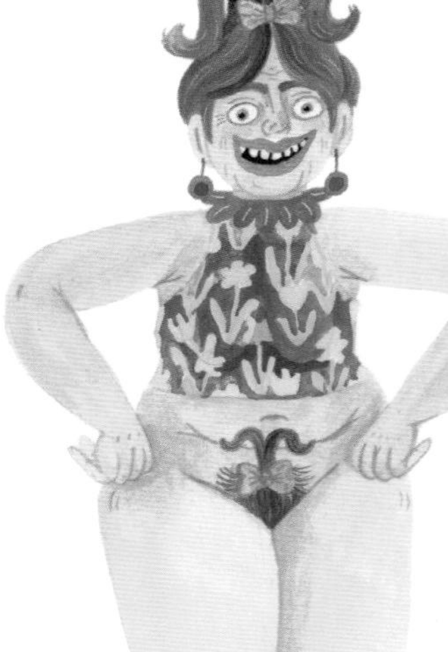
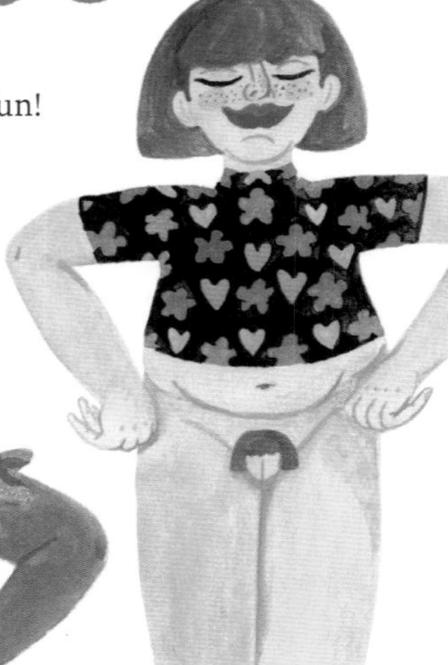
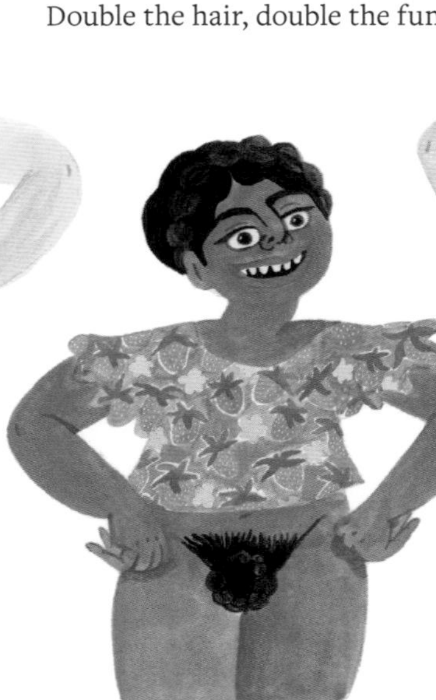

During a year-long (not exactly intentional) hiatus from dating, I began to relate to my pubes in a very different way. Being hairy went from being an emblem of my singledom to a very core and accepted part of being me. Getting a wax just wasn't something I wanted for myself. My unruly, full bush felt right—or so I thought . . .

Come summertime when I would find myself at the beach or a pool, I became self-conscious again. I didn't feel confident walking around with my wild bikini line, and I scurried into the water as fast as I could so as to spare the innocent bystanders around me.

I couldn't help but wonder...

VEGGIE STICK SNACKS ARE MY CIGARETTES AS I CHANNEL MY INNER CARRIE.

Are my pubes purely an act of rebellion? Do I actually feel best with a more polished and pruned bush? Getting a butt crack wax has always been surprisingly satisfying. Is my fully natural look just a feminist statement I'm forcing myself to make to prove a point—a statement that's keeping me from enjoying my body more wholly? Wouldn't it be more empowering to say "fuck it" to the implications and enjoy a smooth body if that's what I want? But then, do I only actually feel compelled to be smooth because I am so deeply conditioned to believe it's more beautiful? Can I still feel like a feminist and **bash the bush?**

the power of PUBES

I don't know where exactly I land on that question, but I know that I've gotten to a better place just by asking it. In taking ownership over my pubes, I've learned to turn to myself for the answers, rather than feel like there is only one way to look and feel feminine.

I try to treat my pubes just as I treat the hair on my head. The way I want to style them will probably change from time to time, and any way I choose to wear my hair is great—as long as I'm into it!

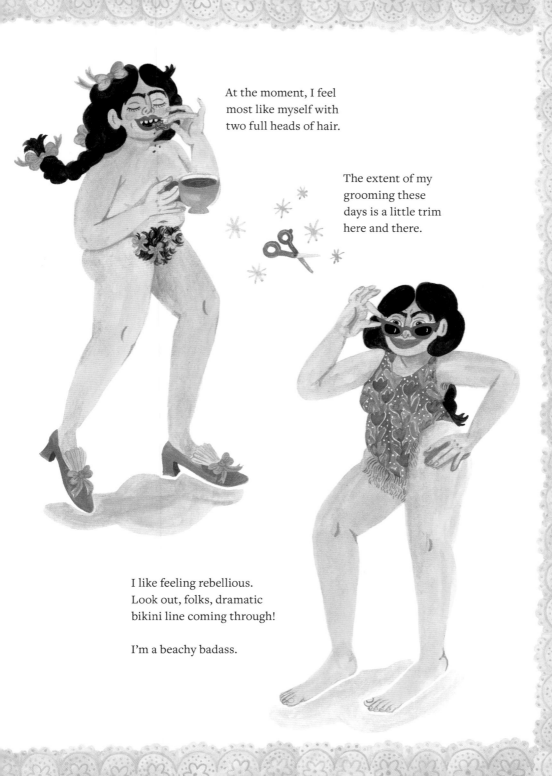

At the moment, I feel
most like myself with
two full heads of hair.

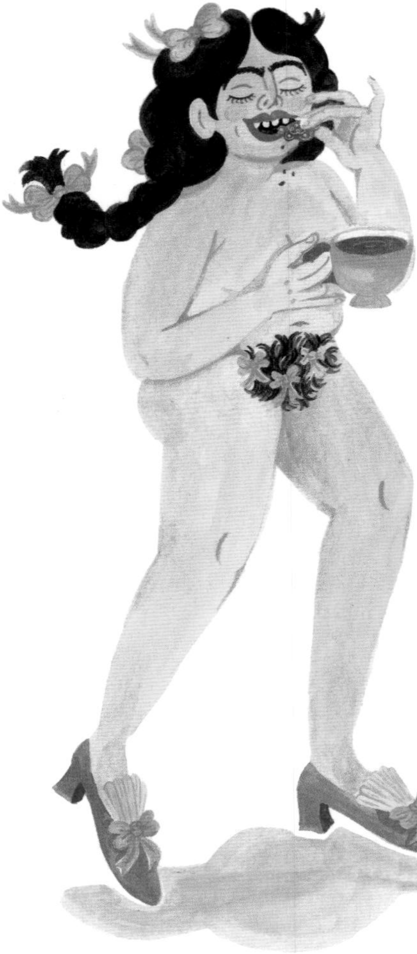

The extent of my
grooming these
days is a little trim
here and there.

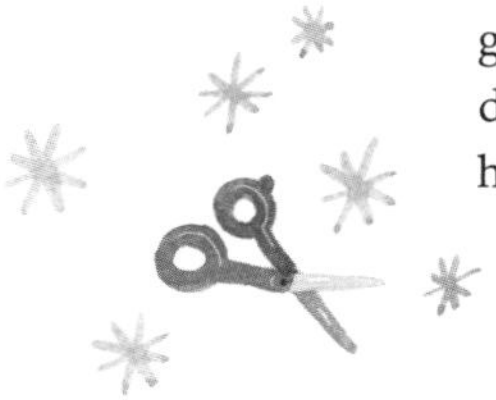

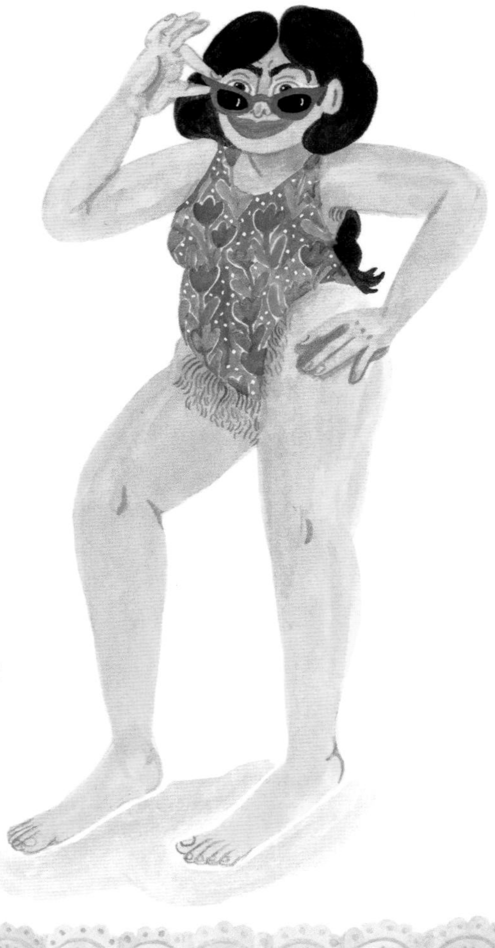

I like feeling rebellious.
Look out, folks, dramatic
bikini line coming through!

I'm a beachy badass.

LEGS & FEET

When I was younger, I had a perpetual scab on my knee from
continually falling on the same spot. My childhood next-door
neighbor Lizzie and I were always running around.

We spent hours digging up our backyards, overturning rocks and logs to play with worms and catch the ever-so-rare salamander.

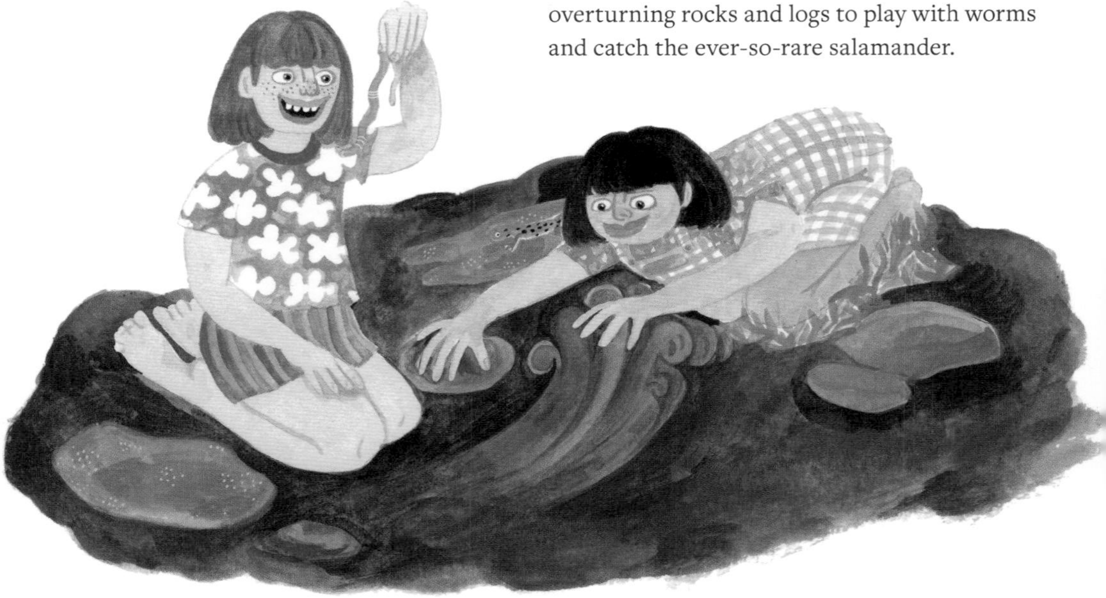

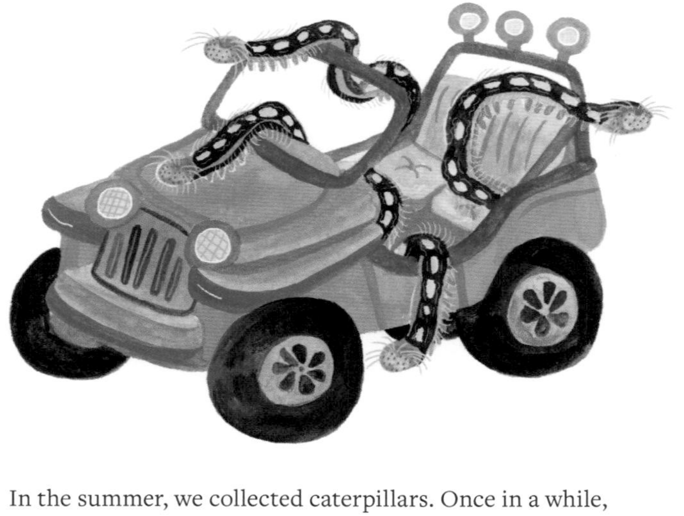

In the summer, we collected caterpillars. Once in a while, we'd give them a treat and push them around in Lizzie's hot pink Barbie jeep.

On a particularly hot summer afternoon, Lizzie and I stripped down to our underwear, covered our entire bodies with paint, and ran around her backyard. I later learned that Lizzie's mom created this activity because she was very pregnant and it was very hot and she wanted us to be occupied for hours. Genius.

"THUNDER" THIGHS

YOU WON'T BELIEVE HOW **JIGGLY!**

The carefree joy with which I gleefully ran around my yard came to an abrupt halt one summer at camp. I was sitting at the lake waiting for my swim class to start when I overheard some boys discuss a girl's jiggling thighs as she walked on the dock.

I hated to think anyone would ever talk about me in the same way, and it became starkly clear to me in that moment that I was fair game. My body was open to judgment, and moving around made me more vulnerable to harsh criticism.

I became minutely aware of every inch of my legs:

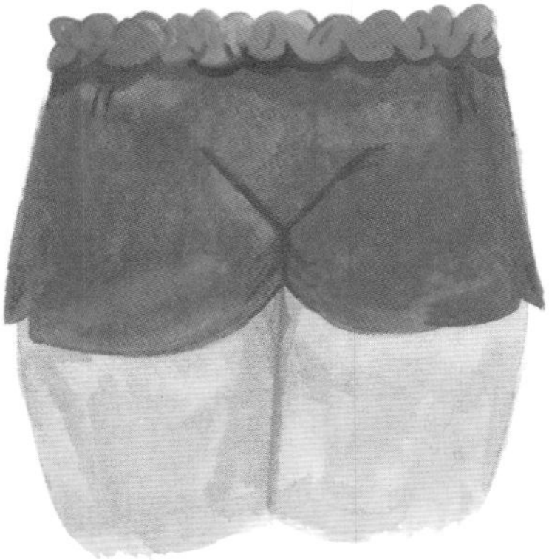

I hated how my thighs rubbed together when I walked and how the rubbing pushed up my shorts.

JUST THE THOUGHT OF WEARING SOFFE SHORTS MAKES ME CRINGE

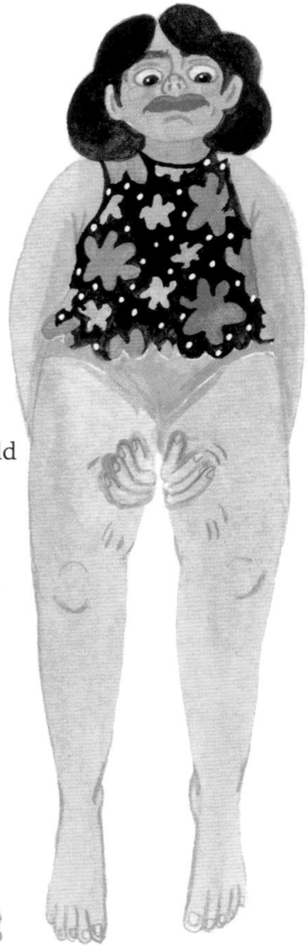

I'd stand in front of the mirror and pull my inner thighs back from behind to see what it would look like if I was thin enough that they wouldn't touch.

I HAVE A FOLD IN MY KNEECAP AND ALWAYS THOUGHT IT MADE MY LEGS LOOK LAZY AND DROOPY. I WANTED SKINNY, SHARP-LOOKING KNEES.

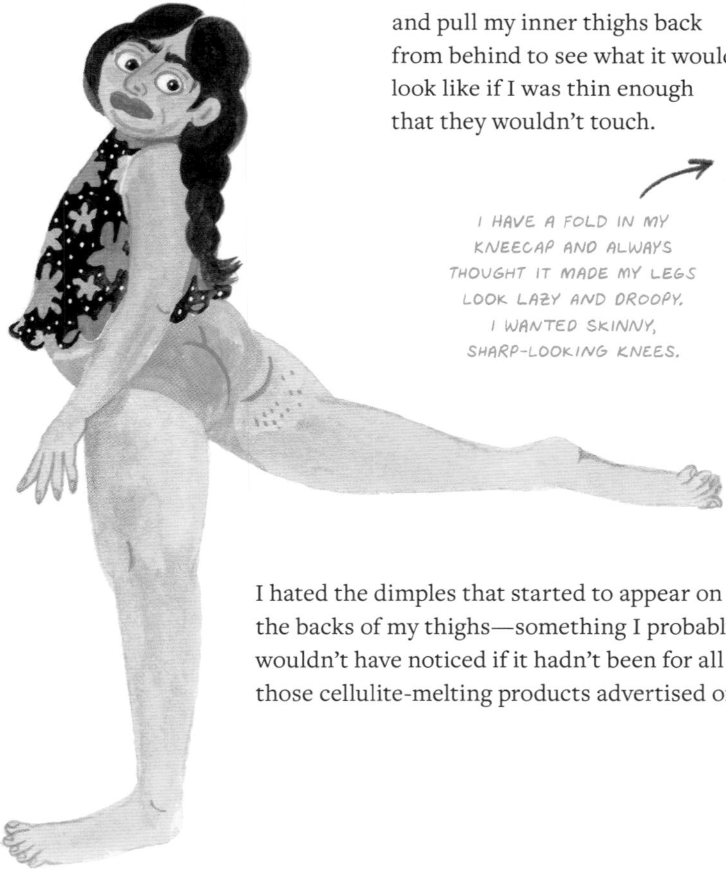

I hated the dimples that started to appear on the backs of my thighs—something I probably wouldn't have noticed if it hadn't been for all of those cellulite-melting products advertised on TV.

And just when I thought I had racked up enough issues with my thighs:

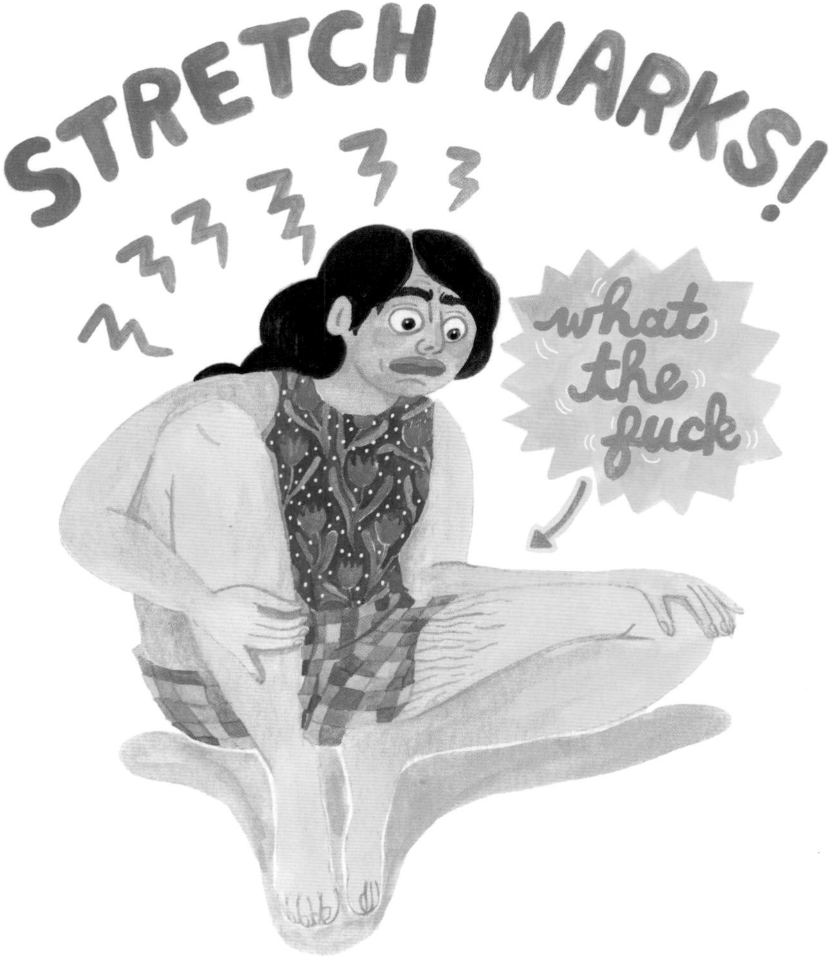
STRETCH MARKS!
what the fuck

I first discovered mine in eighth grade. One afternoon during gym class, I spotted pinkish-purple lines streaked across my upper inner thighs. I had no idea where they had come from or what they even were. Had I scratched myself in my sleep? Or maybe I had been attacked by some sort of nightmarish, clawed creature?

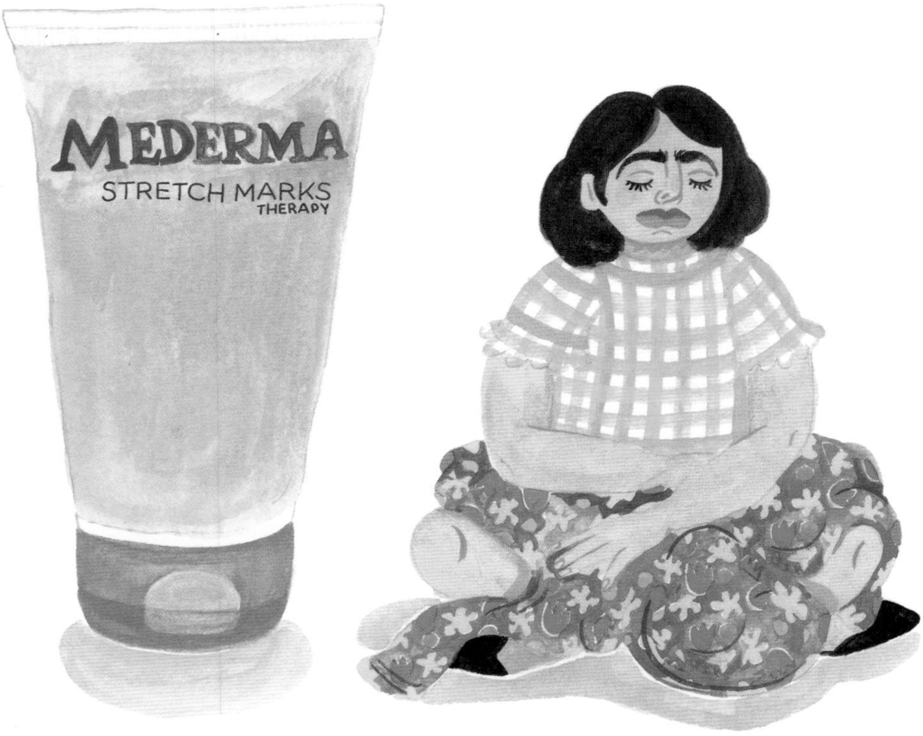
MEDERMA
STRETCH MARKS
THERAPY

I was too ashamed to ask my mom what these marks might be, and instead made it my mission to figure out how to get rid of them. I kept them hidden, espectially from myself, at all costs. I hated looking at them and I hated how I could feel the grooves they made in my skin.

look here!

I began to dread summertime because that meant shorts and pool parties.

When there were bathing suits involved, stretch mark exposure was inevitable. On my first family vacation with stretch marks, Alex pointed at me as I was getting into the water and asked what the purplish lines on my legs were. I ran out of the ocean sobbing. I had been found out.

* TO BE FAIR, THE WATER AND MY TANKINI BOTTOMS CREATED THE PERFECT FRAMING DEVICE TO SHOW OFF MY STRETCH MARKS.

My subsequent poolside strategy: I walked around with a towel draped around my entire body at all times. Good thing it was cute and girly to be cold (where did that whole thing come from?), so I could shiver and look like a little fragile bird. This poolside straitjacket made it tough to move around, eat snacks, or participate in any games, but I felt it was the perfect solution. If and when I did get into the pool, I'd keep my towel right next to my entry and exit points so I'd spend as little time exposed as possible.

THE PERFECT SETUP

HUNCHED OVER TO
ENSURE THAT BRA
WILL STAY IN PLACE.

BRA PULLED DOWN
OVER BUBBLE OF TOP
TUMMY FAT, SIDE FAT,
AND BACK FAT.

SHORTS AND LEGS
POSITIONED TO HIDE
STRETCH MARKS.

With all these "imperfections" to keep hidden, moving freely in front of other people really felt out of the question. Getting dressed was about adjusting my clothing to hide all of my least favorite features. Once I got situated with every fat roll in place and stretch marks covered, the last thing I wanted to do was run around and reverse all of that careful work.

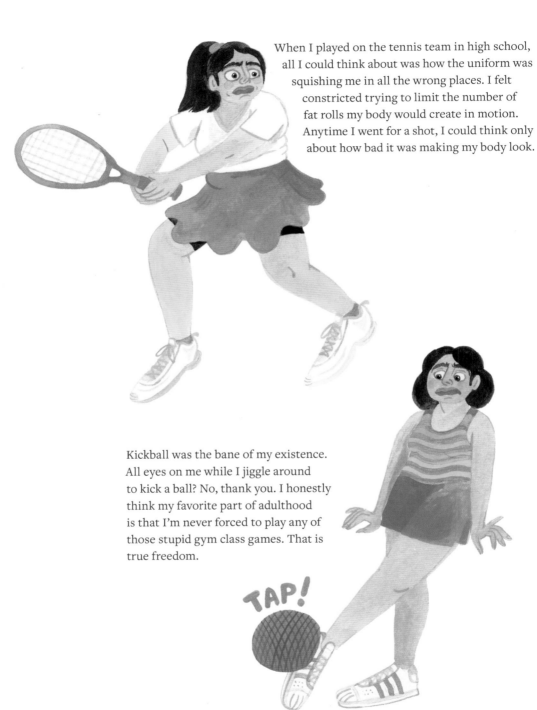

When I played on the tennis team in high school, all I could think about was how the uniform was squishing me in all the wrong places. I felt constricted trying to limit the number of fat rolls my body would create in motion. Anytime I went for a shot, I could think only about how bad it was making my body look.

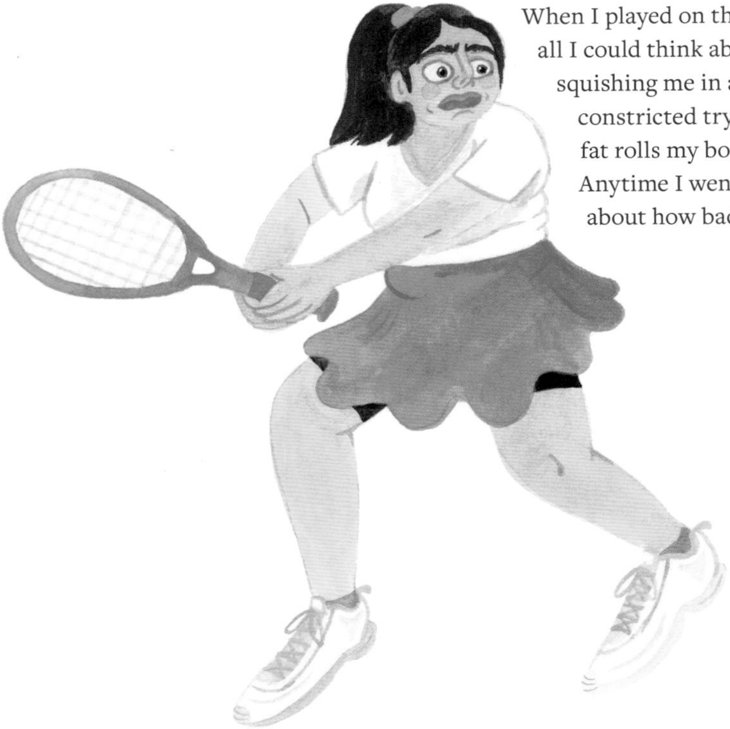

Kickball was the bane of my existence. All eyes on me while I jiggle around to kick a ball? No, thank you. I honestly think my favorite part of adulthood is that I'm never forced to play any of those stupid gym class games. That is true freedom.

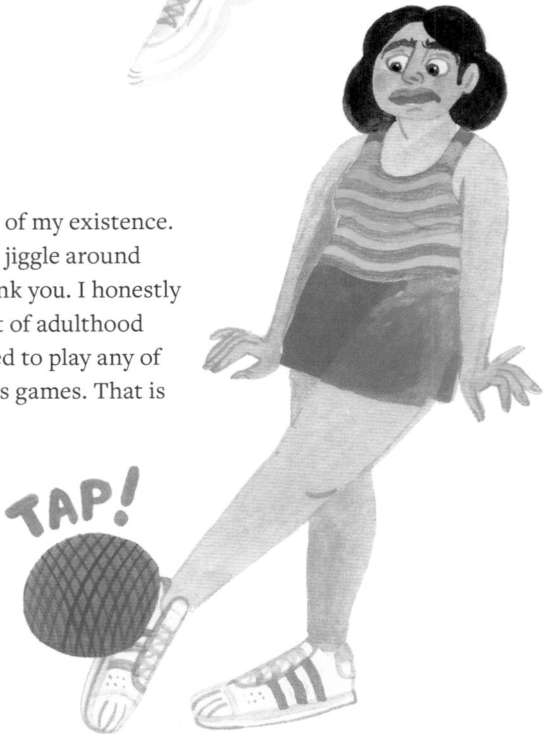
TAP!

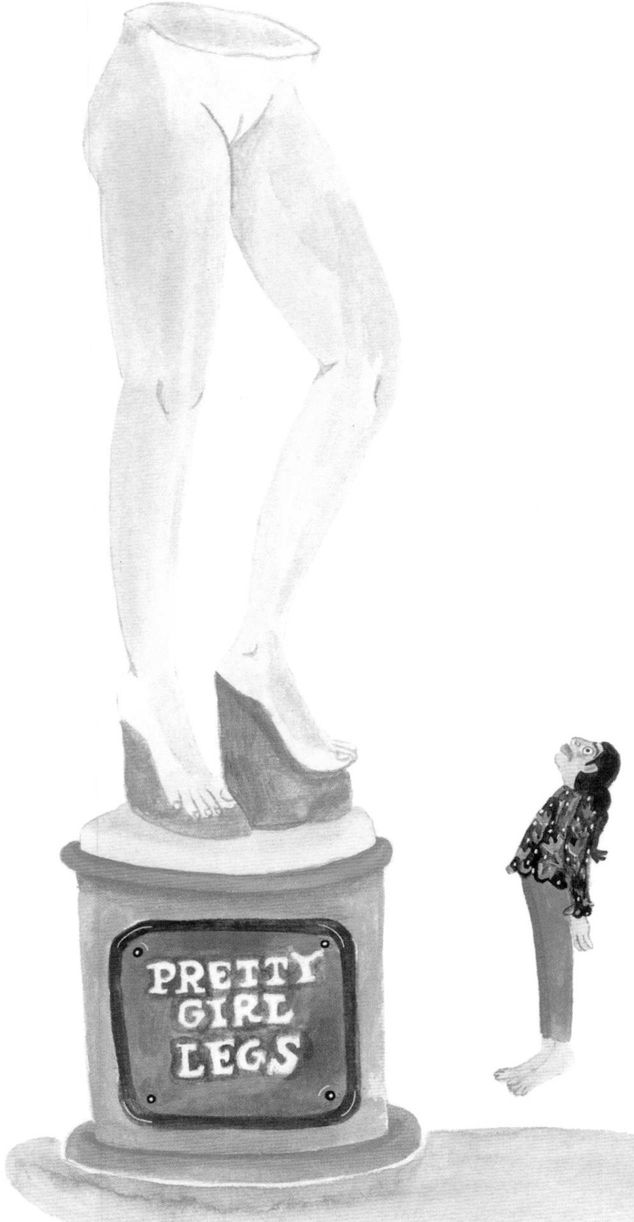
PRETTY
GIRL
LEGS

I wanted good legs, and in my mind there was only one kind: long and lean.

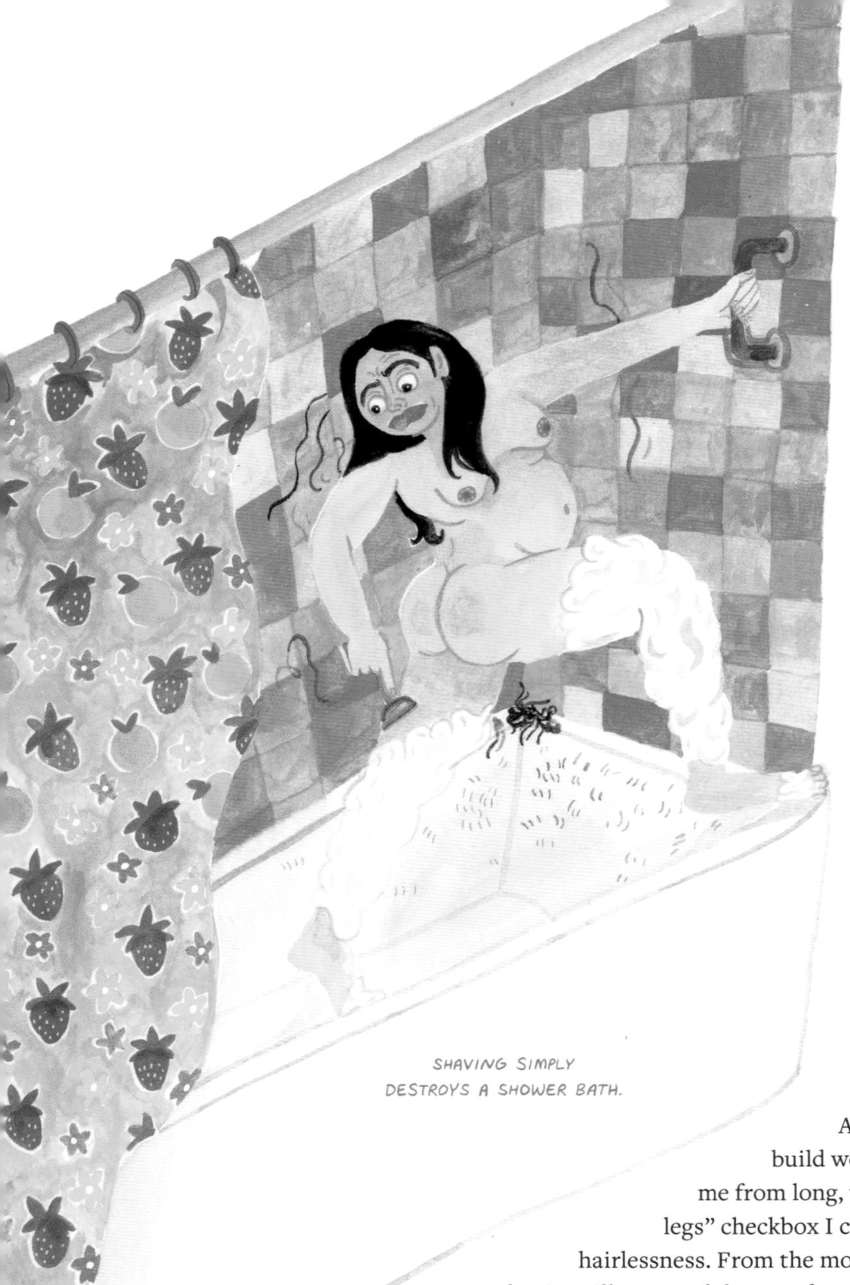

i'm your venus, i'm your fire, your desire!

SHAVING SIMPLY DESTROYS A SHOWER BATH.

Accepting that my genetic build would most likely preclude me from long, thin legs, the one "pretty legs" checkbox I could actually tick off was hairlessness. From the moment I picked up a razor, having silky smooth legs made me feel more like a woman than anything else ever had. And thus shaving became just another part of my shower routine—specifically, while my hair soaked up conditioner.

ALEX ONCE SAW ME SHAVING MY BUTT CHEEKS AND WHEN SHE TOLD MY MOM I WAS DEEPLY MORTIFIED. MY HAIR JUST KEPT GOING! IT WOULD BE WEIRD TO SUDDENLY HAVE HAIR ON MY BUTT CHEEKS!

& THE HAIR DOESN'T STOP THERE!

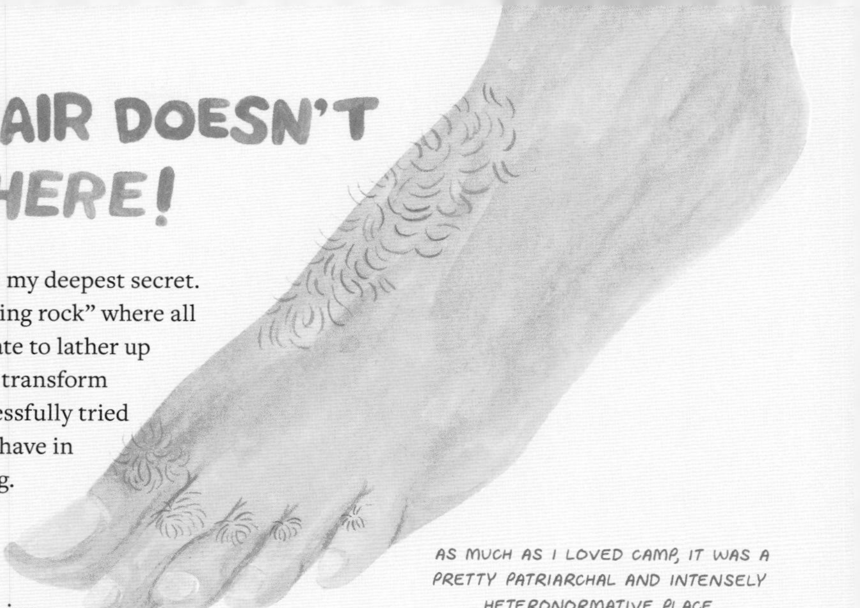

The hair on my toes was my deepest secret. At camp, we had a "shaving rock" where all the girls would congregate to lather up with shaving cream and transform into elegant ladies. I stressfully tried to sneak a foot and toe shave in while no one was looking.

While we girls were busy shaving our legs, the guys were either playing on the tennis courts that were conveniently right outside their bunks, or grilling.

AS MUCH AS I LOVED CAMP, IT WAS A PRETTY PATRIARCHAL AND INTENSELY HETERONORMATIVE PLACE.

*THAT'S A WHOLE OTHER BOOK, SO I'LL JUST LEAVE THAT HERE FOR NOW.

nair interlude!

* GAS MASK NOT INCLUDED.

I tried Nair for a day. The stuff is diabolical and genuinely smells like a burning carcass.

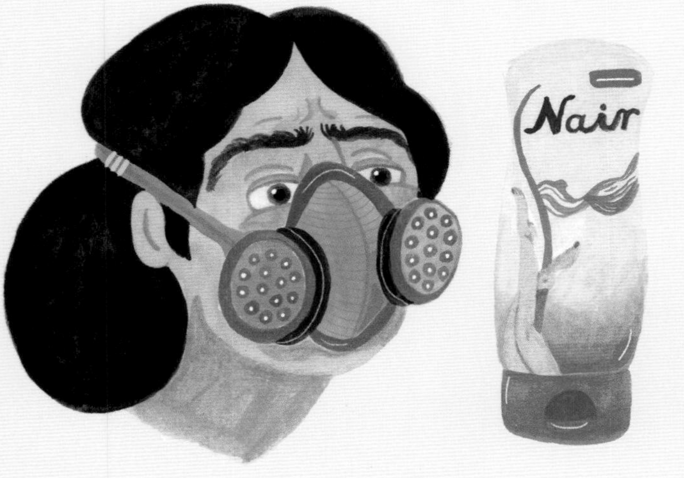
Nair

CIRQUE DU SOSHAVE

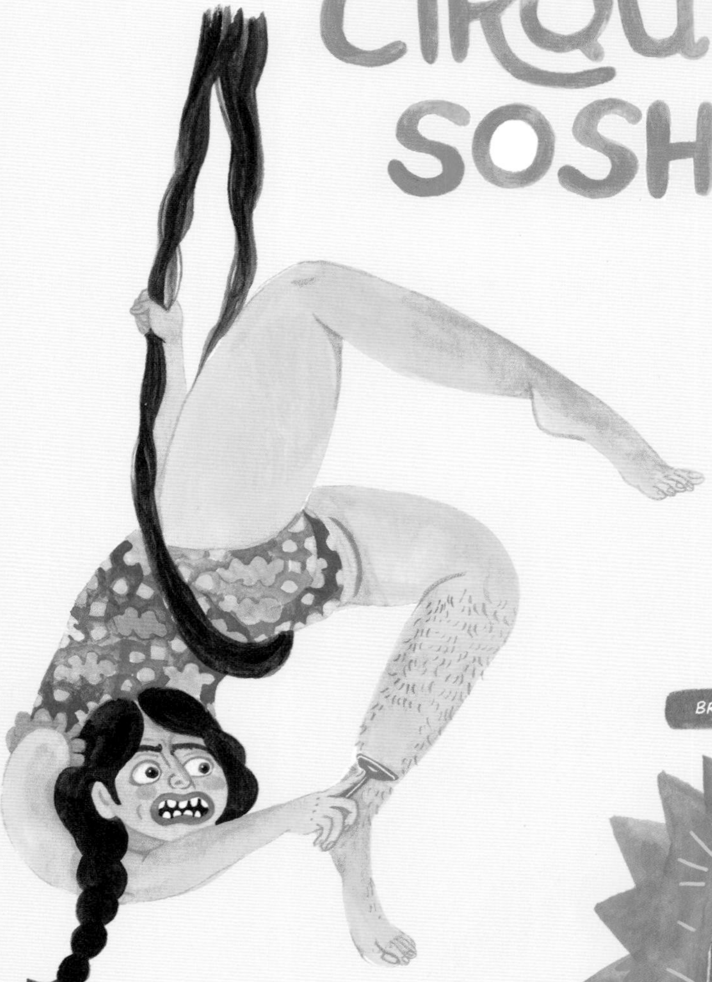

BROUGHT TO YOU BY:

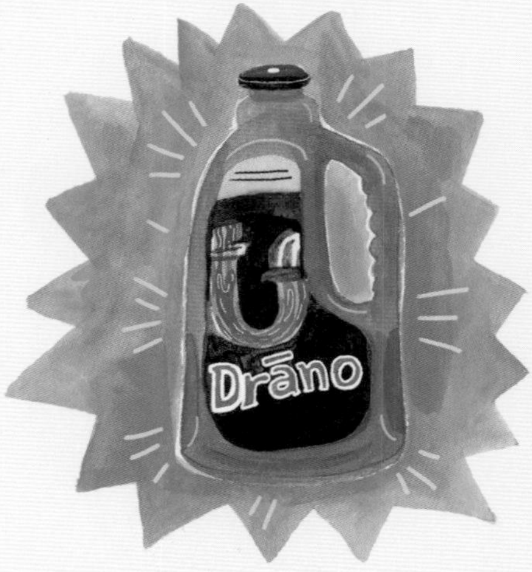
Drāno

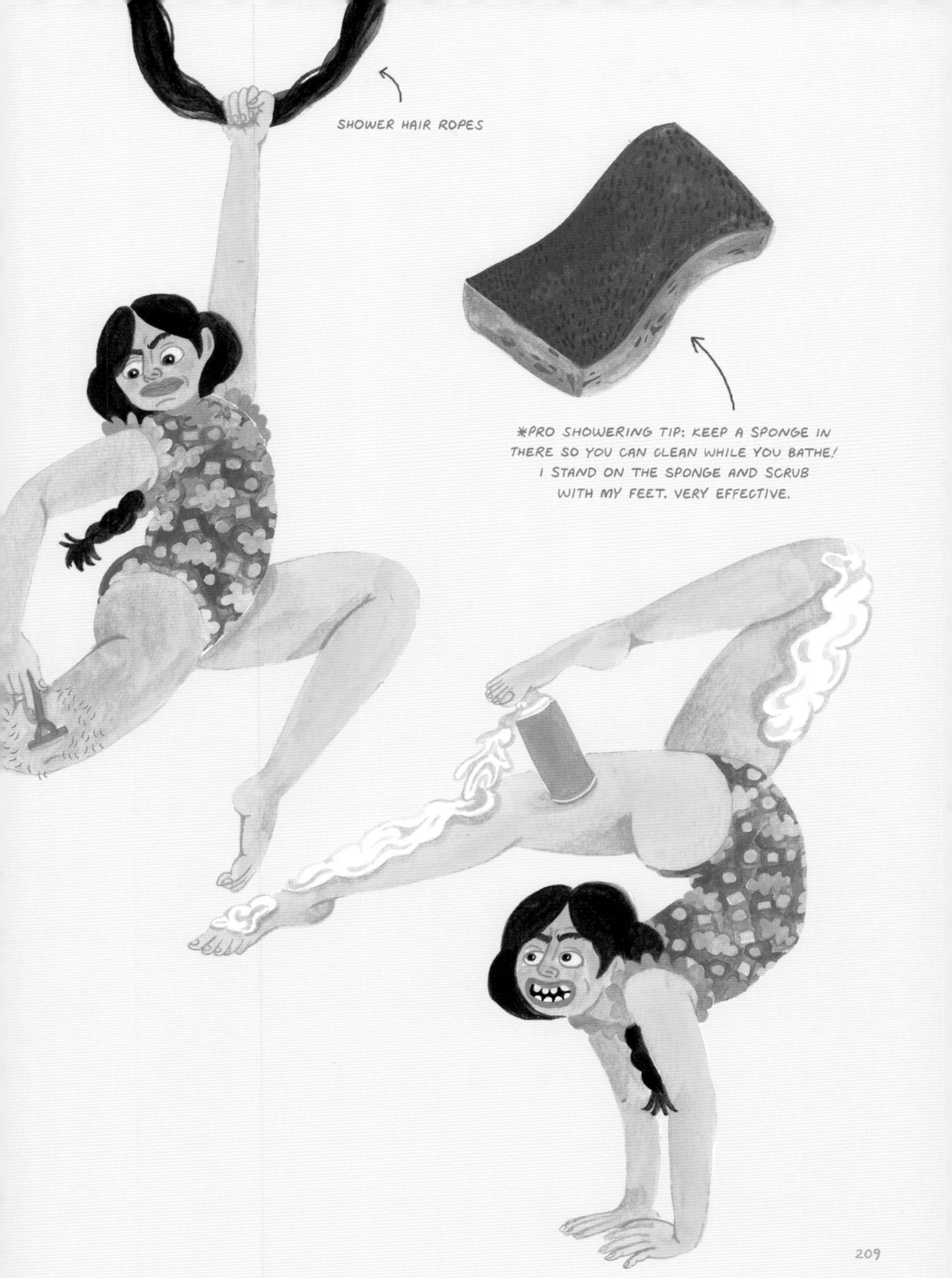
SHOWER HAIR ROPES
*PRO SHOWERING TIP: KEEP A SPONGE IN THERE SO YOU CAN CLEAN WHILE YOU BATHE! I STAND ON THE SPONGE AND SCRUB WITH MY FEET. VERY EFFECTIVE.

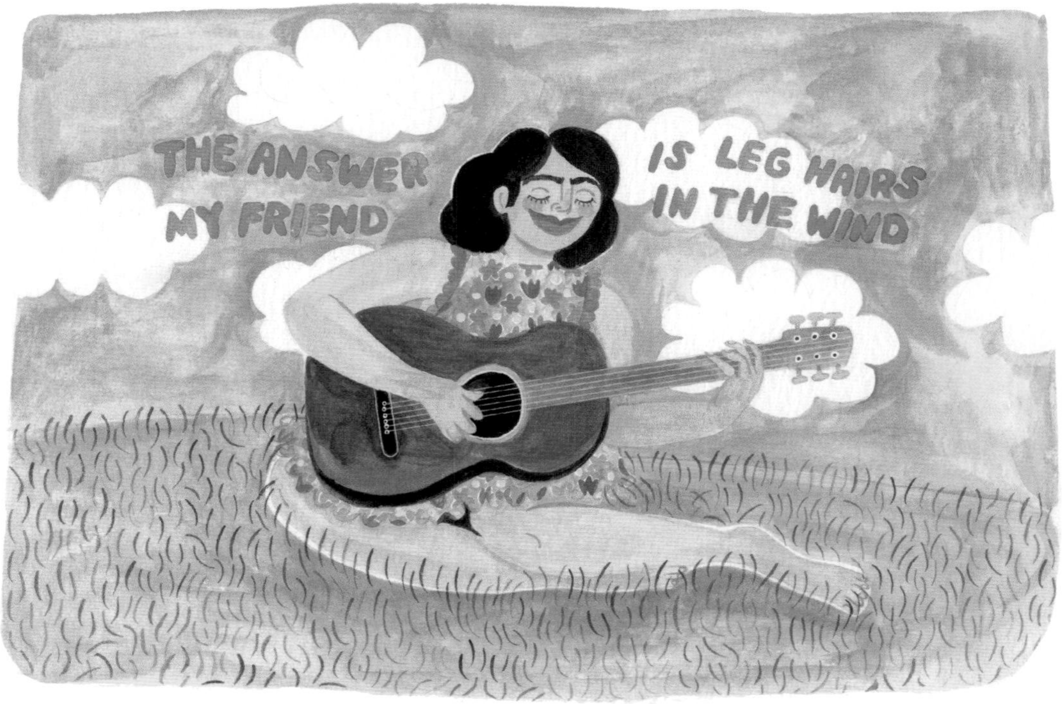
THE ANSWER MY FRIEND
IS LEG HAIRS IN THE WIND

Flash forward to my twenties living in New York when I finally decided it was okay to grow out my leg hair in the winter. I'd save my poor overworked shower drain and use Drano less often. My legs weren't seeing the light of day, so why even bother? One morning as I was walking to the gym, I kept feeling something caress my leg. I kept stopping in the middle of the street to see what was touching me, but nothing was there. I eventually realized that the gentle tickling I'd been feeling was just my newly grown out leg hairs caressing my own leg (cute!!!). My legs hairs were blowing in the wind. I started singing to myself "the answer my friend / is leg hairs in the wind / the answer is leg hairs in the wind." I texted the Yentas immediately.

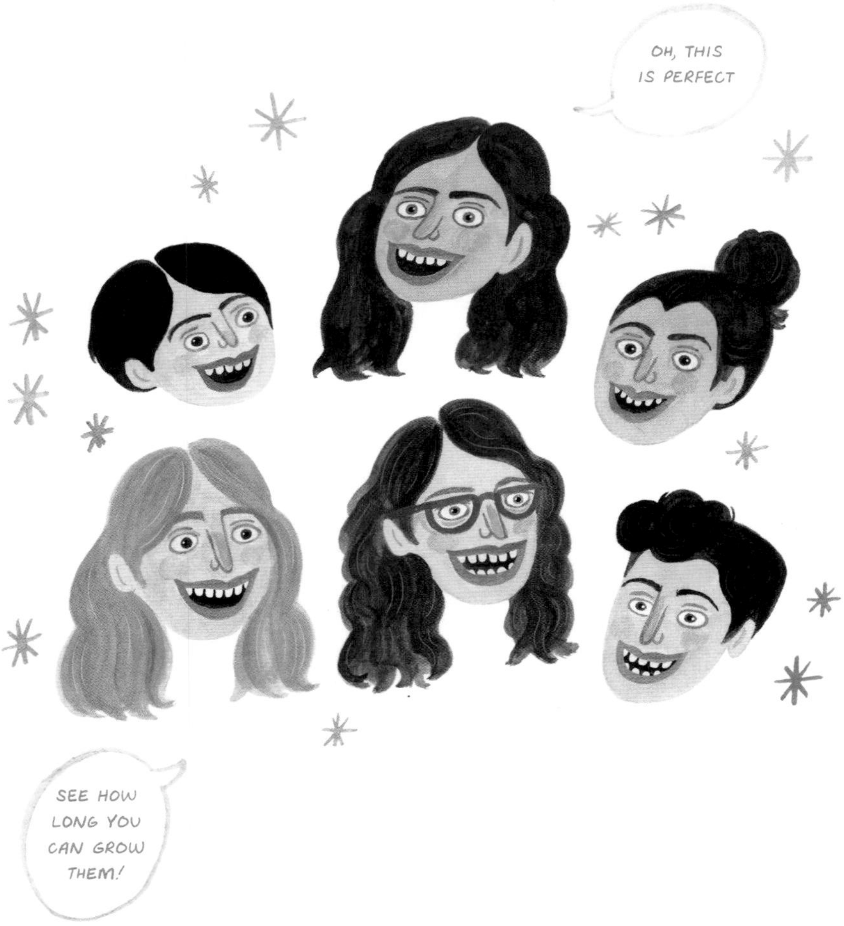
OH, THIS IS PERFECT
SEE HOW LONG YOU CAN GROW THEM!

That silly little moment on the street corner was invigorating, and was actually a big step toward embracing my hairy legs.

heels : A PERSONAL HISTORY

I inferred at a young age that heels signified womanhood. Whenever I'd dig through my mom's closet to find a pair to try on, my clumsy trip to the nearest mirror was always totally erased the moment I caught sight of myself in these grown-up "real woman" shoes. The effect is still the same anytime I find myself in a DSW—all of a sudden I can take on myriad hyper-feminine personas.

The dress-up fun typically stops there. Heels aren't in my everyday rotation. Comfort has always been nonnegotiable for me. When I was little, I hardly was able to wear socks because I could feel the seams folding in on themselves inside my shoes—I called them "pokies." Needless to say, I was never thrilled at the prospect of squeezing my toes into stiff, hard, stilted shoes. But, of course, I did spend some time in heels over the years—they are my birthright as a woman after all!

OK, I'M A MODEL

My first heel: a sensible shoe from Payless for Bat Mitzvah season. Even though the heel was quite modest, I was incredibly relieved to learn about the great Bat Mitzvah party tradition of doing away with shoes all together and wearing socks instead.

A quick pause to pay tribute to the other stars of Bat/Bar Mitzvahs: these shoes. For those unfamiliar, there are sometimes hired dancers at Bar/Bat Mitzvah parties to get the crowd going. They always wear these shoes—and bedazzled vests.

Took these monster heels for a spin in college. They ate my feet.

In my early online dating days, I went on a date with a finance bro and wore platforms because I thought that would make me look more like the type of girls he usually went out with. The night was catastrophic.

I bought this pair for a friend's wedding under the supervision of my sister Alex. She is always my phone-a-friend when shoe shopping. These look scary, but were shockingly comfortable. Not one blister!

PEDICURES

I used to think open-toed shoes simply demanded a pedicure. I got my first one for prom in high school and decided then and there that it was the only acceptable way for the world to see my toes.

At this point, though, they quite honestly feel like a waste of time and money. Objectively speaking, pedicures probably are one of the nicest treat-yourself moments one can have, it's just not my choice of treat. I'd rather allocate that time and money to a massage, an order of takeout noodles to eat in bed, or to go see a heartwarming movie by myself and happy cry a lot.

the leggy awards

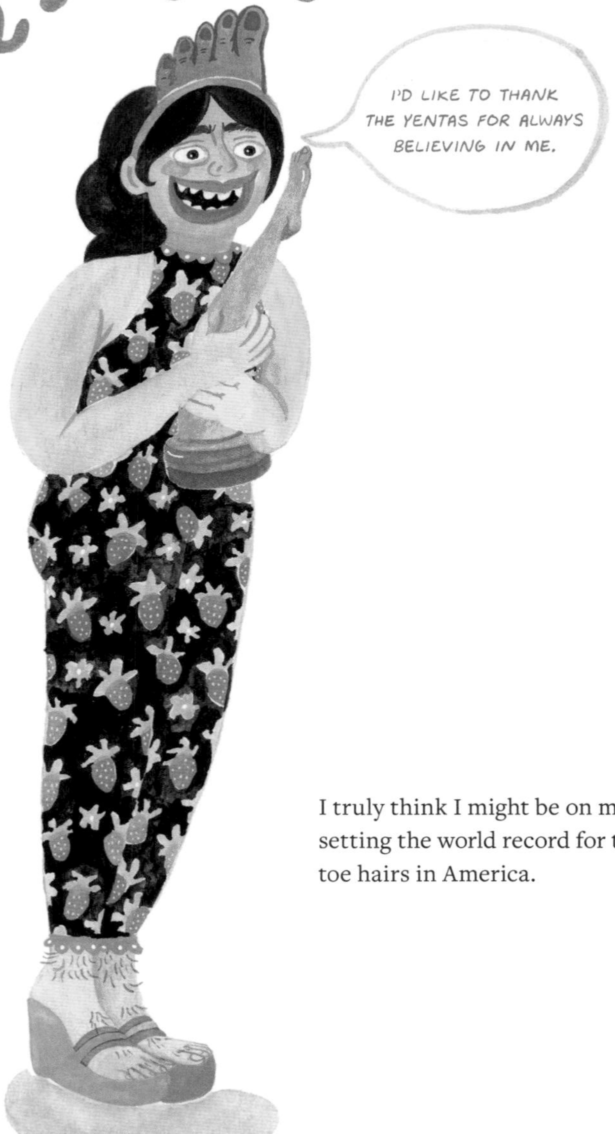
I'D LIKE TO THANK THE YENTAS FOR ALWAYS BELIEVING IN ME.

I truly think I might be on my way to setting the world record for the longest toe hairs in America.

Once in a while, I'll get my legs waxed—mostly because smooth legs make my hot yoga classes a little more fun and slippery.

I HAVEN'T QUITE NAILED THIS POSE YET, SO THIS IS ME MANIFESTING THAT BY THE TIME THIS BOOK IS OUT, I WILL HAVE DONE IT.

My hairy legs can be pretty cozy to snuggle up with—especially in the winter.

By repeatedly acknowledging and accepting my legs for who they are, they feel more like a part of me—rather than some alien logs of fat and muscle I am constantly battling—and I have a lot of appreciation for all that my legs can do.

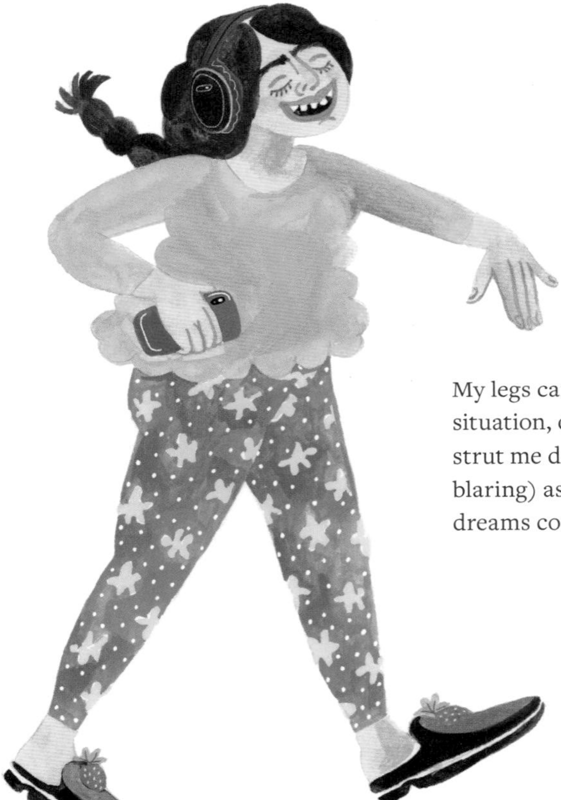

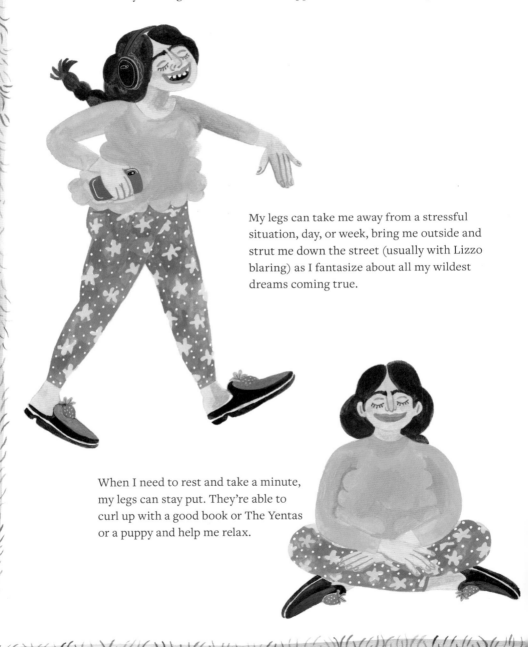

My legs can take me away from a stressful situation, day, or week, bring me outside and strut me down the street (usually with Lizzo blaring) as I fantasize about all my wildest dreams coming true.

When I need to rest and take a minute, my legs can stay put. They're able to curl up with a good book or The Yentas or a puppy and help me relax.

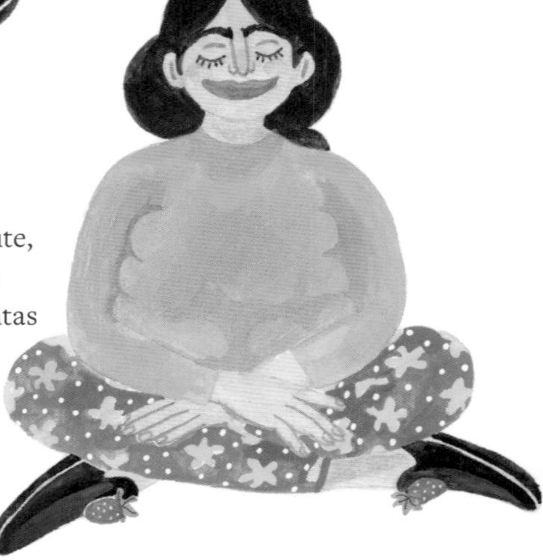

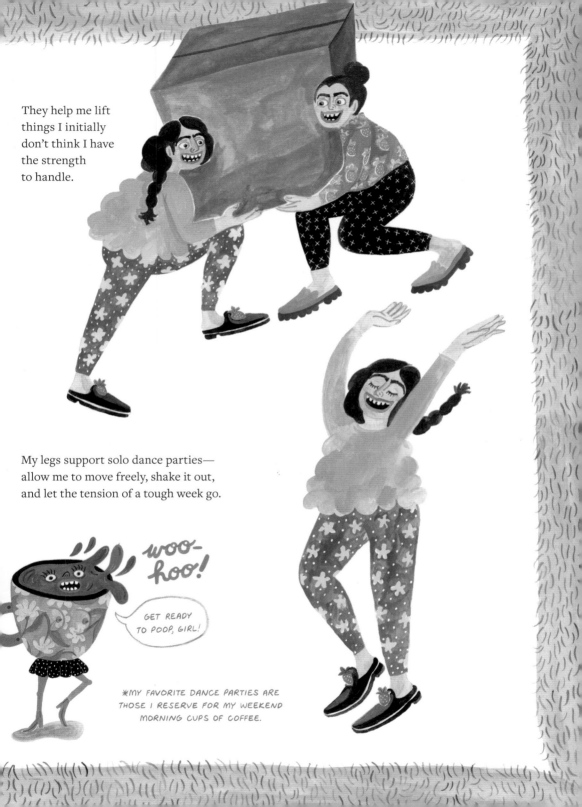

They help me lift things I initially don't think I have the strength to handle.

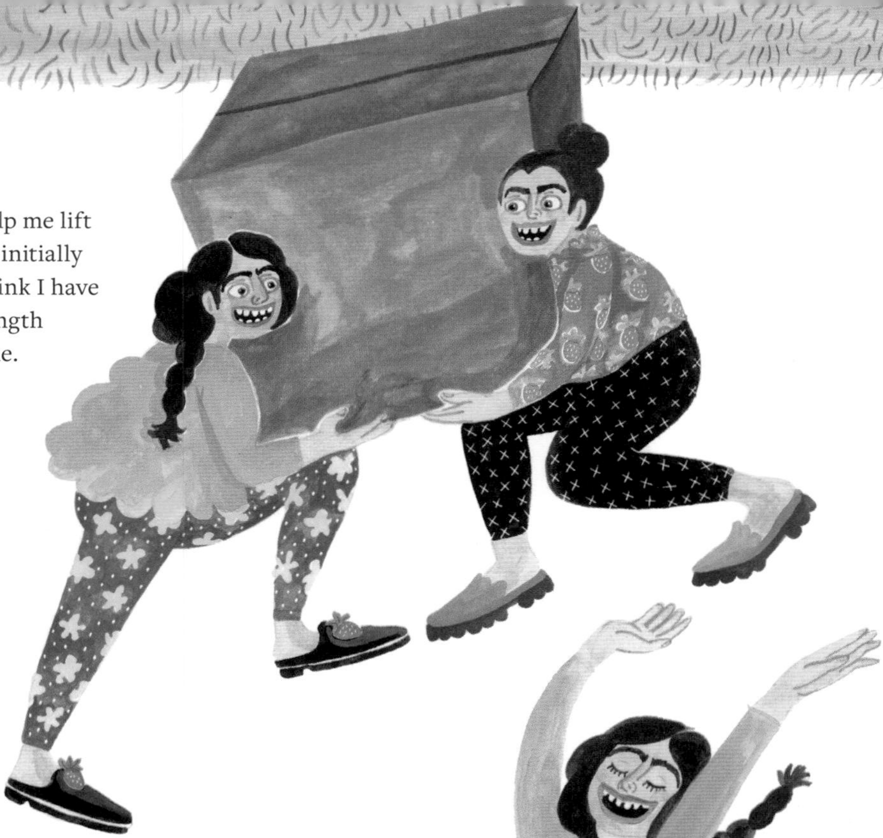

My legs support solo dance parties—allow me to move freely, shake it out, and let the tension of a tough week go.

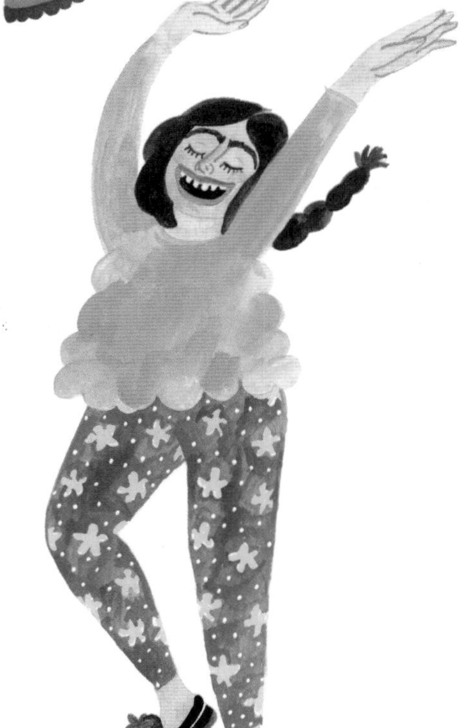

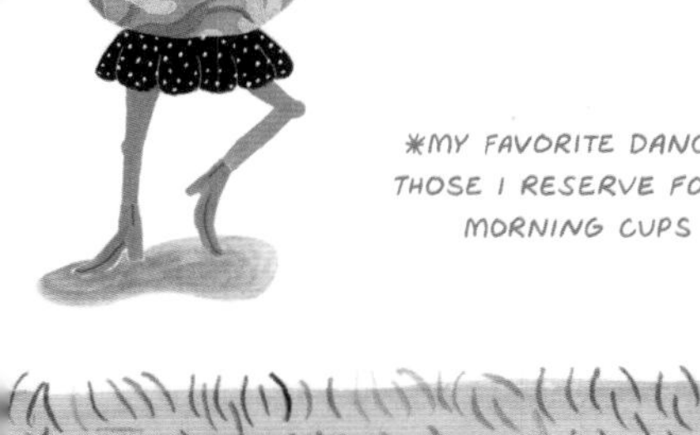
woo-hoo!
GET READY TO POOP, GIRL!

*MY FAVORITE DANCE PARTIES ARE THOSE I RESERVE FOR MY WEEKEND MORNING CUPS OF COFFEE.

SHOULDERS
& BACK

i love myself!

THIS WAS MY ABSOLUTE FAVORITE
OUTFIT IN KINDERGARTEN.
ONE AFTERNOON WHEN I WAS
EATING A SNACK WITH MY
CRUSH, I TOLD HIM TO TAKE
A PEEK AT MY FUNKY PANTS
UNDER THE TABLE.

✳THAT WAS THE FIRST
(AND LAST) TIME I WAS
BOLDLY FLIRTATIOUS.

As a kid, I was incredibly confident and had a strong backbone. I never second-guessed my opinions and was notoriously stubborn, rarely backing down from my stances.

As the oldest of three sisters, I was comfortable taking leadership roles outside my family dynamics. I always jumped at being the group leader for class projects or deciding what games to play at recess.

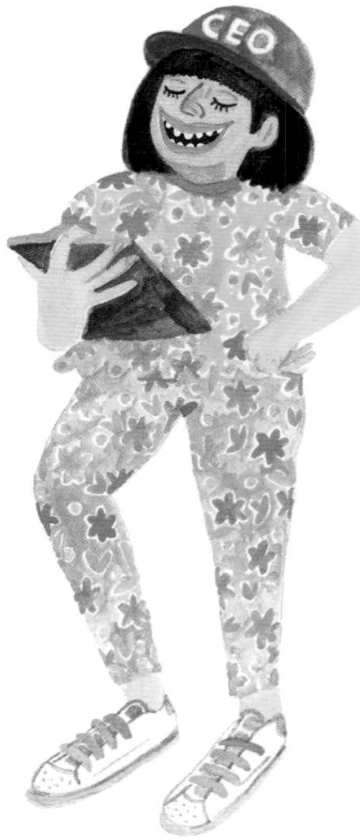
CEO

AS A KID, A CLIPBOARD WAS THE MOST EMPOWERING ACCESSORY TO HOLD, AND I LOVED FEELING IN CHARGE.

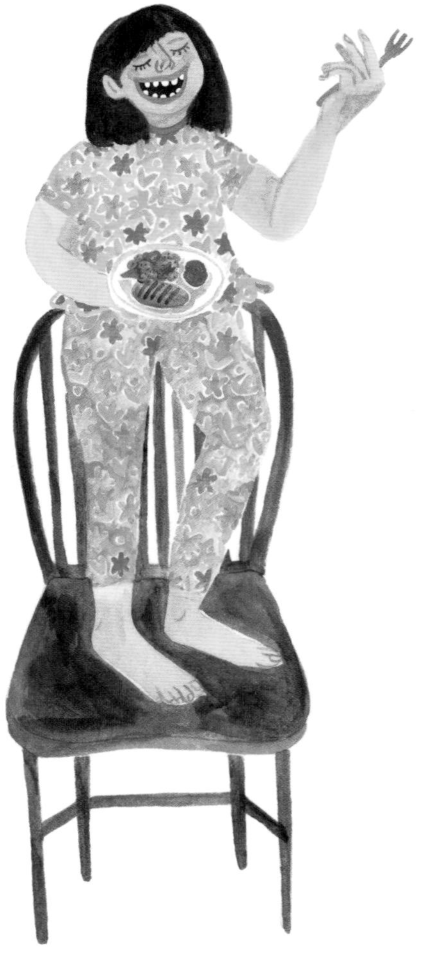

I always had an opinion, and my priority was to have that opinion heard. I eagerly leapt toward any opportunity to debate, and often transformed our family dinner table into a courtroom as I negotiated TV-watching privileges for my sisters and me or lectured my parents on what I believed to be the most appropriate punishment.

Over time my innate self-assuredness and confidence in my thoughts and feelings began to disappear as my focus turned outward. I became weighed down by pressures and expectations—some overtly discussed and others I absorbed over time—dictating how I as a girl should or shouldn't carry myself.

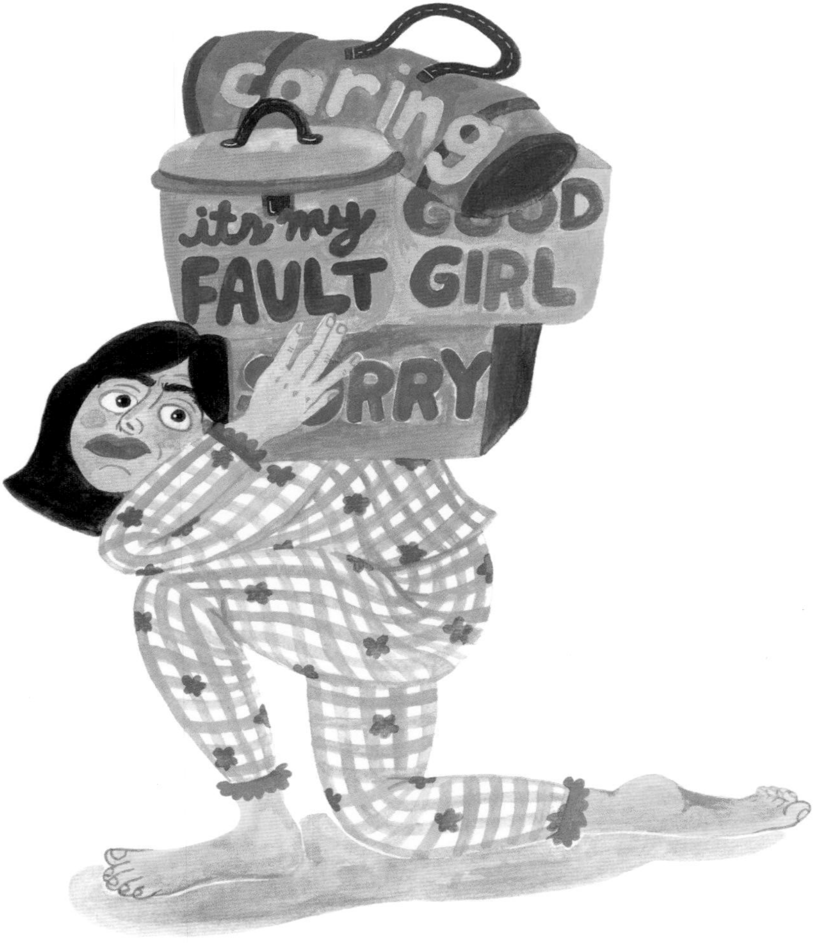
caring
it's my
FAULT
GOOD
GIRL
RRY

My tendency to firmly stand my ground morphed into a quickness to shoulder blame, and I became more comfortable taking on the burden of other people's feelings rather than confronting and calling attention to my own.

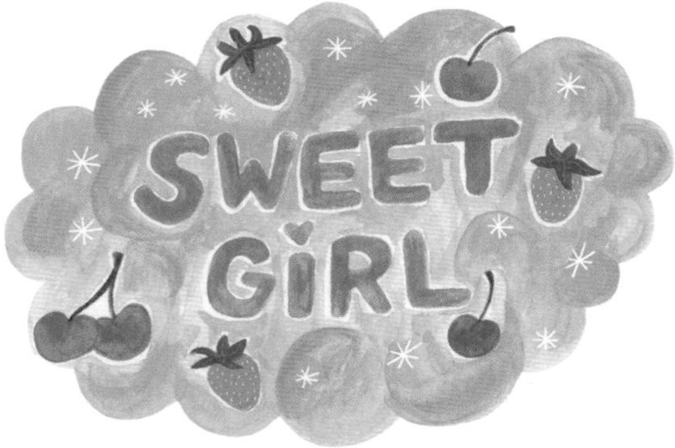
SWEET GIRL

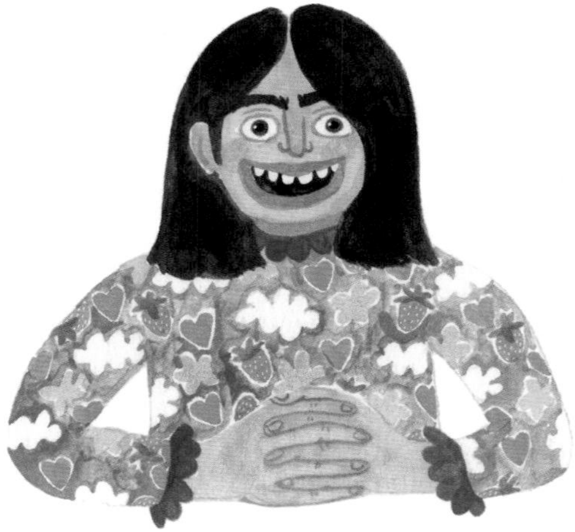

My shrinking confidence and spunk had its first clear plummet in middle school when I learned that the boys in my class had come up with a definitive ranking of the girls. Boobs and certain butt shapes got you extra points. Bossiness was sure to secure you a place at the bottom of the list, and it seemed that kindnesss and generosity could bring you up.

*YES, THE GIRLS HAD FAVORITE BOYS TOO, BUT THAT POPULARITY WAS USUALLY BASED ON PERSONALITY TRAITS OR TALENTS RATHER THAN BODY PARTS OR AGREEABLENESS—FUNNINESS AND ATHLETICISM GOT BOYS MAJOR POINTS.

I vividly remember vowing to myself that I'd be known as a "sweet girl." Subtle, mysterious, and demure. A wonderful complement to my artsy girl persona. Artsy girls are delicate and quiet.

Grease is one of my favorite movies and as a kid, Rizzo was my least favorite chacter. Watching the movie now, I can see that Rizzo is sharp and fiery and undeniably fabulous, but I used to reject her because I was ashamed to feel connected to her brazen persona. Sturdy and stubborn were not attractive qualities, in my mind. That was a side of myself I wanted to shove down. I wanted to be seen more like Sandy. Innocent, kind, and malleable.

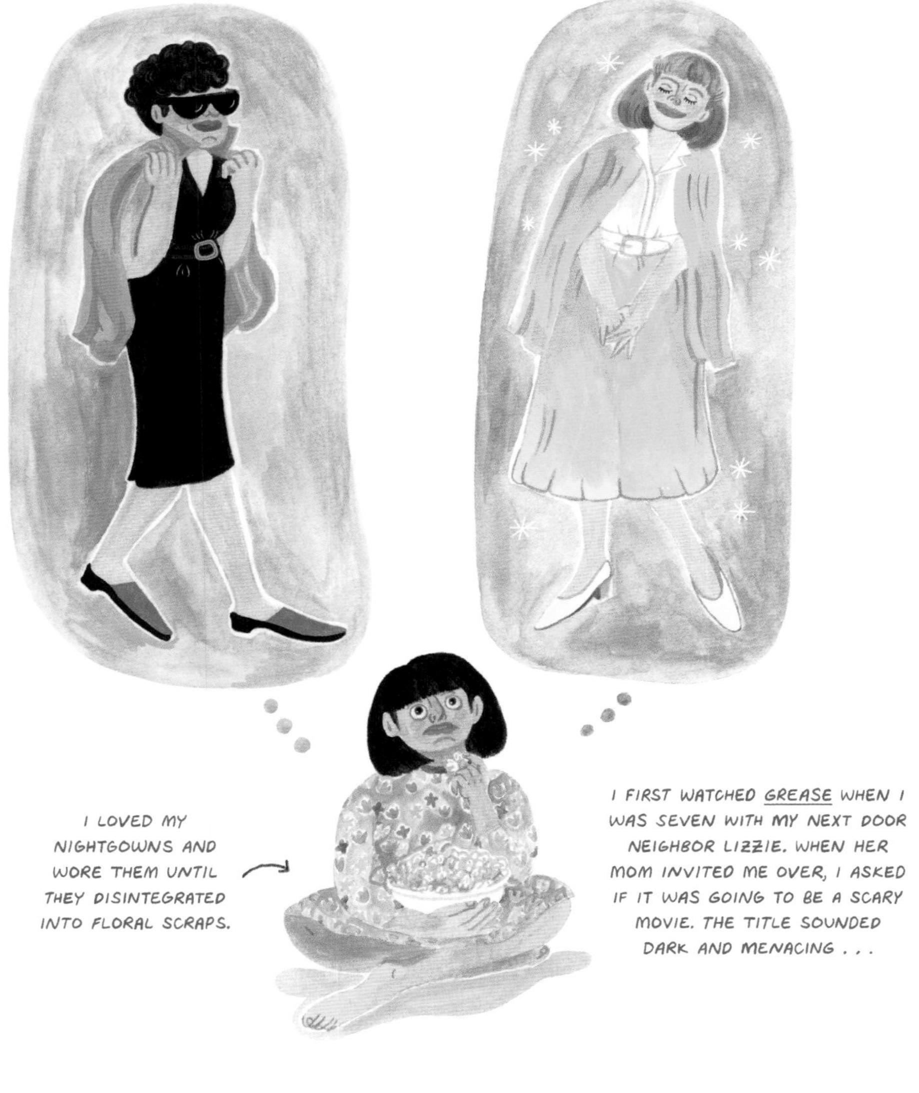
I LOVED MY NIGHTGOWNS AND WORE THEM UNTIL THEY DISINTEGRATED INTO FLORAL SCRAPS.
I FIRST WATCHED GREASE WHEN I WAS SEVEN WITH MY NEXT DOOR NEIGHBOR LIZZIE. WHEN HER MOM INVITED ME OVER, I ASKED IF IT WAS GOING TO BE A SCARY MOVIE. THE TITLE SOUNDED DARK AND MENACING . . .

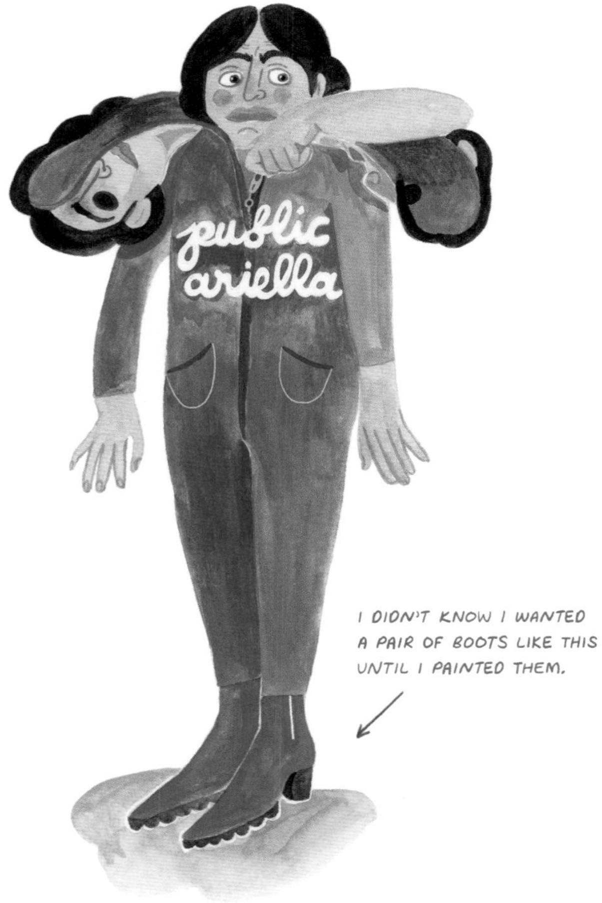
public ariella
I DIDN'T KNOW I WANTED A PAIR OF BOOTS LIKE THIS UNTIL I PAINTED THEM.

I held on to my passionate soapbox tendencies at home, but among my peers I started retreating into myself, putting on a more reserved persona at school, especially whenever boys were around.

Come high school, I had a new label to aspire to:

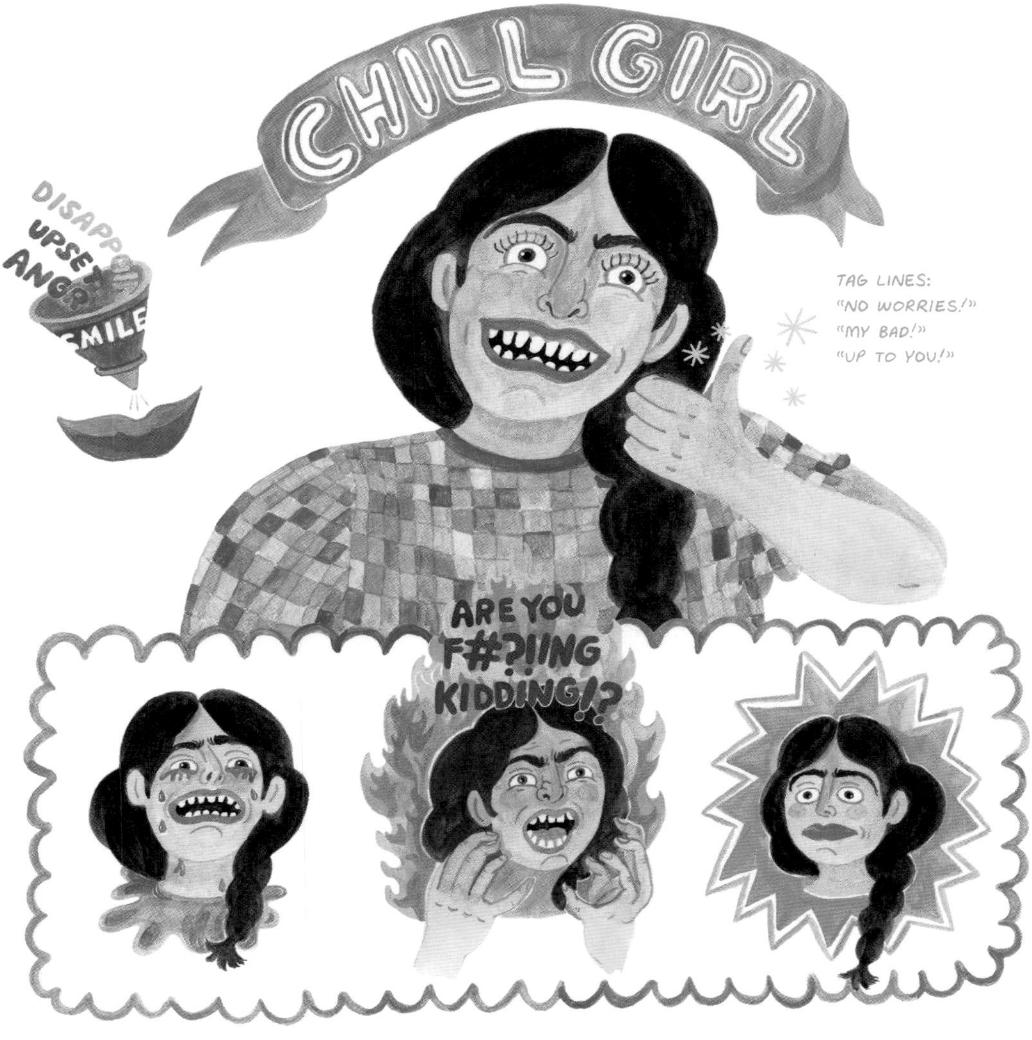

CHILL GIRL
DISAPP
UPSET
ANGR
SMILE
TAG LINES:
"NO WORRIES!"
"MY BAD!"
"UP TO YOU!"
ARE YOU F#?!ING KIDDING!?

Chill girl. The most coveted title for high school girls everywhere. It was cool to be unfazed, have no opinion, have no feelings. The most prized status was to be regarded as "one of the guys," and it felt important for me to reject my femininity so as to avoid being categorized as high maintenance. Absolutely nothing pink, sparkly, or spunky allowed.

I became a

contortionist

twisting and bending over backward to consider others' points of view before consulting my own. I shrunk myself down and held myself back. I grew up less confident. I apologized often. I slumped. I was taught to emphasize how others saw me, and consequently had a hard time prioritizing (or even recognizing) my own needs and desires.

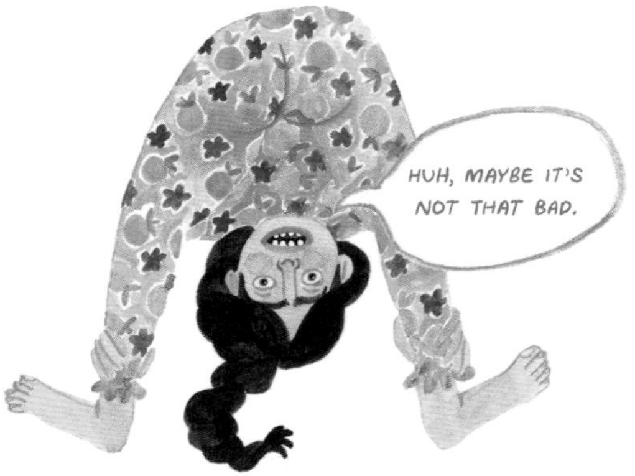
HUH, MAYBE IT'S NOT THAT BAD.

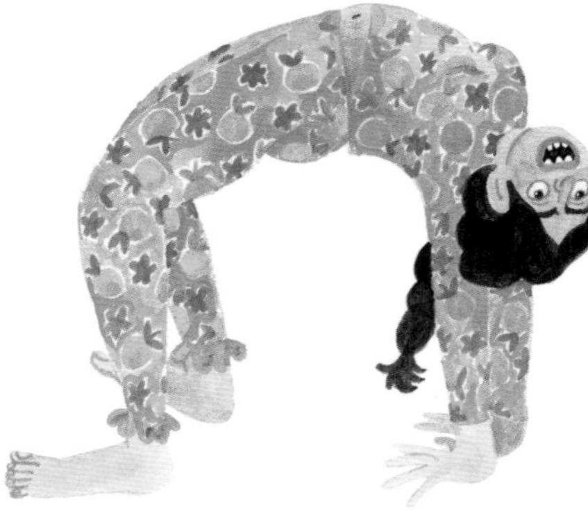

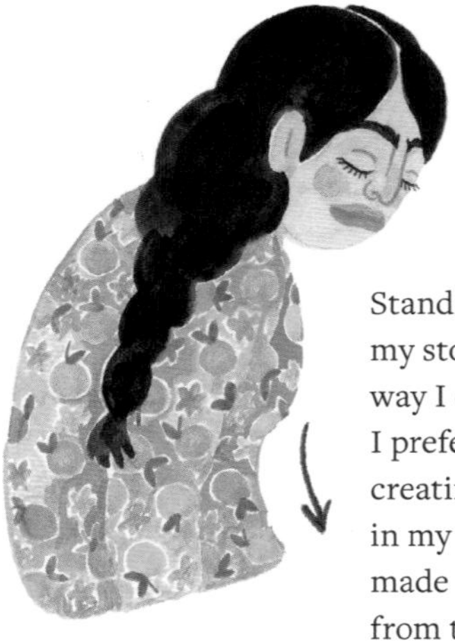

Standing up straight made my stomach jut out in a way I didn't like. Instead, I preferred to slump over, creating a concave curve in my torso that I thought made me look skinny from the side.

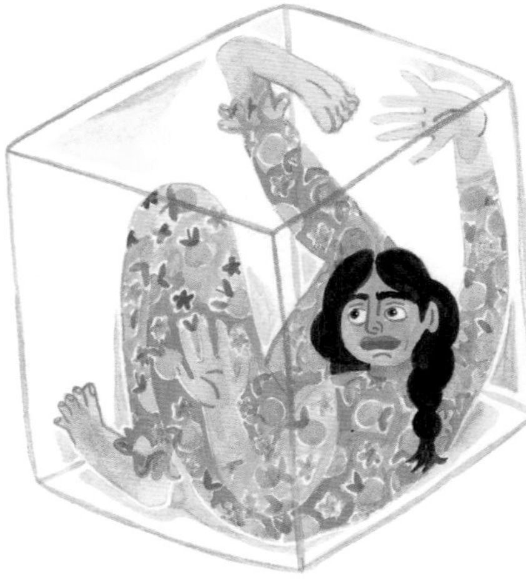

I contorted myself to live within the framework of what it meant to be a "likable" girl, and I generally tried to take up less space.

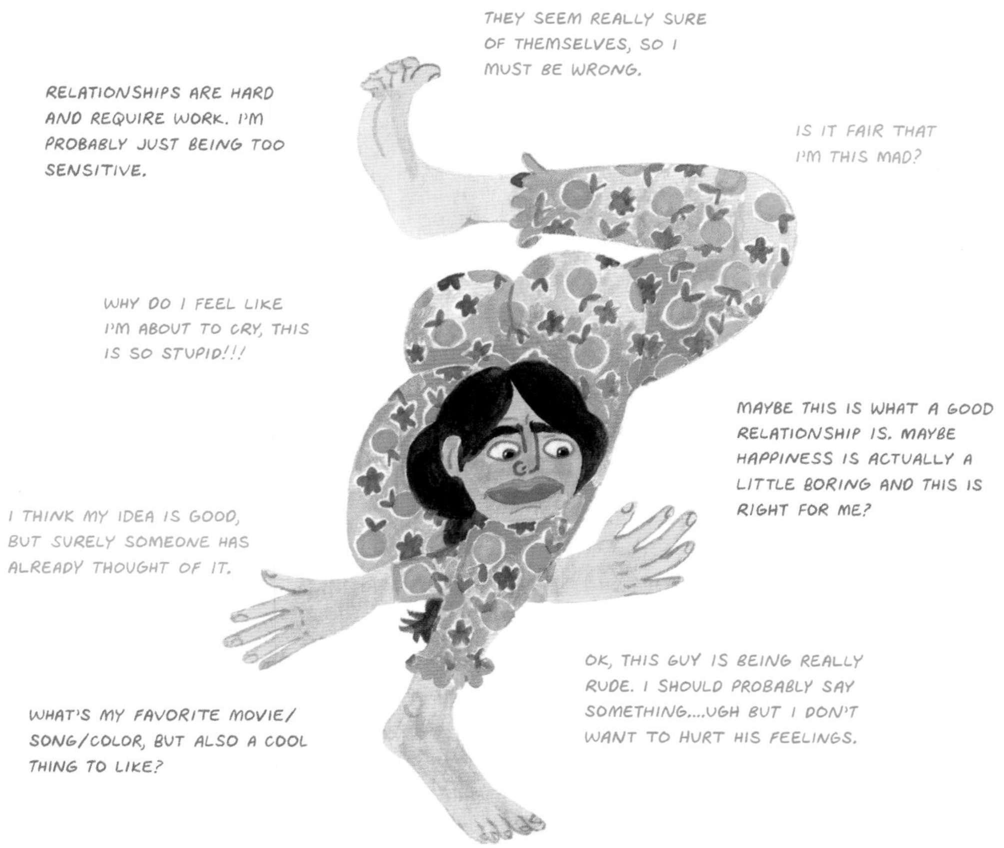
THEY SEEM REALLY SURE OF THEMSELVES, SO I MUST BE WRONG.
RELATIONSHIPS ARE HARD AND REQUIRE WORK. I'M PROBABLY JUST BEING TOO SENSITIVE.
IS IT FAIR THAT I'M THIS MAD?
WHY DO I FEEL LIKE I'M ABOUT TO CRY, THIS IS SO STUPID!!!
MAYBE THIS IS WHAT A GOOD RELATIONSHIP IS. MAYBE HAPPINESS IS ACTUALLY A LITTLE BORING AND THIS IS RIGHT FOR ME?
I THINK MY IDEA IS GOOD, BUT SURELY SOMEONE HAS ALREADY THOUGHT OF IT.
OK, THIS GUY IS BEING REALLY RUDE. I SHOULD PROBABLY SAY SOMETHING....UGH BUT I DON'T WANT TO HURT HIS FEELINGS.
WHAT'S MY FAVORITE MOVIE/SONG/COLOR, BUT ALSO A COOL THING TO LIKE?

By pretending to be laid-back, and by constantly training myself to push down my gut reactions to make way for others' perspectives, I got pretty tangled up. Before I knew it, it was genuinely hard for me to connect with how I was actually feeling. Similar to how a sucked-in stomach began to feel natural, the shoving down and second-guessing of emotions became an everyday exercise, barely detectable.

The women in my life acted as my compass, leading me back to that centered little Ariella mindset.

SELF-LOVE TRAINING WHEELS

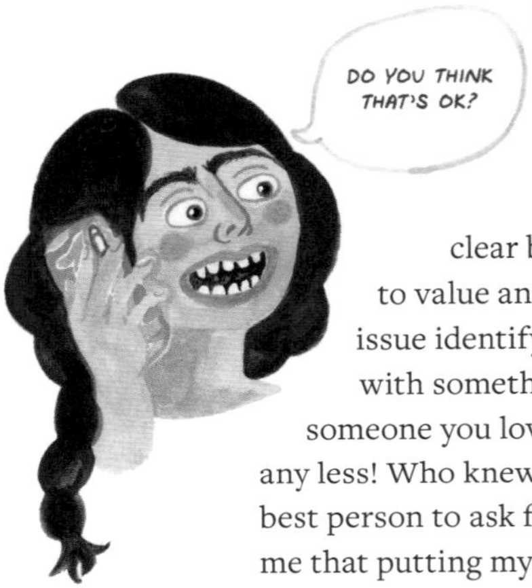
DO YOU THINK THAT'S OK?

My middle sister, Elisha, and I are polar opposites. Elisha has a degree in computer science and her thought process is black and white. She's incredibly decisive and is able to draw clear boundaries—a skill I have really grown to value and admire over time. She has no issue identifying when she is uncomfortable with something and opting out. Saying no to someone you love doesn't mean you love them any less! Who knew! All of that makes Elisha the best person to ask for advice. She reminds me that putting myself first doesn't make me a bad person.

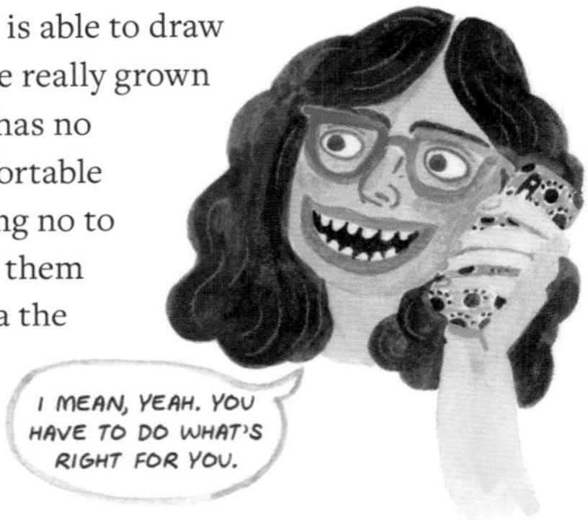
I MEAN, YEAH. YOU HAVE TO DO WHAT'S RIGHT FOR YOU.

My youngest sister, Alex, is six years younger, six inches taller, has long legs, and had lots of boyfriends well before I had my first. I've always thought of her as more cool and "womanly" than me. Her ability to wear full-length gowns with plunging necklines has never held her back from being goofy and hilarious, though. Last year, Alex went to a cool Halloween party dressed up as Guy Fieri—goatee and all (which, by the way, resulted in a goatee-shaped rash). Alex reminds me that we can be the funny girl and the "hot" girl all at once, on different days, or do away with the funny or hot alogether. We don't have to typecast one another or ourselves.

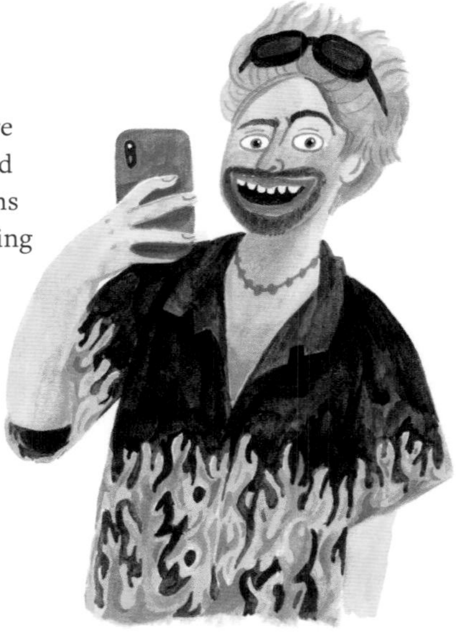

CHILL GIRL IS DEAD!

WE'RE BOTH TOO AMAZING TO PUT UP WITH ANY OF THIS BULLSHIT!

My Yenta Jesse reminds me to take my own advice with dating—to give myself the same honesty I give her. If something isn't working, talk about it. If someone pisses you off, don't just let it slide. We should never put up with someone who doesn't treat us the way we want to be treated.

My Grams has taught me self worth. She doesn't put up with bullshit and she inspires me to do the same. Grams is one of the most confident people I know, and her self-assuredness continually inspires me to recognize my own greatness. Her biggest message to me is to not let others define me—and she leads by example on that one. At eighty-three, she's out more nights than me in a given week, runs through the street to catch MTA buses or hail cabs, is a true fashion icon, and has impressive biceps.

231

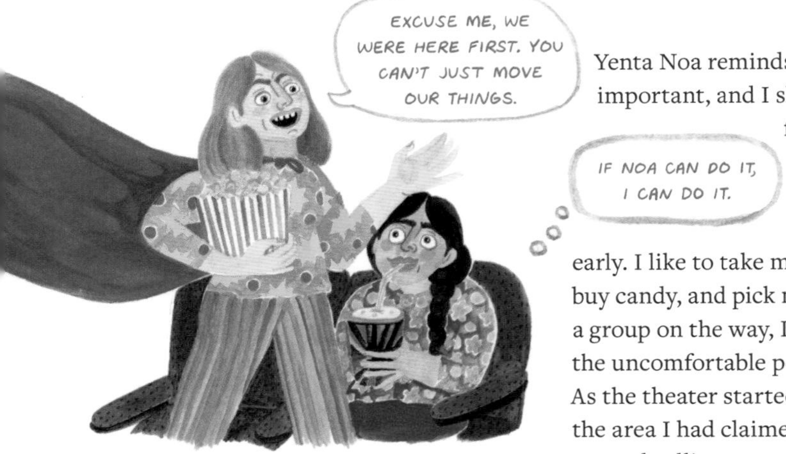
EXCUSE ME, WE WERE HERE FIRST. YOU CAN'T JUST MOVE OUR THINGS.
IF NOA CAN DO IT, I CAN DO IT.

Yenta Noa reminds me that my needs are important, and I shouldn't be afraid to stand up for myself. One night, I was meeting my friends for a movie and I, per usual, got there about half an hour early. I like to take my time, go to the bathroom, buy candy, and pick my seat. Being that early with a group on the way, I had also thrust myself into the uncomfortable position of having to save seats. As the theater started to fill, a girl approached the area I had claimed with my coat and bag and started yelling at me, saying I had no right to save those seats. She began moving my things to make room for herself and her boyfriend, just as Noa swooped in to save the day.

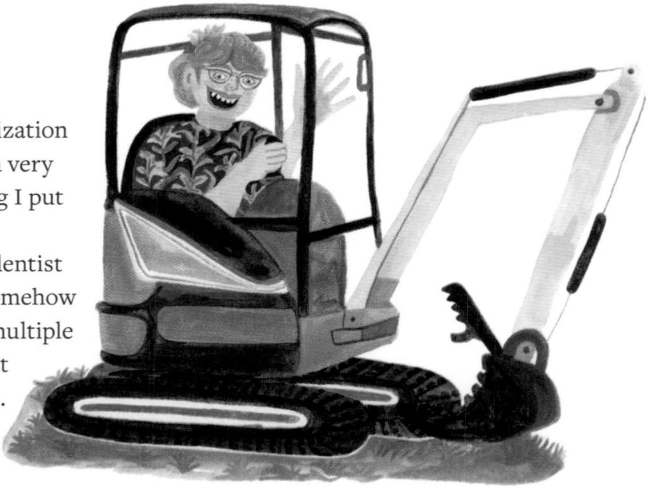

My mom is the epitome of self-actualization and confidence. She taught me from a very young age that I can truly do anything I put my mind to, and I should never think anything is out of my reach. She is a dentist and owns two dental practices, yet somehow finds the time and energy to pursue multiple other activities and hobbies (ones that most people would find intimidating). A few summers ago, she decided to take up gardening. One thing led to another and she rented a Bobcat tractor and excavated our entire backyard to landscape and build a pond with a waterfall. She breeds fish (in our home!), keeps bees, and competes in agility trials with her three golden retrievers.

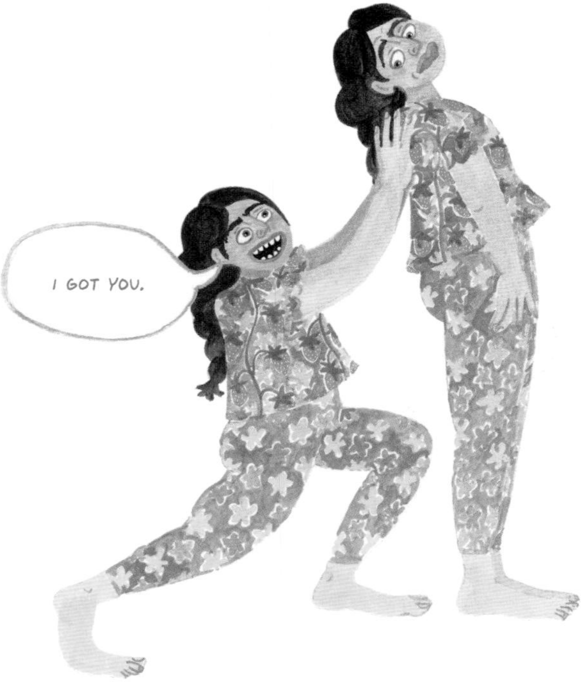
I GOT YOU.

With the women in my life leading by example and validating my feelings, I've begun to slowly, vertebrae by vertebrae, roll up to standing and show up for myself. To do away with that imagined framework of what it meant to "act like a woman." To be my own best advocate and support system.

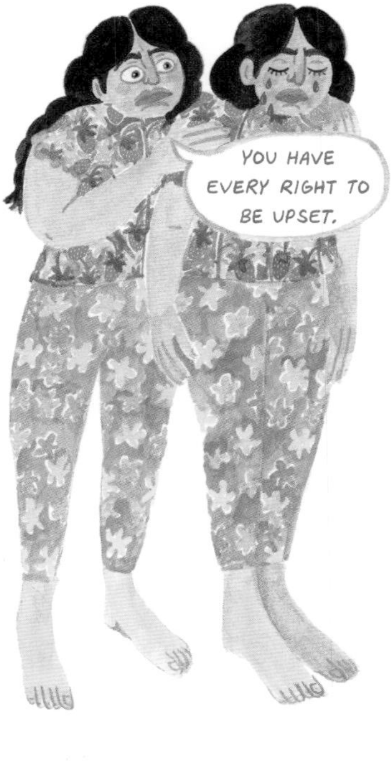
YOU HAVE EVERY RIGHT TO BE UPSET.

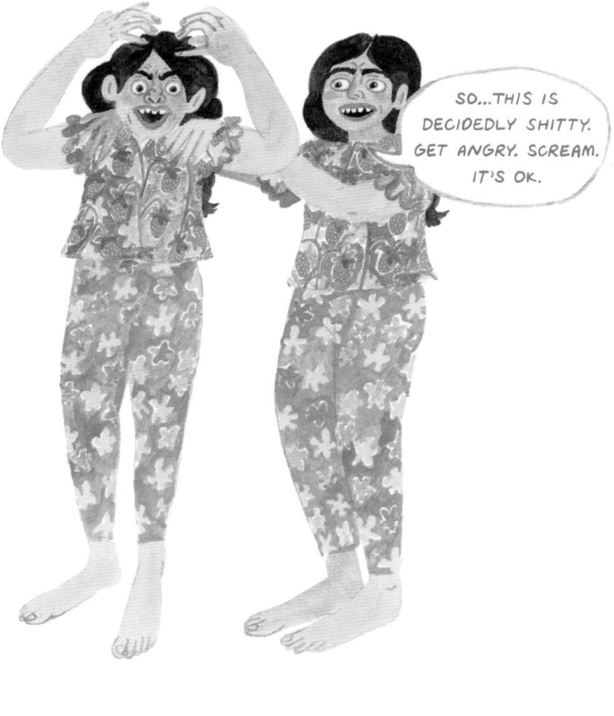
SO...THIS IS DECIDEDLY SHITTY. GET ANGRY. SCREAM. IT'S OK.

The caveat to all this growth and empowerment is that self-love is totally not linear, and there are moments and stretches of time where I majorly lack compassion for myself (and for others). As I grow into becoming my own Yenta, I'm learning to recognize those funks and just allow them to exist. I'm a human and there's no way I'm going to actively like myself every moment of the day—bodies are (wonderfully) gross and our brains can be (fascinating) trash—but I am growing to unconditionally love myself. No matter how yucky I might feel, I'm starting to trust that at the end of the day I'll always have my back.

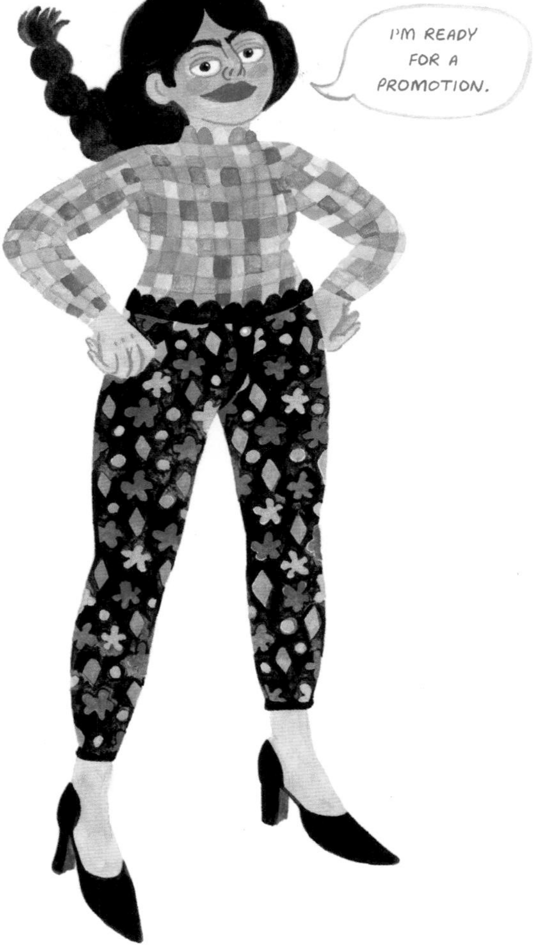
I'M READY
FOR A
PROMOTION.

My greatest accomplishment thus far? I finally gathered up enough courage and (at first somewhat faked) confidence to proactively ask for a raise and promotion at my day job. I wrote up a document, practiced my pitch in the shower for three days, and was shaking during the entire meeting with my manager, but I did it. I got what I asked for, and it felt incredible. Listing my strengths and accomplishments used to feel like bragging, and asking for more used to make me feel like an ungrateful brat. Now that I got over that hurdle, advocating for myself doesn't feel as scary. It gives me an adrenaline rush.

ME!

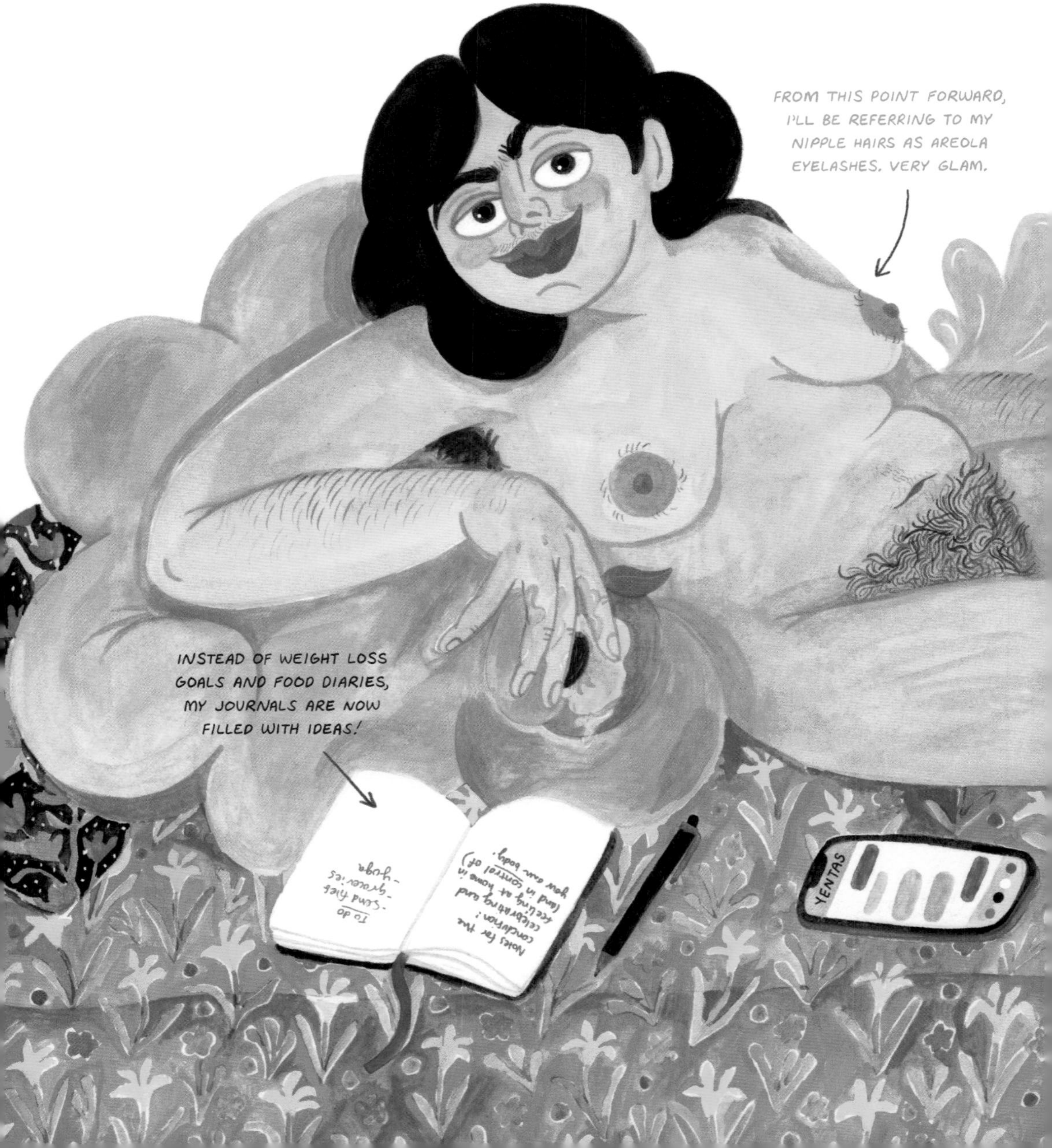
FROM THIS POINT FORWARD, I'LL BE REFERRING TO MY NIPPLE HAIRS AS AREOLA EYELASHES. VERY GLAM.
INSTEAD OF WEIGHT LOSS GOALS AND FOOD DIARIES, MY JOURNALS ARE NOW FILLED WITH IDEAS!
Notes for the conclusion: celebrating and feeling at home in (and in control of) your own body.
To do - send files - groceries - yoga
YENTAS

I hope that as you've joined me on my journey through my every nook and cranny, you've been inspired to appreciate and even cherish all of your own hairs and jiggles and bumps and smells too. Along with your brain and hopes and dreams, those lovely little details are what make you human and uniquely you! May your morning farts be celebrations of life welcoming a new day, and your "stray" hairs a reminder that you're the one calling the shots—you don't have to look or behave any certain way. Your body is yours to feel at home in, enjoy, take care of, and love.

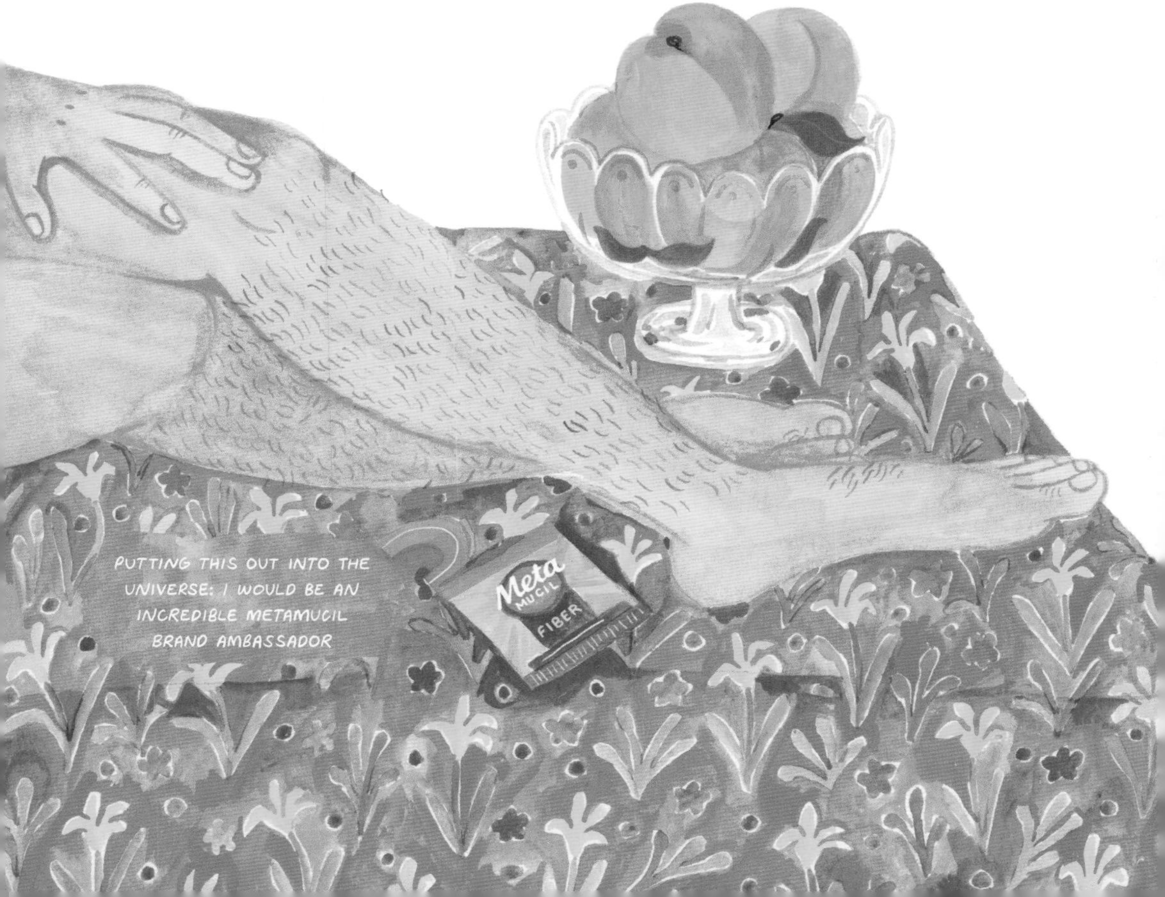
PUTTING THIS OUT INTO THE UNIVERSE: I WOULD BE AN INCREDIBLE METAMUCIL BRAND AMBASSADOR
Meta MUCIL
FIBER

♥ ACKNOWLEDGMENTS ♥

For those who are first meeting me through this book, you might not know that *Cheeky* started on Instagram (if you did meet me through Instagram, thank you for being part of the community that made this book possible!). A couple of years ago, I got the suggestion to start a blog and see what would grow from posting my work on bodily topics online (thank you, Mom and Zooey, for that advice; look what happened!). After lots of brainstorming to find the perfect name for the project, I painted my first juicy peach and @thecheekyblog was born. The Instagram account took off in ways I never imagined it would and, before I knew it, I was knee-deep in paintings of my naked body and chasing my dreams of becoming an author.

I'm probably sitting somewhere still happy crying about having written this book—it's my favorite and most challenging project I've taken on so far—and I've got lots of folks to thank who supported me along the way.

Thank you, Chantal, Richard, Lauren, Ali, Michael, Rosie, Grant, Anthony, Jacob, Steven, and Rachel for reading my early book iterations about my IBS and being my first sounding boards.

To the folks who got *Cheeky* from the start: Overwhelming amounts of love to my lifelong Yenta and friend Jordan Rodman for being the first to encourage me and insist that this work become a book. You've gone above and beyond to help make my dreams come true and I am so grateful to have you in my life, you talented genius. Thank you, Meredith Kaffel Simonoff, my brilliant agent, for being a wise and thoughtful guiding light. It's a dream to work with and learn from you. Thank you to my editor, Nancy Miller, for being my biggest cheerleader and always being spot on. To Katya Mezhibovskaya, for generally kicking ass on the design for this book and being a constant support. Thank you, Laura Phillips, Marie Coolman, Laura Keefe, Rosie Mahorter, Elizabeth Ellis, and the entire Bloomsbury team. Thank you, Lea Beresford, Jason Richman, and Addison Duffy.

To my friends in New York who make me feel at home: lots of gratitude for the teachers and community at YOBK. Special shout-out to Riji Suh; your classes teach me so much about taking care of my body and mind. To my design team at Paperless Post: it's a rare thing to genuinely love your coworkers—thank you for being such an empowering group of friends. Sophie, Miriam, Avital, Eva, and Becca, you probably get it by now, but I would not be me without you. Start saving up for the compound we're going to buy and live in together. To my honorary Yentas Lauren, Tzvia, Maddie, Jenni, Jake, and Pilar, thank you for your friendship, humor, and for sharing your bodily stories over delicious food (and Lactaid pills).

For my family: Grams, thank you for being my New York City mentor and always encouraging me to keep writing. Saba and Chava, thank you for giving me such a deep appreciation for art and for teaching me the importance of sharing your own stories. Savta Illana, I think of you and miss you always. Alex and Elisha, I couldn't ask for a better pair of sisters to grow up and become real people with. Cheers to a lifetime of diarrhea song lyrics. I love you. Thank you, family dogs past and present.

Last and most important, thank you, Mom and Dad, for heartily encouraging my imagination and love for drawing from day one. You both consistently make me feel supported in following my wildest dreams, to the point where those dreams don't feel wild at all.

An extra scoop of thank you to you, Mom, for being such an awesome female role model. I grew up in a home where being a woman meant being strong, ambitious, opinionated, and powerful. Our culture has a sneaky way of undermining that from time to time, but you've given me an incredible example to turn back to. Thank you, too, for being such an open book about all things bodily. Even though your candidness mostly embarrassed me when I was younger, I grew up knowing that you were a safe place to turn (or send insane "does this look normal" photos to). I wouldn't be cheeky without you.

A NOTE ON THE AUTHOR

ARIELLA ELOVIC holds a BFA
in Communication Design from
Washington University in St. Louis
and is the founder of @thecheekyblog,
an online platform through which
she seeks to combat the shame so
many of us feel in relation to our bodies.
Her work has been featured by *Teen
Vogue*, *Buzzfeed*, *KAAST*, and *Womanly
Magazine*. Ariella has collaborated
with various female-interest brands,
including Lunette Cup, What's In Your
Box?, Lunapads, and Cora for Women.
She lives in New York.

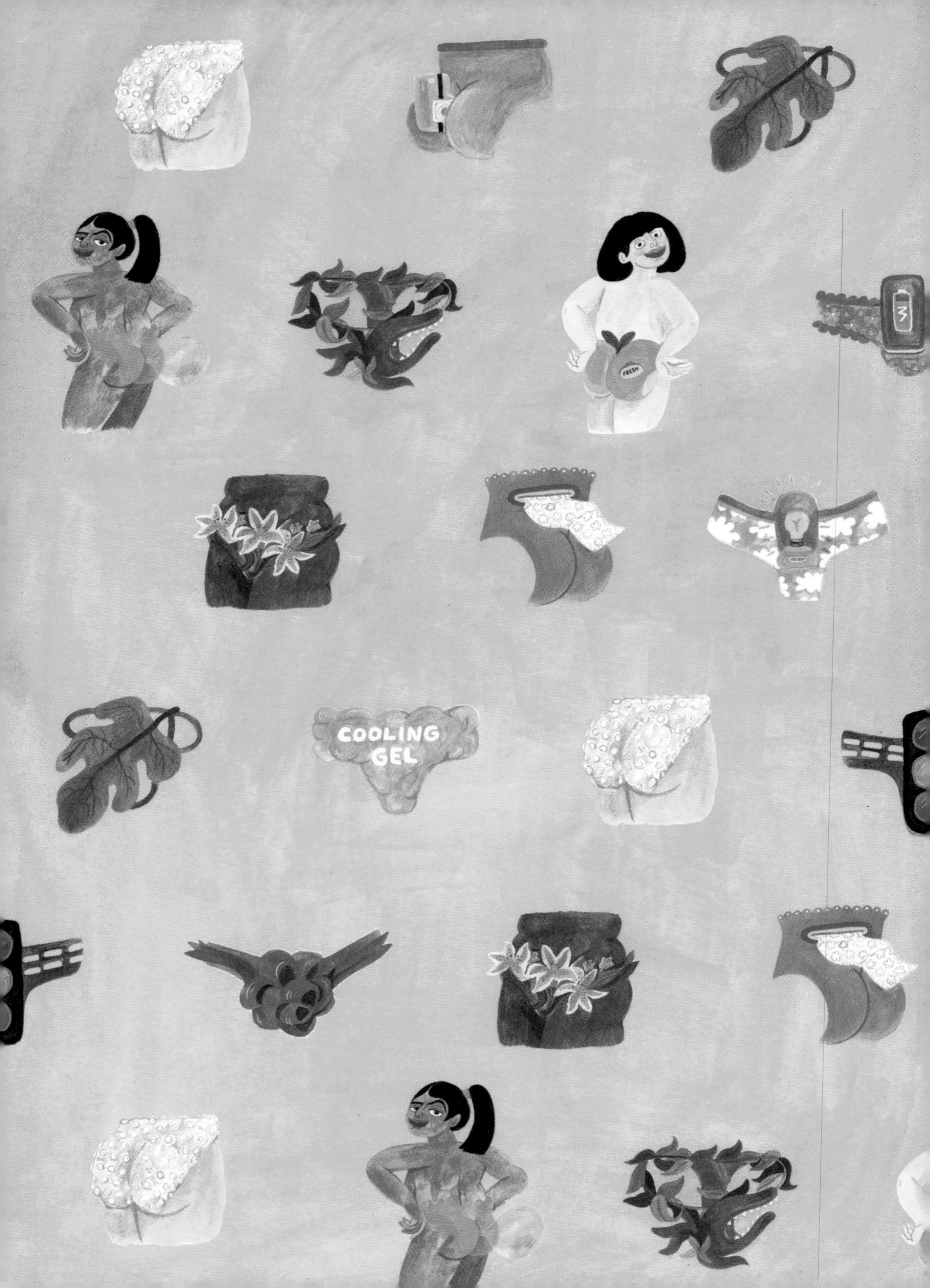
FRESH
COOLING GEL